SIDE 1
MELLOW MOOD
BOB MARLEY
PLUS TWO

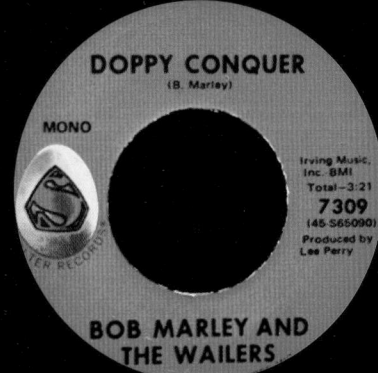

DOPPY CONQUER
(B. Marley)
MONO
Irving Music,
Inc. BMI
Total—3:21
7309
(45-S65090)
Produced by
Lee Perry
BOB MARLEY AND
THE WAILERS

Beverley's
RECORDS
135th ORANGE STREET,
KINGSTON, JAMAICA W.I.
CAUTION
(R. Marley)
THE WAILERS

DREAM LAND
WAIL WAILERS
SOLOMONIC
SIDE 1
SC....
50,001
R.P.M.
TIME
TUFF GONG
ALL RIGHTS RESERVED UNAUTHORISED COPYING PROHIBITED

STUDIO
ST 711
Peter TOSH
SHAME & SCANDAL
THE WAILERS

WINCOX
Records
BRENTFORD RD.
THERE SHE GOES
THE WAILERS
THE MIGHTY VIKINGS
RECORDED AT JAMAICA RECORDING STUDIO

SMILE JAMAICA
45 R.P.M.
Part One
BOB MARLEY & THE WAILERS
© TUFF GONG 1976

MU-SIK
CITY
HABITS
(R. Marley)
THE WAILERS
RECORDED BY JAMAICA RECORDING STUDIO 13 BRENTFORD ROAD

Tuff Gong
A WAIL N SOUL
PRODUCTION
Dub
Side 2 SUN IS SHINING
VR. 3

CoxSone
RECORDS
Side 1 T.G.001
TEENAGER IN LOVE
THE WAILERS
MANUFACTURED B
RECORD MFG. CO. LTD. JAMAICA W.I.

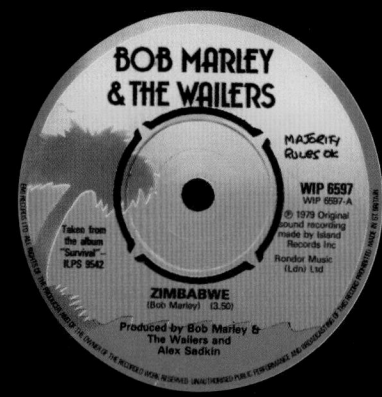

BOB MARLEY
& THE WAILERS
MAJORITY
RULES OK
WIP 6597
WIP 6597-A
Taken from
the album
"Survival"
ILPS 9542
ZIMBABWE
(Bob Marley) (3.50)
℗ 1979 Original
sound recording
made by Island
Records Inc
Rondor Music
(Ldn) Ltd
Produced by Bob Marley &
The Wailers and
Alex Sadkin

Tuff Gong
A WAIL N SOUL
PRODUCTION
Side 2 T.G.002

FAM'S
Tuff Gong
Records
127 King St. K
All rights are reserved for the owner of this record
Prod. by
A. Barrett
TROUBLE DUB
Wailers

TUFF GONG
RECORDS
TG-5005-B
Rec. In Jamaica
GUAVA JELLY
(Bob Marley-Bunny Livingston)
BOB MARLEY & THE WAILERS
Prod. by Bob Marley

COLUMBIA
45
RPM
COLUMBIA MARCAS REG.
CBS S 8114
CBS 8114B
Rondor Music
(London) Ltd
℗ 1972
CBS Records
OH LORD, GOT TO
(B. Marley/J. Nash)
BOB MARLEY
Arr. & Prod. by Johnny Nash
A Jad Cayman Prod.
A U.K. Production
2:15
MFD & DIST BY RECORD SPECIALISTS LTD KGN JA
MAN TO MAN
(B. Marley — L. Perry)
BOB MARLEY & THE WAILERS

D1068803

BOB MARLEY

songs of
freedom

BOB MARLEY

songs of freedom

EXECUTIVE EDITOR

RITA MARLEY

ADRIAN BOOT
AND
CHRIS SALEWICZ

VIKING
STUDIO
BOOKS

VIKING STUDIO BOOKS
Published by the Penguin Group
Penguin Books USA Inc., 375 Hudson Street,
New York, New York 10014, U.S.A.
Penguin Books Ltd, 27 Wrights Lane,
London W8 5TZ, England
Penguin Books Australia Ltd, Ringwood,
Victoria, Australia
Penguin Books Canada Ltd, 10 Alcorn Avenue,
Toronto, Ontario, Canada M4V 3B2
Penguin Books (N.Z.) Ltd, 182–190 Wairau Road,
Auckland 10, New Zealand

Penguin Books Ltd, Registered Offices:
Harmondsworth, Middlesex, England

First published in 1995 in the United States of America by Viking Penguin,
a division of Penguin Books USA Inc. and in Great Britain by Bloomsbury Publishing plc

1 3 5 7 9 10 8 6 4 2

Copyright © Adrian Boot and Chris Salewicz, 1995
All rights reserved

Photograph credits appear on page 284.

ISBN 0-670-85784-X (hc.)
ISBN 0 14.024413 1 (pbk.)

CIP data is available from The Library of Congress.

Printed in Great Britain
Designed by Bradbury and Williams

FOR DENISE MILLS

CONTENTS

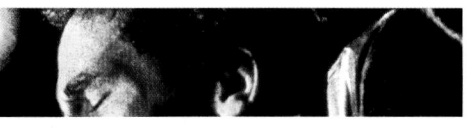

ACKNOWLEDGEMENTS

Working on this book about the great Bob Marley has not only been the highest possible honour, but also an inspiration and a blessing.

We could not help but note the manner in which photographs, information or assistance flowed to us at the least expected moments, almost as an indication that we were on the right course. The help offered by virtually every individual we contacted went way beyond the call of duty.

Everyone named here, and many others besides, played a very significant part. On many occasions Bob's family has welcomed our intrusions with open arms and forthrightness. Mrs Cedella Booker, Bob's mother, shared intimacies of experience and emotion that deeply touched us. Rita Marley, Bob's wife, similarly laid open to us to her innermost secrets, truths that would sometimes leave you stunned. His children, Cedella and Ziggy, also moved us with their willingness to assist.

Chris Blackwell, for many years, has given his time unstintingly, opening his heart about the life and career of his beloved artist, for which we are truly grateful.

Aston 'Family Man' Barrett revealed the secrets of the early days of the Wailers to us; Junior Marvin expanded on hitherto unknown details of recording and touring with the Tuff Gong; Judy Mowatt enlarged on the physical detail and psychic vibrations of working as one of Bob's I-Threes backing singers.

Mortimer Planner, wise beyond belief, illuminated the natural mystic of Rastafari for us. Cosmo Ben Imhotep, with his erudition, filled in many of the missing gaps, as did Jah Stone and Granny Ivy, followers of the doctrine of Rastafari since time. Pepe Judah and Alan 'Skill' Cole also offered wise counsel, particularly on the world of the Twelve Tribes organisation.

To elucidate Bob's position in Jamaican music, many individuals offered their help. Notably, Prince Buster, without whom none of this would have come into being, and Ernest Ranglin, who was also there at the beginning; but also, and no less significantly, Roland Alphonso, Jah Jerry Haines and Johnny Moore, all members of the seminal recording group The Skatalites, who backed Bob on countless occasions. Alton Ellis, Dobbie Dobson and Phyllis Dillon also provided invaluable help and time in untangling the labyrinthine, largely unchronicled story of the early years of Jamaican music. Similarly, the great producers Bunny Lee and Lee Perry have offered unique insights over the years, as has Pauline Morrison. Sylvan Morris and Harry 'J' Johnson have equally illuminated Bob's methods of studio work. Linton Kwesi Johnson fused together the disparate parts with his consummate knowledge, and likewise Neville Garrick, with his experience of hanging with the Gong. To Bob's trusted adviser, Diane Jobson, we are eternally grateful, and our respects to her brother, Dickie.

For the truth about life in Trench Town we give our thanks to Tartar, Bragga and Georgie, and to Mick Cater, who put the Bob Marley show on the road. To the estimable Timothy White, who lit the path, we cannot express too much gratitude. Stephen Davis's work has proved similarly inspirational. And the professor Steve Barrow's immense knowledge has been enormously helpful, as has Trevor Wyatt's, whose understanding of the minutiae of Bob's work saved much time.

At Island Records the inspirational Denise Mills, the book's first interviewee, and Suzette Newman made everything flow smoothly, with love and complete commitment, as part of their personal crusade to champion Jamaican music. Again, Rob Partridge and Gaylene Martin have offered invaluable assistance, understanding and friendship over the years. And let us not forget Brian Blevins, who sent out those first copies of *Catch a Fire* and the tickets for those first Wailers Speakeasy dates. Or Benjamin Foot, for whom it was no doubt preordained that he should now be living in Addis Ababa. Don Letts, moreover, is living proof of the power of Rastafari to bring about personal change.

At various ends of the media and music business Vivien Goldman, Neil Spencer, Bruno Tilley, Roger Ames, David Corio, Dennis Morris, Trish Farrell, Cathy Snipper and Brent Hansen have given help that was inspired simply by their love of Bob Marley. Both Sting and Mick Jones provided guides to the metaphysical heart of the matter. Carl Bradshaw and Woody made themselves a clearly signposted map of Jamaica. Julian Alexander, our estimable agent, provided a back-up that was unobtrusive but ever-present and deeply appreciated. At Bloomsbury, David Reynolds and Charlie Hartley gave us every freedom, as did the design team of Roy Williams and Laurence Bradbury.

None of this would have been possible, of course, without our families who tolerated us during our flights of madness.

Finally, let us thank the citizens of Jamaica. In spite of all the strife and turmoil that can affect this wonderful country, they remain some of the most exceptional people on this earth. Without them, the extraordinary phenomenon of Bob Marley – and certainly this book – simply could not have occurred.

INTRODUCTION

By Rita Marley

Bob was a servant of God. He would always say that. I would say to him, 'Bob, you're so great, so special,' and he would reply, 'I'm not special: this is Jah works and whatever I'm doing is for Jah.' Other times I would tell him, 'Bob, you're so good: the work you are doing is so different.' And he would always say, 'You're crazy, man: this is not hard.'

The respect I had for Bob was more than just that of a wife. It was because of what I saw him doing for the world. And in himself not even knowing how powerful he was becoming.

I came to acknowledge him as someone who was so different. It wasn't about just being great: it was about being really different. And at that same time being able to maintain a certain humility, which was taken for granted by most of his friends, and by those who would keep coming to him: just nipping, nipping, begging, begging . . . He would always make himself accessible to different types of characters, who would often leave a great burden with him. He would try to please everybody and it was a terrible strain.

I think something came over him where he felt he owed so much to Jah for allowing him to express what the people wanted to hear, that he just gave up on himself. He was saying, 'I don't belong to anybody. I don't have a father on this earth. For me there is only the Father in Heaven.'

Bob was very sensitive, with a lot of hurt inside him because of his past. But he grew up in that Trench Town atmosphere where everybody is rough. Bob had to put up with a lot of resistance there. If he hadn't been so strong in himself, he wouldn't have become

what he is today; he'd be down-trodden and seen as another half-caste who could never make it. So it's important he knows that there are people who care and who will strive to see that his works are established all over the world.

With Bob people often just look on the fame and the achievements and they think,'Bwai, it sure must be nice being Bob Marley.' It wasn't necessarily like that, though. There was a lot of sadness inside him, which would just come over him now and then. Even in some of his pictures you can see it: 'I'm so happy to be happy, but I'm sad.' And you would find he would go overboard to make other people feel happy:

Sometimes people just saw him as a singer. But there were a lot of other things going on in Bob's life that he wasn't able to express to other people. He grew up a loner, yet at the same time he was still able to give and to share whatever he thought he could give to make others happy. If someone's goat was down in a pit, Bob would go down there to get it, just to make them happy. Even to the end that's how he was.

There really had to be something at the end to pay off the sacrifice during the early years of coming up. Because there is a God, and he looks out for us. When I looked at Bob's life I knew he wasn't just an ordinary person. He was one of them that comes every 2,000 years.

Rita

THE ROBERT MARLEY FOUNDATION, 56 HOPE ROAD, KINGSTON 6, JAMAICA

THE END

Bob Marley was a hero figure, in the classic mythological sense. From humble beginnings, with his talent and religious belief his only weapons, the Jamaican recording artist applied himself unstintingly to spreading his prophetic musical message. His departure from this planet came at a point when his vision of One World, One Love – inspired by his belief in Rastafarianism – was beginning to be heard and felt in some quarters. For example, the Bob Marley and The Wailers 1980 tour attracted the largest audiences at that time for any musical act in Europe.

Bob Marley's story is that of an archetype, which is why it continues to have such a powerful resonance: it embodies, among other themes, political repression, metaphysical and artistic insights, gangland warfare and various periods in a mystical wilderness. It is no surprise that Bob Marley now enjoys an icon-like status more akin to that of the rebel myth of Che Guevara than to that of a pop star. And his audience continues to widen: to westerners Bob's apocalyptic truths prove inspirational and life-changing; in the Third World his impact is similar, except that it goes further. Not just among Jamaicans, but also among the Hopi Indians of New Mexico and the Maoris of New Zealand, in Indonesia, in India and even – especially – in those parts of West Africa from which slaves were taken to the New World, Bob Marley is seen as the redeemer figure returning to lead this planet out of confusion. Some will come out and say directly that Bob Marley is the reincarnation of Jesus Christ long awaited by much of the world. In interpreting his life as that of the Messiah, the cancer that killed him is inevitably described as a modern version of a crucifixion.

Although the disease possibly did have its origins in a barely treated football injury, conspiracy theories still abound. Was Bob's body poisoned still further when going for medical check-ups in Babylonian cities like London, Miami and New York? Were his hotel rooms or homes bombarded with cancer-inducing rays? Or, more simply, was Bob's system slowly poisoned by the lead from the bullet that remained in his body after the 1976 attempt on his life?

Certainly the argument that the cancer probably originated from the football injury seems convincing. But then, remember that this was a time when the forces of darkness thought nothing of killing a woman like Karen Silkwood who was endeavouring to expose a nuclear risk. Would such forces not have been far more threatened by a charismatic, alternative world leader who, in widely accessible popular art, was delivering warnings about the wickedness of the world's institutions?

Thanks to the tireless efforts of Timothy White, the author of Catch a Fire, the wonderful Bob Marley biography, the extent of the CIA files on Bob has become widely appreciated. Chris Blackwell, who signed Bob to his Island Records label, had personal experience of this. 'There are conspiracy theories with everything, especially out of Jamaica, because Jamaicans have such fertile imaginations. The only thing I will say is that I was brought into the American ambassador's office in Jamaica, and he said that they were keeping an eye on me, on what I was doing, because I was working with this guy who was capable of destabilising. They had their eye on him.'

Bob's end was very sad. After his collapse while jogging in New York's Central Park on 8 October 1980, he received radiation treatment at the city's Memorial Sloan-Kettering Cancer Center; his locks fell out, like a portent. While undergoing therapy, Bob made the decision to be baptised into the Ethiopian Orthodox Church. A priest came to his hotel and performed the ceremony. Bob was overwhelmed with emotion, tears pouring down his face.

'I am not the angel of death. I am the angel of life.'

Even confronted by a future of such grim uncertainty, Bob managed to retain his wry view of life. Two weeks after his collapse, his death was being inaccurately reported in the US media; Bob put out a statement in which his characteristic dry sense of humour was clearly still in evidence: 'They say that living in Manhattan is hell, but . . .'

With a similar attitude he tried to make light of his illness to his children. While he was being treated in New York, they flew up from Jamaica to see him at the Essex House hotel. 'He told us what was wrong with him,' said Cedella, his eldest child. 'His hair was gone. We were like, "Where's your hair?" He was making it to be such a big joke: "Oh, I'm Frankenstein." "That's not funny," we said.'

Eventually, by November 1980, the doctors at the Sloan-Kettering Center admitted they could do no more. A number of alternative cures were considered: the apricot kernel cancer cure in Mexico that the actor Steve McQueen had attempted; a spiritual cure by journeying to Ethiopia; a simple return home to Jamaica – although this plan was abandoned as the island was in the aftermath of the most violent general election it had ever known.

After the options had been weighed up, Bob travelled to Bavaria in West Germany, to the Sunshine House Cancer Clinic in Bad Wiesse. A holistic centre, it was run by the controversial Dr Josef Issels, a former SS officer. Issels only took on cases that had been diagnosed as being incurable, and he claimed a twenty per cent success rate.

The environment, however, was hostile and alien. Bob, who had always tried to avoid touring Babylon during the winter months, was living in a house surrounded by thick snow. Bob would go to Issels's clinic for two hours of treatment each day, and then return to spend time with the visitors who had flown in to be with him – his mother, his wife, members of The Wailers, old friends. Much of his time was spent watching video-tapes of soccer matches, particularly those played by the Brazilian team.

Bob never stopped writing songs. He seemed to think he could make it. His weight went up and for a time he seemed in better spirits. But

the sterile, picture-postcard atmosphere of Bad Wiesse hardly nurtured Bob's soul. 'It was a horrible place,' Chris Blackwell recalls. 'It must have been very disorientating for him. He had virtually no hair, just scraggly bits, and was so thin: he must have weighed a hundred pounds or something like that. He looked terrible. But there was something . . . He was still so proud. He would say, Hi, and chat for a bit. He was somehow still very strong.'

The atmosphere around Bob was even worse: vicious psychological warfare had broken out between two branches of Rastafari, the Orthodox and Twelve Tribes factions. It seems demeaning to everyone involved, Bob included, to describe this in further detail. Sufficient to heed the words of the Rastafarian elder, Mortimer Planner. 'A terrible misunderstanding has gone on. For all these people loved Bob.'

He developed a craving for plantain tarts, and it was arranged for a carton of them to be flown up to him from Jamaica. Before they arrived, however, he decided he wanted to go home. He had had enough of Bad Wiesse. He knew what was going to happen.

A private plane was hired. Accompanied by two doctors, Bob was flown across the Atlantic.

He made it no further than Miami, where he arrived in the early hours of 10 May. By this time Bob's condition was judged sufficiently serious for him to be immediately checked into the city's Cedars of Lebanon hospital.

That afternoon his children Cedella and Ziggy visited him in his private room. They were uplifted by the sight of a group of evangelists who had flown up from Jamaica to be with him; they seemed very holy as they surrounded Bob's bed, praying and speaking comforting words 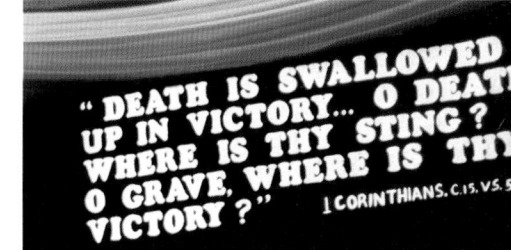 to him. Confident that their father was in safe hands, that he would come through this great trial, the children left the hospital and returned to the Miami house of their grandmother, Mrs Cedella Booker, Bob's mother.

Shortly after 11.30 a.m. the next morning, Cedella heard the telephone ring. Picking it up at the same time as her uncle Gibson, she heard

OFFICIAL FUNERAL SERVICE OF THE LATE HON. ROBERT NESTA MARLEY O.M.

perhane selassie

Bob Marley's funeral service was held in Kingston's National Heroes Arena. He had been given radiation treatment to fight the cancer invading his body, and as a result his dreadlocks had fallen out. Rita, his wife, had kept the locks and they were woven into a wig which was placed on his head. Sharing Bob's coffin with him were his worn copy of the Bible and his Gibson guitar.

the voice of Diane Jobson, Bob's lawyer and a close friend of the family, telling her uncle that Bob Marley had passed on to the next life.

As she still held the receiver to her ear, her attention was caught by a movement across the room: on the mantelpiece she saw a framed photograph of her father shift slightly. Cedella looked across at it, and Bob's eyes gazed deeply into her own.

Back in Jamaica, on the morning of 11 May 1981, Judy Mowatt, one of the singers in Bob's I-Threes backing group, was at home when she had a similar experience. A little after 11.30 a.m. there was a loud clap of thunder and lightning flashed through a window on to a picture of Bob on the wall. Judy knew exactly what this foretold: Bob Marley had surrendered his soul to the Almighty Jah.

AT THE STATE FUNERAL THERE WERE READINGS FROM THE BIBLE BY FLORIZEL GLASSPOLE, JAMAICA'S GOVERNOR GENERAL, AND BY MICHAEL MANLEY, THE LEADER OF THE OPPOSITION PARTY. EDWARD SEAGA, THE PRIME MINISTER, DELIVERED A SERMON IN PRAISE OF THE HONOURABLE ROBERT NESTA MARLEY: THE PREVIOUS MONTH, IN RECOGNITION OF HOW HE HAD BENEFITED THE CULTURE OF JAMAICA, BOB MARLEY HAD BEEN AWARDED THE ORDER OF MERIT, JAMAICA'S HIGHEST HONOUR.

OFFICIAL FUNERAL SERVICE

FOR THE

HON. ROBERT NESTA MARLEY O.M.

(BOB MARLEY - BERHANE SELASSIE)

(Light of the Trinity)

AT

THE ETHIOPIAN ORTHODOX CHURCH
HOLY TRINITY

89 MAXFIELD AVENUE, KINGSTON, JAMAICA

8. 00 — 9. 00 a.m.

AND

THE NATIONAL ARENA

11. 00 a.m.

THURSDAY MAY 21, 1981.

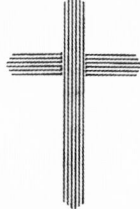

OFFICIATING:-

HIS EMINENCE ABOUNA YESEHAQ
ARCHBISHOP OF THE ETHIOPIAN ORTHODOX CHURCH
IN THE WESTERN HEMISPHERE

Assisted by Priests and Deacons of the Ethiopian Orthodox Church in Jamaica.

SERVICE WILL BE PERFORMED IN GEEZ, AMHARIC AND ENGLISH

g

*AFTER VARIOUS
DIGNITARIES HAD MADE
SPEECHES, THE WAILERS
PLAYED SOME OF BOB'S
SONGS, WITH THE
I-THREES (RIGHT) ON
VOCALS. HIS MOTHER, MRS
CEDELLA BOOKER, SANG
'COMING IN FROM THE
COLD', A TUNE FROM
UPRISING, HER SON'S LAST
ALBUM. THE MELODY
MAKERS, A GROUP
CONSISTING OF SEVERAL OF
BOB'S CHILDREN ALSO
PERFORMED, LED BY
ZIGGY (ABOVE), BOB'S
ELDEST SON.*

A JOYOUS, CELEBRATORY OCCASION, THE FUNERAL OF BOB MARLEY WAS THE MOST SIGNIFICANT DAY OF NATIONAL MOURNING THAT THE ISLAND HAD EXPERIENCED.

THE COFFIN WAS THEN DRIVEN ACROSS THE ISLAND TO NINE MILES, BOB'S BIRTHPLACE, A TINY HAMLET IN THE MIDDLE OF JAMAICA. HALF THE ISLAND FLOCKED THERE TO PAY THEIR RESPECTS.

ENTERING THE KINGDOM

*ALL THOSE PRESENT WERE
UNITED BY THE OCCASION.
FROM NOW ON BOB'S
MESSAGE AND INFLUENCE
WOULD ONLY CONTINUE TO
GROW.*

*THE HUMBLE MAUSOLEUM
AT NINE MILES, BOB
MARLEY'S FINAL RESTING-
PLACE.*

THE BEGINNING

When Cedella Malcolm, who was later to bring Bob Marley into the world, was eight years old, she heard Hubert Hall, a local practitioner of obeah, confess that he had caused her father's car to crash some seven years earlier. On his death-bed, the man struggled to save his soul by admitting the wickedness of his sins. As he spoke, Cedella sensed his terror.

Hall had waited until Omeriah Malcolm's car, packed with relatives, hit a straight section on the winding road that passes through Nine Miles in the parish of St Ann. Hall then summoned up his 'science', as the Jamaican voodoo-like practice of obeah is known, to flip the car over on its side. A truck driver passing through Nine Miles called out the grim news: 'Mr Malcolm's car overturn 'pon the bank and all the people dem dead dere!'

Omeriah's friends and relatives, the tiny Cedella clutched to the bosom of an aunt, hurried to the scene of the accident. Arriving there, they found some consolation; no one was dead, but there were some terrible injuries: the mother of one of Cedella's brothers had had her hair entirely burned off. Trapped in the wreckage, crumpled on top of each other, were the other passengers, moaning from the pain of their broken bones and burned flesh. Sitting dazed by the side of the road, however, with only a slight cut to his face, was Cedella's father, balancing her little brother John on his knee. Omeriah Malcolm's inborn goodness had led God to protect him.

Even as they were taking Hubert Hall's body on a stretcher up to the burial plot, little 'Ciddy' was still mulling over the man's confession, her first direct experience of the force of obeah. This wickedness distressed her deeply – Hall had admitted that he had been in league with others who had sought out his dark talent. They had urged him on to the terrible act with no more lavish a bribe than a meal of goat's head, yam and cho-cho. But for most of the adults who had

Obeah, similar to the African animist traditions found in voodoo, is like an alternative dimension in Jamaica. It is commonplace in the lives of many of the island's inhabitants.

heard Hall's tormented words, such evil was sadly commonplace. Cedella's father, for example, was little surprised at the way the obeahman had distorted the natural mystic that wafts on the breeze through Nine Miles.

The God-given land of Jamaica has drawn comparison with sites from the Garden of Eden to the home of the lost civilisation of Atlantis. Situated in the heart of the Caribbean, the island has a far larger variety of vegetation and plant-life than almost anywhere in the world: birds carrying seeds in their droppings are able to fly to it from North, Central and South America. Jamaica's British colonisers added to this wealth of vegetation, often in an attempt to find new, cheap means of filling the bellies of their slaves: the mango, for instance, was brought in from West Africa.

While this extraordinary, unique country is a strong contender for the most beautiful land in the world, the parish of St Ann is in its turn often considered to be the most beautiful part of Jamaica. The rolling, lush countryside around Nine Miles, deep in the interior of St Ann, is like a microcosm of the region – the heart, even the soul and mystery of the island. Nine Miles is almost as many feet above sea level as the Blue Mountain Peak, Jamaica's highest point at 7,402 feet. As a result, this landlocked region enjoys a temperate climate, cooler and less oppressive than that of the marshy plains in the south of the island.

The Malcolms were the oldest and most respected family in the area of Rhoden Hall, where Nine Miles is located, owning or renting a considerable amount of land and local properties. Omeriah's father was Robert 'Uncle Day' Malcolm, who was descended from the Cromanty slaves shipped from the Gold Coast – what is now Ghana – some 200–250 years earlier: as tenant slaves the Malcolms had lived in this bush region long before slavery was abolished in 1838.

Cedella's grandmother, Katherine Malcolm, known only as Yaya, lived 'down the bottom', away from the road over on the other side of a steep hill. Her home was the family residence known as the 'Big House', although it consisted

JAMAICA

The Caribbean island of Jamaica has had a far greater impact on the rest of the world than one would expect from a country with a population of under three million.

Jamaica's history, in fact, shows that ever since Columbus discovered the island in 1494, it has had a disproportionate effect on the rest of the world.

In the seventeenth century, for example, Jamaica was the world centre of piracy. From its capital of Port Royal, buccaneers led by Captain Henry Morgan plundered the Spanish Main, bringing such riches to the island that it became as wealthy as any of Europe's leading trading centres; the pleasures that money brought earned Port Royal the reputation of being the 'wickedest city in the world'. In 1692, four years after Morgan's death, Port Royal disappeared into the Caribbean in an earthquake. Such a karmic sense of poetry is Jamaica; it is a land where magic realism, interwoven with the common belief in obeah, the local voodoo, seems the norm.

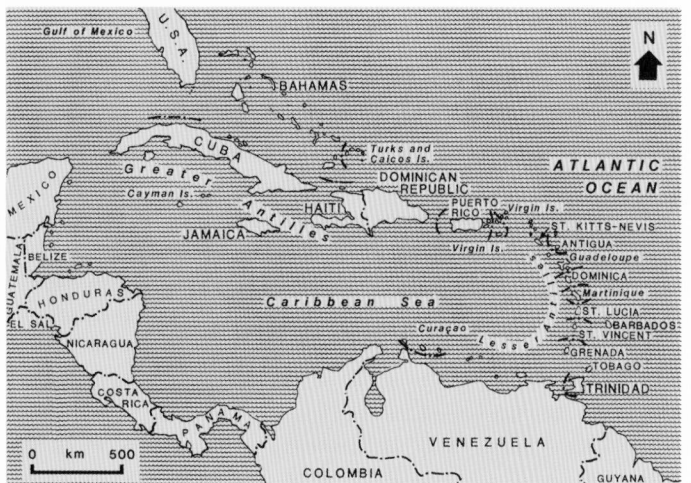

A piratic, rebellious spirit has been central to the attitude of Jamaicans ever since. This is clear in the lives of Nanny, the woman who led a successful slave revolt against the English redcoats in 1738; of Marcus Garvey, who became the first prophet of black self-determination in the 1920s, founding the Black Star shipping line, intended to transport descendants of slaves back to Africa; and of Bob Marley, the Third World's first superstar, with his musical gospel of love and global unity.

Jamaica was known by its original settlers, the Arawak Indians, as the Island of Springs. And it is in the high country that Jamaica's unconscious resides: the primal Blue Mountains and hills are the repository of most of Jamaica's legends, a dream-like landscape that provides ample material for an arcane mythology.

It was here, to the safety of these impenetrable hills, that bands of former slaves fled, after they were freed and armed by the Spanish to fight the English when they seized the island in 1655. The Maroons, as they became known, founded a community and underground state that would fight a guerrilla war against the English settlers on and off for nearly eighty years.

When peace was eventually established, the Maroons were granted semi-autonomous territory both in Portland and Trelawney, to the west of the island. It was in Moore Town that the great Maroon queen, Nanny, was buried. Honoured today as a national hero of Jamaica, Nanny's myth is so great that it is said she was able to catch the musket-balls fired at her.

Jamaica has always been tough. The Arawak Indians had to ward off invasions by the cannibalistic Caribs, who were taking over most of the neighbouring islands. Jamaica was an Arawak island when Christopher Columbus discovered it in the fifteenth century, claiming it to be 'the fairest island that eyes have beheld; mountainous and the land seems to touch the sky' - although he may have felt differently nine years later, on his fourth voyage to the New World. In St Ann's Bay, Columbus was driven ashore by a storm, and his rotting vessels filled with

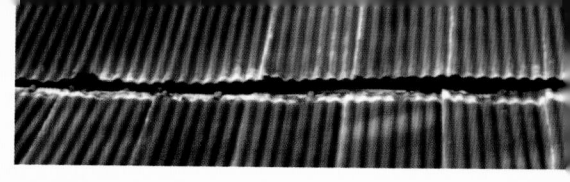

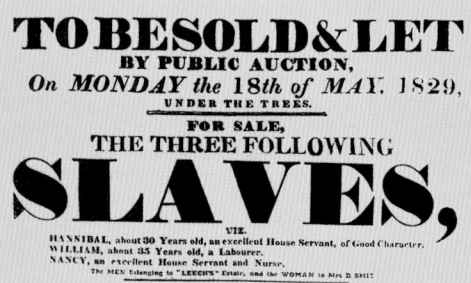

water until they sunk to the sea-bed. He was stranded on the island for a year before being rescued.

Later the Arawaks were placed into slavery by the Spaniards, and were shockingly abused, many committing suicide; others were tortured to death in the name of sport. By 1655, when the English captured the island, the Arawaks had been completely wiped out.

Even after the 1692 earthquake, piracy remained such a powerful force in the region that in 1717 a King's pardon was offered to all who would give up the trade.

Those Jamaican settlers who wished to trade legally could also make fortunes. It was soon discovered that sugar, which had been brought to the New World by Columbus on his first voyage, was the most profitable crop that could be grown on the island. Because of their importance as sugar-producing islands, the British West Indies had far more political influence with the English government than all the other thirteen American mainland colonies.

Sugar requires a large labour force, and it was this that led to the large-scale importation of African slaves. For the rest of the eighteenth century Jamaica's wealth was secured with the 1713 Treaty of Utrecht which terminated the War of Spanish Succession: one of its terms was that Jamaica became the distribution centre of slaves for the entire New World. The

first slaves shipped to the West Indies had been criminals or prisoners of war, purchased from African chiefs in exchange for European goods. When demand increased, raiding parties used the pretext of tribal wars to launch attacks all along the West Coast of Africa. Slaves had to endure the horrors of the middle passage before they were auctioned, £25-£75 being the average price.

Although the money that could be earned was considerable compensation for the white settlers, life in Jamaica was often troublesome. There were slave revolts and tropical diseases; war broke out frequently, which left the island vulnerable to attacks by the French or the Spanish (Horatio Nelson, when still a midshipman, was stationed on the island). Hurricanes, which invariably wiped out crops, were not infrequent, and earthquakes not unknown. Inhabitants of the south coast of the island also ran the risk of being devoured by crocodiles: in the late seventeenth century Kingston Harbour was infested with them.

Slavery was eventually abolished in 1838. From the 1860s indentured labour was imported from India and China, the Indians bringing with them their propensity for smoking ganja. In the 1880s a new period of prosperity began after a crop was found to replace sugar-cane – the banana. In 1907, however, this affluence was partially unhinged by a devastating earthquake that destroyed much of Kingston. But the economy recovered and the next wave of financial problems occurred in the late 1930s, as the worldwide depression hit the island.

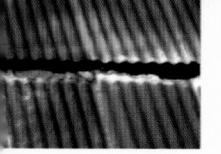

IN THE LATE SEVENTEENTH CENTURY PORT ROYAL, THEN THE CAPITAL OF JAMAICA, HAD THE REPUTATION OF 'THE WICKEDEST CITY IN THE WORLD'. THE BASE FOR CARIBBEAN PIRACY, IT WAS RULED OVER BY SIR HENRY MORGAN; FOUR YEARS AFTER HIS DEATH IN 1688, A COLOSSAL EARTHQUAKE CAUSED IT TO TOPPLE INTO THE SEA.

Nevertheless, a consequence of this was the founding of the two political parties – the Jamaica Labour Party (JLP) under Alexander Bustamente and the People's National Party (PNP) under Norman Manley – which would spearhead the path towards independence in 1962.

On 6 August 1962 Jamaica became an independent nation. The Union Jack was lowered and the green, gold and black standard of Jamaica was raised. Three months previously the JLP had won a 26-seat majority and taken over the government under Prime Minister Bustamente. Paradox is one of the yardsticks of Jamaica, and it should come as no surprise that the Jamaica Labour Party has always been far to the right of its main opposition, the People's National Party.

Beneath this façade of democracy, however, the life of the 'sufferah', downcast in his west Kingston ghetto tenement, remained essentially unchanged. In some ways things became more difficult, with the jockeying for position created by self-government bringing out the worst in people. Soon the MPs from each of the ghetto constituencies had surrounded themselves with gun-toting sycophants, anxious to preserve their positions: back the wrong candidate in a Jamaican election and you can lose not only your means of livelihood, but also your home – political patronage is the ruling principle in Jamaica.

Jamaican youth, who felt particularly disenfranchised, sought refuge in the 'rude boy' movement, an extreme precursor of the teenage tribes surfacing throughout the world. Dressed in narrow-brimmed hats and the kind of mohair fabrics worn by American soul singers, rude boys were fond of lethal 'ratchet' knives, and bloody gang fights were common. Independence for Jamaica also coincided with the birth of its music business; in quick succession ska, rock steady, and then reggae music were born, the records often being used as a means of broadcasting news that the *Daily Gleaner* would not print.

In 1972 the JLP was voted out of office after ten years in power. Michael Manley's PNP was to run Jamaica for the next eight years. Unfortunately Manley's efforts to ally with other socialist Third World countries brought down the wrath of the United States on Jamaica. This was especially the case after the Prime Minister nationalised the country's bauxite industry, which provides the raw material for aluminium, and which had previously been licensed to the American conglomerate Alcan.

A period of destabilisation began that turned Jamaica into a battleground, particularly after Manley was returned to power. Soon the country was virtually bankrupt. Bob Marley played a part in attempting to restore peace, making Manley and his opposition rival Edward Seaga publicly shake hands at the 1978 Peace Concert, and bringing opposing gunmen together. But the 1980 election, won by Edward Seaga, in power until 1988, was the bloodiest of them all.

In recent years a measure of peace seems to have been restored to the island. In the 1990s a mood of unprecedented optimism hovers about Jamaica. A positive relationship with the nearby United States has been forged and a new national pride has emerged.

The story of Jamaica is that of an island that can be simultaneously paradise and hell; that suffered the devastating economic bullying of the United States Caribbean basin initiative during the 1970s, but now, against expectations, is experiencing economic growth and a concomitant rise in self-esteem that serves as a model for developing nations as they enter the twenty-first century.

only of one room, a hall and a number of outhouses. Cedella had the impression that Yaya never slept. Every morning, at about three or four, the hour at which many Jamaican country-folk rise, Omeriah Malcolm would walk to his mother's for his morning coffee, bringing with him a big log of wood to stoke up the fire that always blazed at Yaya's; in those days before matches were common, anyone who needed fire would go and beg a blazing lump of wood from her. When he returned home an hour or so later, he would be carrying a covered quart tin full of coffee for the children's breakfast. Set up for the day, Omeriah would then leave for his various pieces of farmland. He was the biggest cultivator of coffee in the neighbourhood, taking it to market at Green Hill in his horse and cart before he bought first a Ford Model T and then a De Soto. But he would also grow pimento and bananas, ensuring that every strip of land he worked had a plentiful supply of banana trees.

Omeriah Malcolm's relative financial success was not his only source of wealth: his father had also taken care to instruct him in the arcane arts, rooted in Africa's animist religions and brought to Jamaica by the Cromanty slaves. Omeriah proved to have an empathy and skill with these God-given positive forces; he was, to all intents and purposes, a white magician, who dealt only with light and high matters; one of his closest friends was an eminent Jamaican 'scientist', so skilled he was said to be able to simultaneously write two letters of the alphabet with one hand. Omeriah Malcolm became what was known as a 'myalman', a healer, and his understanding included the natural medicine and power in the individual plants, such as Leaf of Life and Sinkle Bible, that flourish in the blessed land of Jamaica. When Cedella grew older her father would confide in her about the many powerful spirits lodged in the neighbourhood of Nine Miles. It had always been so, he would say, puzzling why, in this case, so many people there were ready to surrender themselves to the dark forces; why it would always be said that the place was a small garden where a bitter weed grew.

Ten years later, when Cedella Malcolm was pregnant with her son Nesta, her father or her grandmother would show her which herbs to take to ease any potential problems in the pregnancy; which blend of bush tea would ease high blood pressure or back-ache; which bush was the best cleanser for the coming baby's skin. Her father, in fact, was more nervous about this imminent birth than his daughter. He would scold her: 'You runnin' around hearty, but you sicker than the rest of your sisters.' 'Always remember,' he would add, 'you are between life and death until you give birth to that baby' – a piece of Jamaican folk wisdom that never failed to unnerve his daughter.

'Take up your doctor book and read it,' he would say. 'But I was young. I didn't know any better. I was happy, everything was lovely. The pregnancy was great.' Cedella would even find it within her to ignore those malicious souls in the neighbourhood who cursed her as she passed, angry at her for having taken up with a white man.

Two years previously Captain Norval Marley, a white Jamaican, had proudly ridden into Nine Miles on his horse. The man was employed by the colonial government: he was involved in yet another attempt by the authorities to persuade locals to farm or even to settle in Jamaica's vast acres of uncultivated bush, the region around Nine Miles being this man Marley's particular terrain. At first he boarded in Yaya's Big House. Then one day he asked Omeriah if he could oversee the building of a small house for him to stay in: Omeriah complied, knocking up a wooden shack in a weekend.

It was in this little house that Captain Marley, a fifty-year-old man, began an affair with the foolish girl, then only seventeen: he would joke about how their destinies were linked because of the way both their surnames began with the letters MA. The relationship had an unexpected consequence by the standards of Jamaican society at that time: Cedella was married to Captain Marley on a Friday in June 1944, not long after they had learned of her pregnancy; the following day he left Nine Miles for Kingston, having bestowed legitimacy on his unborn child. Cedella was surprised, but her youthful innocence protected her from grief. Norval Marley had explained, after all, that he was ill and needed to have an operation – his long days in the saddle had caused a hernia to develop. This was the reason for his move back to Kingston: for the sake of his health he was taking another, more humble job, as an overseer of the bridges being built to carry water into Kingston.

The pregnancy was problem-free. On the first Sunday of February 1945, Cedella Marley, as she was now called, went to church as usual. The next day she hoped to fast, rejoice and give testimony in the church in the evening, as Elder Thomas encouraged his flock to do each Monday. But Cedella's pregnancy appeared to have run its allotted time and, feeling the first twinges of labour, she stayed behind at one of her father's properties, a vacant shop, where she had set up her bedroom. The next morning Auntie Missus, as they called the great-aunt who doubled as local midwife, was called to Ciddy, who was now in considerable pain. Auntie Missus pointed at pictures of pretty women from magazines that Cedella had pasted up on her bedroom wall. 'All these women go through the same thing,' she reminded her. Auntie Missus had brought food – some yam, some sweet potato, some rice. But now the contractions were coming more powerfully, and Ciddy had to time each mouthful in between them.

The baby boy was born at around 2.30 in the morning of Wednesday, 6 February 1945. He weighed seven pounds four ounces, and the name he was given was Nesta Robert Marley, the Robert at the request of Norval, whose brother had the same name. The afterbirth was taken and buried at the foot of one of Omeriah's coconut trees. The child had been conceived in Yaya's Big House, and after the birth Cedella returned there to live with him.

Nesta was a healthy child. Running on the rock stone, 'him not have no time fe sick'. As he

started to grow bigger, Cedella would feel a twinge of sadness from time to time that she didn't hear more regularly from his father. Some help, some support, would have been nice, that was all. Even when he sent money – for a time four or five pounds would come most months – the envelope would be addressed to her father. As time went by, the money supply began to dwindle until Cedella scarcely ever heard from her husband.

Still, Nesta was happy. They would always say that Bob loved to eat, and the boy was

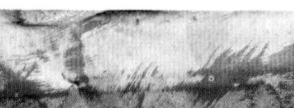

especially fond of his uncle Titus, who lived up by Yaya and who always had plenty of surplus banana leaf or calaloo cooking on his stove. For a long time Nesta's eyes were bigger than his stomach: it became a joke in the area how he would take up a piece of yam, swallow the first piece and almost immediately fall asleep: one piece just fill up his belly straight away.

Early on there were signs that the child had been born with a poet's understanding of life, an asset in a land like Jamaica where a kind of magic realism is almost commonplace. When he was around four or five, Cedella would hear stories from relatives and neighbours about how Nesta had claimed to read their palms, but she took them for a joke. How could this little boy of hers possibly do something like that? But she felt slightly shaken when she first heard that Nesta's predictions about people's futures had come true. There was District Constable Black from Stern Hill, for example: he told Cedella how the child had read his hand and everything he said had come to pass. Then another woman confirmed this, forcing his mother to accept this strange talent her son possessed.

If Nesta perceived what was to be the pattern of his own life, he never told his mother. When he was almost five, however, Omeriah received an unexpected visit from Norval Marley. What Cedella should do, he suggested, was give up Nesta for adoption by Norval's brother, Robert. She should also guarantee not to see the boy any more. 'It's like he wouldn't be my child no more! I said, "No way."'

Norval came out to Nine Miles on another visit. He had had another idea: what if Bob was to come and stay with him in Kingston for a time? He would pay for his education and provide him with all the opportunities available to his own large, affluent family – Marley and Co., also known as Marley and Plant, was Jamaica's largest plant-hire company.

Cedella could see the advantages for her son in this. She felt she could go along with the plan. Nesta was duly delivered to her husband in Kingston. Hardly had the boy arrived, however, when he was taken downtown, to the house of a woman called Mrs Grey. Norval Marley left his son with her, promising to return shortly. He never did.

All communication was then broken with the Malcolm family at Nine Miles. Cedella was deeply worried, fearing her son had been stolen from her – as indeed he had. After almost a year, however, when Cedella had moved to Stepney, a village two or three miles past Nine Miles, a woman friend of her's went to Kingston to see her niece. The woman and the niece were on Spanish Town Road when they ran straight into Nesta. 'Ask my mother,' the boy said, 'why she don't come look for me.' And he told the woman his address.

When Cedella's friend returned to Stepney that night, she reported all that had happened. Nesta looked healthy and happy, she told Cedella. A colossal sense of relief came over Cedella. But there was one problem: her friend had not had a pen or pencil with her. She had forgotten the address where Nesta was living.

A solution was suggested: that Merle, the niece, might remember the address. Cedella wrote to her, and Merle replied straight away that, although she couldn't remember the number of the building, she knew Nesta was living on Heywood Street, in a poor downtown neighbourhood. If Cedella came up to Kingston, Merle added, she would help her look for the missing child.

Accompanied by another friend from Nine Miles, Cedella arrived in Kingston one evening. Meeting Merle as arranged, Cedella discovered Heywood Street off Orange Street, filled with stores. All these businesses were closed, but

MRS CEDELLA BOOKER; AS CEDELLA MARLEY SHE GAVE BIRTH TO A SON, ROBERT NESTA MARLEY, ON 6 FEBRUARY 1945.

outside the first building that she came to, Cedella saw a man sitting on the sidewalk. 'I asked him,' she said, using the name by which her son's father called him, 'if he knew a little boy who lived round there by the name of Robert Marley.'

'Yeah, mon,' came the reply. 'He was jus' here a minute ago.'

Following the man's eyes, she suddenly spotted her son. 'There he was, just on the corner, playing. Nesta just bust right round: when he see it was me him just ran and hugged me so. And he say, "Mummy, you fatty!" I say, "Where you live?" He was very brisk, very bright. He say, "Right here. Her name is Mrs Grey: come and I'll introduce you to her."'

Mrs Grey was a heavy-set woman. She did not look at all well: she had lost almost all of her hair, and the skin peeled away in thin scales from both sides of her hands, one of the symptoms of 'sugar', as diabetes is known in Jamaica; Mrs Grey also suffered from chronic high blood pressure. Nesta, she told Cedella, had been her strength and guide, running errands for her, going to the market to fetch coal, as he had been on the day he was seen on Spanish Town Road. He was going to school, Cedella discovered, though somewhat irregularly, it appeared. Norval Marley, said Mrs Grey, had brought Nesta to her; but from the moment he left he had never once returned. All the while, Mrs Grey continued, she would find herself looking at Nesta and wondering, 'What happen to your mother? How is it that your mother never come to see you?'

'I told her that I had to take him. And you could see how much she love him. She said she was going to miss him because he's her right hand, he do any little thing for her. But she know

that he have to leave. Then Nesta and I just go home. And we come back and everybody was glad to see him at his school, everybody.'

Once Nesta was back at school he started to become very thin, suffering an inexplicable weight loss. On his teacher's advice, Cedella began to feed the boy a daily diet of goat's milk. Whether it was the additional food supplement, or merely the healthier life he was living, he soon began not only to recover but also to grow stronger and tougher.

That was the only occasion on which Cedella could remember sickness coming near her son. Not long after he returned to Nine Miles, however, Nesta suffered a physical injury, perhaps a portent of a future problem: running along the road one day, he stepped on some splinters of broken glass with his right foot. At first not all the glass could be dug out from the sole, hard and tough from years of barefoot walking. Then the wound would not heal. Tears would well up in Cedella's eyes as she watched her young son hobble up the rocky path to Yaya's, trying to place his weight on the side of his foot. Eventually, Nathan, Cedella's cousin, baked a poultice, and the foot finally healed.

One more event of significance occurred around this time. When a woman asked him to read her hand, the boy shook his head. 'No,' said Nesta, 'I'm not reading no more hand: I'm singing now.'

'He had these two little sticks,' Cedella recalls. 'He started knocking them with his fists in this rhythmical way and singing this old Jamaican song:

"Hey Mr, don't you touch me tomato
Touch me yam, pumpkin, potato
All you do is feel up, feel up
Ain't you tired of squeeze up, squeeze up
Hey Mr, don't you touch me tomato
Touch me yam, pumpkin, potato."

'And it just made the woman feel so good, and she gave him two or three pennies. That was the first time he talked about music.'

During this period Nesta was a pupil at the Stepney All Age School, where he had first been enrolled when he was four, before going to

Kingston. Now that she had brought him back, Cedella continued to live in Stepney. She set up a small grocery shop there, carrying the mortar and grout, and building most of it herself. Its stock was never more than the local people required: bread, flour, rice, soft drinks, which she used to go and collect on a donkey. One day as she was walking along the road, the donkey's rope held loosely in her hand, the animal reared up on its hind-legs and ran down a hill, mashing up all the bottles it was carrying. Cedella cried and cried, and was only somewhat placated when people who had witnessed the incident assured her they had also seen the cause of it: a spirit that had come from Murray Mountain to frighten the beast. But it set Cedella thinking: wasn't there an easier way of ensuring some small measure of prosperity for her and her pickney?

There was another new grocery shop in the area, owned by a man from Kingston called Mr Thaddius 'Toddy' Livingston. He had a son named Neville, who had been born on 23 April 1947. Like Nesta, Bunny, as Neville was more generally known, was a pupil at Stepney All Age School, and he and Bob became friends. Cedella remained only on nodding acquaintanceship with her business rival, Mr Toddy, who after a while sold up his business and moved back to Kingston.

Soon Cedella made a similar decision, and a relative bought the shop from her.

Cedella was now in her mid-twenties and was becoming restless. Although she deeply loved her son, she felt her life was slipping away in Nine Miles. More and more, she had been travelling to Kingston, taking jobs as a domestic help and leaving Nesta in the care of her father, Omeriah, who cherished the boy and was happy to look after him. Inevitably, Nesta began to learn from his grandfather's arcane wisdom. Another relative, Clarence Malcolm, who had been a celebrated Jamaican guitarist, playing in dance-halls during the 1940s, would also spend time with the boy, letting him get the feel of his guitar. He was delighted when Nesta won a pound for singing in a local talent contest held at Fig Tree Corner. So began a pattern of older wise

Cedella Booker: 'How he do things and prophesy things, he is not just by himself – he have higher powers, even from when he is a little boy. The way I felt, the kind of vibes I get when Bob comes around . . . It's too honourable. I always look upon him with great respect: there is something inside telling me that he is not only a son – there is something greater in this man. Bob is of a small stature, but when I hear him talk, he talk big. When it comes to the feelings and reactions I get from Bob, it was always too spiritual to even mention or talk about. Even from when he was a small child coming up.'

men taking a mentor-like role in the life of the essentially fatherless Nesta Robert Marley; this was something that would continue throughout his life.

From Nine Miles Nesta would walk the two and a half miles to school at Stepney, dressed in the freshly pressed khaki shirt and pants that comprise the school uniform of Jamaican boys. The journey was not considered excessive – some children walked to the school from as far as Prickle Pole, seven miles away.

When he was ten, Nesta had a teacher called Clarice Bushay; she taught most subjects to the sixty or so children in her overcrowded but well-disciplined class, divided only by a blackboard from the four or five other classes in the vast hall that formed the school. Away from his family circle, Nesta did not reveal the same cheerful countenance, although his wry and knowing smile was still in evidence.

Hidden behind a mask of timidity, his potential was not immediately apparent to Miss Bushay, but as soon as she realised that this particular pupil required constant reassurance, she saw he began to blossom. 'As he was shy, if he wasn't certain he was right, he wouldn't always try. In fact, he hated to get answers wrong, so sometimes you'd really have to draw the answer out of him. And then give him a clap – he liked that, the attention.'

Nevertheless, she felt she should moderate the amount of attention she gave him. 'Because he was light-skin, other children would become jealous of him getting so much of my time. I imagined he must have been very much a mother's pet, because he would only do well if you gave him large amounts of attention. But it was obvious he had a lot of potential.'

Even then, Nesta was involved in extra-curricular interests. After running down to the food vendors by the school gates at lunch-time to buy fried dumplings or banana or fish fritters and lemonade, he would play football – with oranges or grapefruits used as balls – and make music for the rest of the break. But he sang so softly – a further sign of a lack of self-confidence – that his fine alto voice could scarcely be heard. Yet of all the children who attempted to construct guitars from sardine tins and bamboo, it would always be Nesta who contrived to have the best sound. 'He was very enterprising: you had to commend him on the guitars he made.'

He was a popular boy, with lots of friends; very loving, but clearly needing to receive love, too. 'When he came by you to your desk,' Miss Bushay noted, 'you knew he just wanted to be touched and held; he was really quite soft. It seemed like a natural thing with him – what he was used to.' An obedient pupil, he deeply resented the occasion when he and the other children from Nine Miles were flogged by the principal for their consistent late arrival at school; after the beating, falling back on his grandfather's secret world, he was heard muttering dark threats about the power of a cowrie shell he possessed and what he planned to do with it to the principal.

Maths was Nesta's best subject, while his exceptional memory also meant he excelled in General Knowledge. Still, Miss Bushay would have to encourage him to open reading books: for although he would get through all his set texts, he wouldn't borrow further volumes. 'He seemed to spend more time with this football business.'

For a time Nesta stayed with his aunt Amy, who lived in the hamlet of Alderton, some eight miles from Ocho Rios. By all accounts the woman was something of a slave-driver, a strict disciplinarian even by Jamaica's harsh standards. Nesta would be woken at five in the morning to do yard work. He also had to milk the goats and walk miles for fresh water before he went to the nearby school. The only respite from his chores was his friendship with his cousin Sledgo; the pair rebelled together against Amy's regime, and were considered by her to be troublemakers.

One Sunday evening when Cedella was about to set off back to Kingston after a weekend with her family, she got a lift with Toddy Livingston, who had been visiting friends in Nine Miles. It was the first occasion they had spent any time together, and there was a strong mutual attraction. On their return to Kingston they started dating and, notwithstanding Toddy's married status, became lovers.

TRENCH TOWN

In 1957, when Nesta was twelve, Cedella decided that it was time for her son to come and live with her in Kingston. This hardly displeased the boy, who was unhappy living with his aunt. Although the Jamaican capital was a very different world from the rural runnings to which he had become accustomed, Nesta had at least experienced city life when his father had whisked him off to Kingston. At the corner of Beckford Street and Charles Street, near the terminus for buses from the country, his mother had rented an upstairs room from a property-owning family called Faulkner. Living there, however, meant that Nesta's education suffered: there were no good schools in the neighbourhood. The same problem arose at other downtown addresses where Cedella and her son briefly stayed: in Barrett Street, Oxford Street and Regent Street.

Accordingly, Cedella made the decision that Nesta should be privately educated, enrolling him for a time at Ebenezer School, a small establishment on Darling Street. The teacher here adored him. 'Where's Nesta?' she would ask as soon as she arrived in the morning. The boy was now beginning to show an interest in reading – as long as it was linked to his copious knowledge of the Bible, the one text which most Jamaicans know intimately.

Although the school fees were inexpensive – partially a reflection of the education the school provided – Cedella had to hustle and scrape to find the thirty shillings for each term's fees. 'But I never have to beg nobody or borrow from nobody. I could pay his fee, then save again to buy his shoes. I can't remember a time when I was so badly off that I couldn't find food for him. And he was not a child that demand this and demand that. Never have no problem with him: always obedient, would listen to me. Sometimes he get a little mad with me, but it never last fe time.'

Despite the 'lost' year Nesta had spent in

Kingston, he was at first disoriented by being back in the capital. He did, at least, have the comfort of his close friend Bunny, who was living not too far away. With an urgent need for expression, Bunny's soul was also drawn instinctively to music. Down on Russell Road, where Bunny lived with his parents, Bob could be seen with his little home-made guitar, trying to work up a tune with his friend. 'Bob wrote little songs, and then he and Bunny would sing them,' Cedella remembered. 'Sometimes I'd teach him a tune like "I'm Going to Lay My Sins Down at the Riverside."'

Meanwhile, Cedella was becoming more and more involved with Bunny's father, who would frequently come by and visit her, particularly when Nesta was staying elsewhere, which was not infrequent now. Her son's secondary education was becoming a problem, especially since Cedella had moved to the new housing scheme of Trench Town, and had decided that he should return to state education: the schools in this downtown, impoverished area of west Kingston were particularly rough. So, for a while Cedella lodged her son at her brother's home further uptown, so that he could qualify for a better school up by Maxfield Avenue. This served a dual purpose: her brother's girlfriend was also able to care for Nesta and keep an eye on him when he came home at the end of the school day. Sometimes Cedella picked him up in the evenings and took him down to Trench Town or, if she was working in the neighbourhood, she would stay over at her brother's. Still, it wasn't an easy life for either of them.

To all intents and purposes, Cedella was the mistress of Toddy, who was running a rum bar near the bus terminus, and working on odd construction projects during the day. But quirks of Toddy's personality, particularly his quarrelsome nature, meant that it was not an easy love affair. His jealousy had created an unpleasant tension almost from the start: he would only have to hear that Cedella had talked

'Me only have one ambition, y'know. I only have one thing I really like to see happen. I like to see mankind live together – black, white, Chinese, everyone – that's all.'

to another man and he would be ready to box him down. 'When a man is married they are always jealous of the woman they are with more than their own wife, because they know another man might come and take them. And that's how he was handling me. I would get frustrated and upset.'

The liaison, which for Cedella was beginning to take on the features of a classic love-hate relationship, could only get worse. Nesta, who had already suffered pain and loss in his life, would often come in to find his mother crying at the kitchen table, and would attempt to console her.

Meanwhile, Cedella would throw herself on the Lord's mercy: 'I would pray and wouldn't stop praying and asking God to take me out of that man's hands.'

Cedella moved to 19 Second Street in Trench Town, so called because it had been built over a ditch that drained the city's sewage. She took over the downstairs one-room apartment from her elder brother Solomon who was about to emigrate to England; the rent was twelve shillings a month.

Trench Town was a housing scheme, built after the 1951 hurricane had destroyed the area's squatter camps. These camps, which had gradually grown up around west Kingston, had been built around the former Kingston refuse dump, where the country folk and displaced city-dwellers would scavenge for whatever they could find. In the days of the 'plantocracy business', the area had been a sugar plantation, owned by the Lindos, one of the twenty-one families that are said to rule Jamaica.

Originally west Kingston had been a simple fishing village. The fishing beach of Greenwich Farm was only a short walk away, providing a source of nutrition or income for anyone with a hook and line; and if you had the nous to lash driftwood together into a raft, so much the better. Those who became fishermen were also granted an honourable, respected role in the community – fishing, after all, had archetypal associations with Jesus and his disciples.

Trench Town was in the hottest part of Kingston, almost untouched by the breezes from the Blue Mountains that swept through to cool the city's more northerly, uptown reaches. However, Trench Town was considered desirable accommodation for the slum and shanty-town dwellers who lived there. The 'government yards' comprised solidly constructed one- or two-storey concrete units, built around a central courtyard which contained communal cooking facilities and a stand-pipe for water. Few were so ungrateful as to complain that Jamaica's colonial masters had seen fit to build Trench Town without any form of sewerage system.

Alton Ellis, later to become one of Jamaica's·most mellifluous – and, during the 1960s, most successful – vocalists, moved to the area as soon as the first stage of building the government yards had been completed: work had begun at Fifth Street and progressed to Seventh Street, before the overgrown area known as the Dungle was cleared to make way for the construction of the first four streets. Ellis recalls how Trench Town soon became renowned as a haven for outlaw rejects, a reputation that later became well deserved. At the same time, Ellis and others also remember it as a 'peaceful, loving place': 'When I went there, it was a new scheme, government built for poor people.' Each apartment within the individual complexes had two bedrooms; in the communal yard would be four toilets and bathrooms; by each gate a mango or pawpaw tree was planted. 'But even though the place was nice, the poverty still existed. The poverty was so strong that you know what that lead to.'

Near to Trench Town, in Jones Town, lived Ernest Ranglin, a professional jazz guitarist influenced by musicians such as Charlie Christian and Django Reinhardt; originally from a hamlet called Harry Watch in Manchester, Ranglin had been a teenage prodigy, soon employed by the likes of Eric Dean and Val Bennett, who ran big, swinging dancehall bands in the American style; Ranglin had shared the stage in Dean's orchestra with another of Jamaica's musical maestros, Don Drummond, who would later be considered one of the world's top jazz trombonists. Hired by JBC Radio from 1958 as their staff guitar-player, Ranglin

NOTICE
OPEN

SUN. 21st
SAT. 7th AUG. 1973
MUSICALLY YOURS...
SUPER "T"
OPERATION

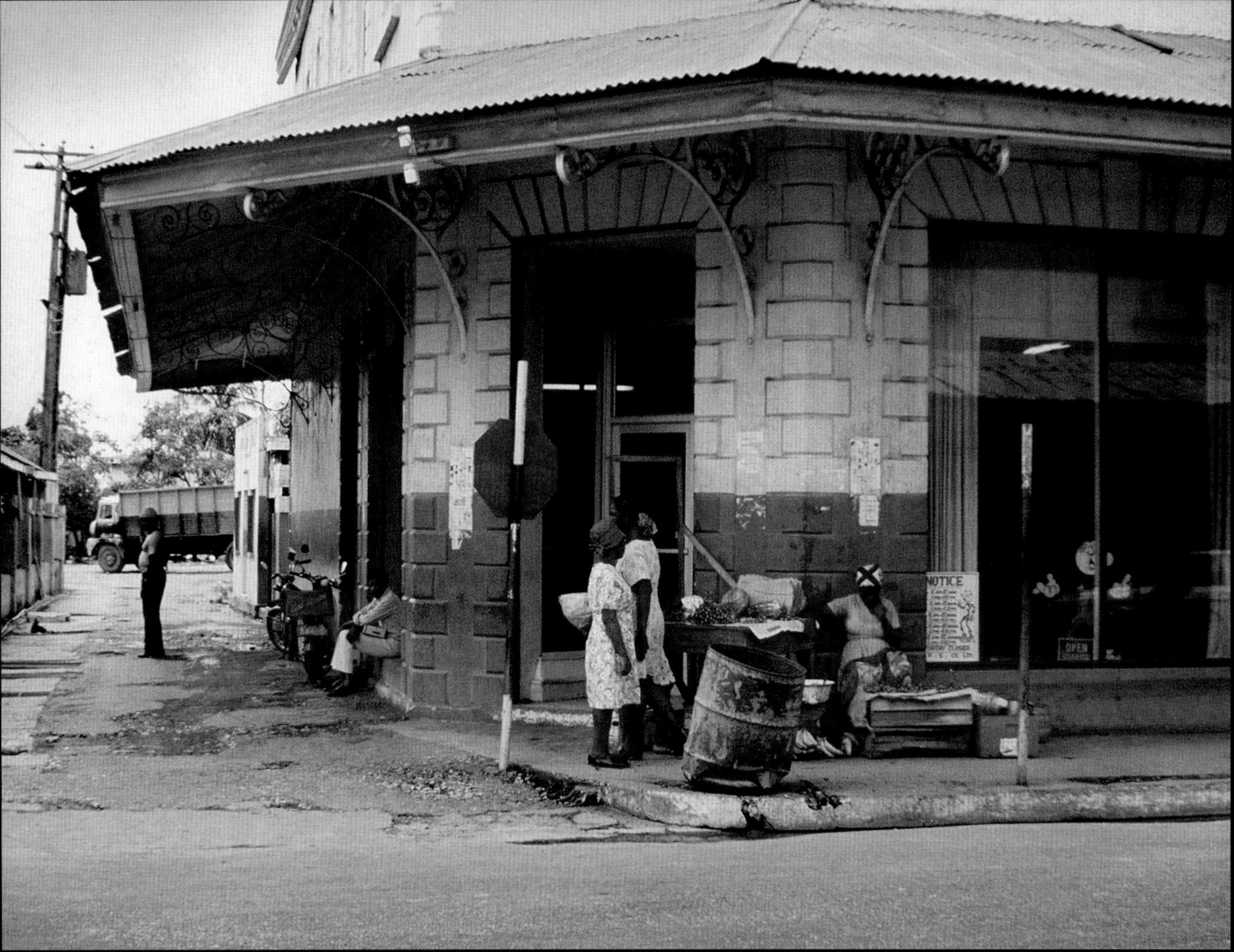

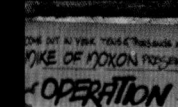

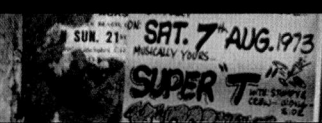

was similarly regarded as the Jamaican master of his particular instrument. He would frequently find himself in Trench Town, sometimes playing cricket with the local youth, including the Marley boy. 'Really, it was still a nice area. And even the parts that weren't, those kids didn't notice: when you're a child you only see the good things.'

Even before the 1951 hurricane had mashed down the zinc-and-packing-case residences of the shanty town, the region was already considered as an area for outcasts. In particular, Trench Town had now become the main home in Kingston for the strange tribe of men known as Rastafarians, who had set up an encampment down by the Dungle in the early years of World War II. Garlanded in acres of matted, plaited hair, these primal figures, permanently surrounded by the funky aroma of marijuana, could appear as archetypal as a West African baobab tree. It all depended on your point of view and upbringing. Mortimer Planner, for example, considered sufficiently elevated in the Rastafarian brethren to meet His Imperial Majesty Haile Selassie I, had first moved to the area in 1939. A very simple reason, he said, had drawn him there – the energy emanating from this part of Kingston: 'Trench Town is a spiritual powerpoint'.

Yet others in the area were not at all happy about the presence of these men with their curious belief that Haile Selassie was God. Why would a young woman called Rita Anderson, a worshipful member of the Church of God, go out of her way to avoid them? Her parents had told her the truth: that Rastafarians lived in the drainage gullies and carried parts of people they had murdered in their bags. No doubt it was such thinking that resulted in the sporadic round-ups of Rastas by the police, who would shove them into their trucks and cut off their locks.

As yet, young Nesta Marley knew almost nothing about the Rastas' religion. He was simply getting through his schooldays, perhaps in a more perfunctory manner than his mother realised. Later he would come to realise that his secondary education had been almost non-existent. With no permanent male role model to act as a guide, the transition from childhood to adolescence was even more awkward for Nesta than for most teenagers.

There were too many unanswered questions, not least those surrounding his parenthood. Why did he never see his father? Why had he been cursed with light skin, a clear indication of white blood flowing in his veins. (This became the taunt of boys jealous of his talents, especially football, at which he excelled.) So much moving around from place to place, from home to home . . . As Nesta roamed around Kingston, often playing truant, he would sometimes find himself in the area where he had spent time that year in the capital; and at those times he would feel an inexplicable chill run through him. There was a sense of unease within him, a fear of opening himself to others. No wonder he could appear timid one moment, and then take on the screwface façade of the ghetto youth the next. As he grew older he seemed to wear a more or less permanent frown.

Rita Marley: 'Sometimes he'd come across the resistance of being half-caste. There was a problem with his counterparts: having come through this white father caused such difficulties that he'd want to kill himself and thinking, "Why am I this person? Why is my father white and not black like everybody else? What did I do wrong?"

'He was lost in that: not being able to have anyone to say it's not your fault, or that there's nothing wrong in being like you are. But that was the atmosphere he came up in, that Trench Town environment where everybody is rough. He had to show them that although he didn't know his father, at least he knew there was a God and he knew what he was feeling.

'Bob had to put up with a lot of resistance. If he wasn't that strong in himself he wouldn't be what he became today. He would be down-trodden and seen as another half-caste who would never make it.'

RASTAFARI

The source of Rastafarianism lies in a specific geographical area, the Nile valley, a huge region that includes Egypt in the north and Ethiopia in the south. The philosophy at the heart of Rastafari is gathered from the soul of this part of Africa. For example, it acknowledges Ra, revered by the Egyptians as the god of the sun, as a life-giving force, and accepts that mankind is not separate or different from God, or Jah, an abbreviation for Jehovah.

Rastafari believes that within man there are three different levels: the animal stage, where he is controlled by his passions; a second stage, where he has recognised and is governed by his will to command his emotions; and the third stage where he is able to commune peacefully with the inner depths of his being: such an individual is considered a 'Godman', and only such a person is capable of sitting on a throne.

If mankind's origins are traced back to the Lake region of Africa, then the migration system across the African continent shows how these ideas were carried. To this day such thinking exists up and down Africa, within various families who have commanded their animal instincts and followed the path.

The notion of the shaman derived from this spiritual well-spring. Essentially it meant one thing: God Is Love. There was a more than acceptable logic at work here: love makes life so much easier than hate.

At the heart of Rastafari lie the Egyptian mysteries, the sort that may be found in *The Egyptian Book of the Dead*. The elements of Judaism within Rastafari are themselves an offspring of Egyptian mysticism. This became institutionalised by Moses; when adopted by the High Priest's daughter in Egypt, he was taught the principles of Osiris, Isis and other Egyptian gods. For his final initiation he travelled to Ethiopia. The source of Judaism was the teaching of Moses. As tradition has it, Moses was author of the first five books of the Bible (the sixth and seventh books of Moses are considered to be too complex for the common man to comprehend; there is a famous obeah textbook entitled *The Sixth and Seventh Book of Moses*).

In the time of King Solomon, Queen Makeba ruled over the empire of Sheba, which consisted of Ethiopia, Egypt and parts of Persia.

The Queen's visit to the wealthy and wise Solomon in Jerusalem had been planned for many years. In Jerusalem, Solomon converted her to the God of Abraham; she had until then worshipped the sun in the person of Ra the sun-god. When she returned to her land, Queen Makeba changed the religion of her empire to Judaism.

On her return, Makeba was pregnant by Solomon; she had promised him that if she bore a son she would send the boy to Jerusalem for instruction by his father. Accordingly, her son Menelik journeyed, as a young man, to meet Solomon, having sworn to his mother that as heir and successor to the kingdom he would return to Ethiopia.

When Menelik was leaving Jerusalem, King Solomon saw to it that he was accompanied by the sons of his priests: he wanted to ensure that the religion of Abraham would continue in Ethiopia. As a result, this religion existed there in an undiluted form.

During the time of Christianity, however, Paul the Apostle converted an Ethiopian eunuch to Christianity. This eunuch was a high-placed, respected rabbi of orthodox Judaism. When he returned to Ethiopia, he in turn converted the country to Christianity.

So began the Ethiopian Orthodox Church, a pure form of Christianity that kept its connection with its Judaic and Egyptian pasts, all elements within

An official family portrait of His Imperial Majesty Haile Selassie I, his wife and two sons.

Rastafarianism. This church had considerable influence on the 225th king (descended directly from King David, who, in turn, was descended from Moses). This member of Ethiopian royalty was Ras Tafari, Emperor Haile Selassie I. Before his visit to Jamaica on 21 April 1966, Haile Selassie, which means Power of the Trinity, had already established the Ethiopian Orthodox Church there, in answer to a request from the island's Rastafarians.

In order to become Emperor of Ethiopia, His Imperial Majesty Haile Selassie I had had to rise above squabbling and infighting. For centuries Ethiopia had been divided by warrior barons whose only allegiance was to themselves. Attempting to turn Ethiopia into a modern nation by importing Western expertise, Haile Selassie set about bringing unity to his country.

Rastafarianism, as it has been practised in Jamaica since around 1930, is a rejuvenation of this very ancient religion. Rastafarians acknowledge that their religion is the blending of the purest forms of both Judaism and Christianity; they also accept the Egyptian origins of both these religions. In affirming the divinity of Haile Selassie, their religion rejects the Babylonian hypocrisy of the modern church. The church of Rome, and even the council of Rome, are considered to be particularly Babylonian: was it not from this city that Mussolini invaded the holy land of Ethiopia in 1935? Religions always reflect the social and geographical environment out of which they emerge, and Jamaican

Rastafarianism is no exception: for example, the use of marijuana as a sacrament and aid to meditation is logical in a country where a particularly potent strain of 'herb' grows freely.

According to Mortimer Planner, the honoured Rastafarian elder who greeted Haile Selassie, the destiny and purpose of the religion were certainly known by certain select Jamaicans at the beginning of the twentieth century, if not before. The Egyptian Masonic order known as the Great Ancient Brotherhood of Silence may have played a part in this, but so did the Jamaicans' habit of assiduously studying and reasoning about the Bible, a book which, as any Rastafarian can tell you, will take three and half years to complete from Genesis to Revelations if you read a chapter a day.

Jamaica's followers of Rastafarianism are aware that we are living in the last days of the present global order. Only the righteous will move forward through the apocalypse into the new era; only those who have battled to save the world from the perpetrators of the Babylonian greed and destruction that are all around, will flourish.

In the 1920s Marcus Garvey, the colourful prophet of black self-determination, added his rhetoric to the argument. Garvey, who had been born in St Ann in 1887 and founded the United Negro Improvement Association, spoke to an audience at Madison Square Garden in New York of 'Ethiopia, land of our fathers', and proclaimed that 'negroes' believed in 'the God of Ethiopia, the everlasting God'. Most significantly, he announced, 'Look to Africa for the crowning of a Black King; He shall be the Redeemer.' (Later there

'*Marcus Garvey was a prophet, mon. He tell that we must look to the east, to a king. A lot of things Marcus Garvey say, and a lot of it come to pass. Some still heed, and everyone see it. I mean, it get you more stronger, in reality. And everyone see it happening. Well plain.*'

was some debate about this: was it Garvey who said these words? An associate of his, the Reverend James Morris Webb, the author of *A Black Man will be the Coming Universal King, Proven by Biblical History*, had spoken to the same effect at a meeting in 1924.)

In 1930 Ras Tafari Makonnen, great-grandson of King Saheka Selassie of Shoa, was crowned Emperor of Ethiopia and given the name of Haile Selassie, King of Kings, Lord of Lords, Conquering Lion of the Tribe of Judah. Garvey's prophecy had surely been fulfilled. Even more so, the prediction of Revelations 5 had now come into being: 'See, the Lion of the Tribe of Judah, the Root of David, has triumphed. He is able to open the scroll and its seven seals.'

In Jamaica, as elsewhere in the world, the 1930s were years of social upheaval. Labour unrest on the island culminated in the vicious suppression of striking sugar-cane workers in Westmoreland: four strikers were shot dead, and dozens rounded up and jailed, including Alexander Bustamente, the leader of the new Jamaican labour movement.

It was a perfect context for the rise of a band of islanders who had divorced themselves mentally from an oppressive social system. This cult, Rastafarianism, thus became cast as a religion of the dispossessed among those who failed to acknowledge the intellectual rigour of many practitioners (the depth of Biblical and historical knowledge displayed at a

Rastafarian reasoning is intense).

In the hills of eastern Jamaica, Rastafarian encampments sprang up; a life of asceticism and artistry became the armour of the religion's followers against Babylon. Leonard Howell, one of the island's chief propagators of the religion, founded the Pinnacle encampment in an abandoned estate between Kingston and Spanish Town. Eventually taking thirteen wives, Howell finally decided that it was not Haile Selassie who was Jah but himself. In 1954 he was thrown into a mental home, and Pinnacle was closed down. The dreads, as Rastafarians became known colloquially, spilled out into the ghettoes of west Kingston.

Around the time of independence in 1962, there were a number of violent incidents involving fire-arms between Rastas and the police, making headlines in the *Daily Gleaner*. The movement was now travelling with the speed of a bush-fire into the popular psyche of Jamaica.

But it took the unceasing efforts of one man who had grown up in Kingston, hearing the orations of dreads in the Dungle and Back a Wall, to popularise the apparently crazy idea that the emperor of Ethiopia could be the living Deity.

That man, of course, was Bob Marley. Many of his brethren in the Rastafari faith felt that this was why he had been blessed with this talent. Others believed that Bob Marley was capable of such a task because of his spiritual closeness to His Majesty himself, on whose right-hand side he deserved to sit.

In the late 1950s there was a growing undercurrent of opportunism in Jamaica: people were redefining themselves, working out who they were with a new confidence. The guilty, repressive hold of the British colonialists was becoming increasingly uncertain; already there were whispers of independence being granted to the island. A new era was beginning.

This sense of optimism was reflected in the music. Jamaicans had developed a taste for American popular music when US troops were based on the island during World War II. During the late 1940s a number of big bands were formed, including those of Eric Dean, who employed both Don Drummond and Ernest Ranglin, and Val Bennett, for example. Audiences would dance until dawn to tunes they drew on from American artists like Count Basie, Duke Ellington and Glenn Miller.

By 1950 the big bands in the USA were being superseded by newer outfits: the feisty, optimistic new sounds of bop and rhythm and blues. 'Since 1945,' says Steve Barrow, the British expert on Jamaican music, 'Jamaica has adopted and adapted American popular music forms – swing, bebop, R&B and soul – making them serve its own ends.'

There had always been a large traffic of Jamaicans to the United States, a country always eager – as was the United Kingdom for fresh supplies of manual workers to undertake the jobs its more successful citizens disdained. Ambitious, musically inclined Jamaicans would return from the USA with piles of the hottest, most underground 78s; to conceal the tunes' identities, the labels would be scratched off before they were used by sound systems. Sound systems were like portable discos for giants: they would consist of up to thirty or forty speakers, each as large as about six tea-chests stuck together, and linked by a vast network of cables. Through these the music would thud at spine-breaking volume, interspersed with eccentric comments from the disc jockeys spinning the records. (Disc jockeys bore little resemblance to the British or American understanding of the term: these people were performers who would extemporise on rhythm about anything, from current issues to topics of a highly sexually charged nature.)

The sound-system dances took over Jamaica. Few people owned radios and the only way to hear the latest rhythm and blues was to go to the big outdoor dances held at 'lawns' in locations like Chocomo on Wellington Street and Jubilee on King Street. Setting up in 1950, Tom the Great Sebastian was the first significant sound-system operator. Many believe Tom the Great Sebastian was the all-time giant of sound systems. 'He is the man,' said Prince Buster, who later ran his own system and became one of Jamaica's most innovative musicians. Goodies, Count Smith the Blues Blaster, Count Joe and Sir Nick the Champ were among the other leading contenders, but they never triumphed over Tom the Great Sebastian. This would be apparent at the dances, billed as sound system battles, in which two or more systems would compete, each playing a record in turn: Tom, with his unique tunes straight

off the plane from the USA, the originality of his DJ-ing and the sheer power of his equipment, would inevitably mash up the opposition.

Although there was clearly an ironical purpose in the adoption of such aristocratic titles, it was also the only way non-white Jamaicans could possibly hope to aspire to such heights. Duke Reid the Trojan's nickname came from the Bedford Trojan truck he used to transport his equipment. His wife had previously won the national lottery, which enabled them to open the Treasure Isle liquor store and provide the financing for his battery of equipment.

Reid was a particularly contentious figure. Sporting a trio of revolvers in his belt, from which he would indiscriminately fire shots, he was more inclined to destroy the opposition through violence than talent. Having set up a couple of years after Tom the Great Sebastian,

much of the gangland-like behaviour that later became a feature of the Jamaican music business can be attributed to Duke Reid. Ironically, his former occupation as a policeman placed him in close contact with many of the tough characters he would use to threaten the competition – instead of mashing up the sound-system opposition by playing the heaviest, loudest tunes, he would simply charge into rival dances with his gang, beating up or stabbing people and destroying their equipment. And if that didn't work, he could always resort to a spot of obeah. Reid would even have gangs of tough, sexy women, all dressed in the same uniforms, and controlled by a female lieutenant called Duddah, at dances. But he also had tons of boxes, tons of 'house of joy', as sound-system speakers were referred to.

This was a world in which Tom the Great Sebastian desired to play no part. He packed up his sound system and moved his headquarters from Pink Lane, off Beat Street – one of the worst corners in Jamaica – to a less violent venue called the Silver Slipper in Crossroads, where he found he made far more money.

Soon there came another contender for Duke Reid's crown: the Sir Coxsone Downbeat sound system, which took its name from the Yorkshire cricketer Coxsone and was run by Clement Seymour Dodd, whose family was also in the liquor-store business. Coxsone, as he became known, employed Prince Buster as one of his main DJs; his former occupation as a boxer also ensured he was a sizable deterrent to the gangs run by Reid.

The first two dances at which the Sir Coxsone Downbeat sound system played were in Trench Town; and the first of these was an event put on by Jimmy Tucker, a leading Jamaican vocalist.

Both Coxsone and Duke Reid soon began recording songs by local artists to use on their respective sound systems. The law of supply and demand proved to be inescapable, and out of this – as well as Coxsone's realisation that American record companies like Imperial and Modern didn't seem to notice when he blatantly pirated their material – was born the Jamaican recording industry.

By 1958 Prince Buster was running his own sound system; Reid and fifteen of his thugs went to a dance at the Chocomo lawn on Wellington Street looking for him. But Buster wasn't there: he was playing dice down on Charles Street. Hearing that Reid and his gang were up at Chocomo, Prince Buster hurried up there, and a man immediately pulled a knife on him. In the mêlée that followed, another of Reid's hoods split Buster's skull open with a rock. Later he and Reid became good friends: 'He became a nice man: he was just possessed by what was going on.'

The cauldron of Trench Town epitomised one of the great cultural truths about Jamaica – and other impoverished Third World countries: how those who have nothing, and therefore nothing to lose, are not afraid to express their talents. These people seem to have a pride and confidence in their talents – a pride and confidence that western educational and employment systems seem to conspire against. The pace of life in Jamaica also seems to be

'When we were all right, living in Trench Town, I have mi acoustic guitar. We would go over where we stay, to our yard, where we smoke herb and t'ing, and everyone is there. Music start to play. Everyone influenced communally. A man might hear you sing something who is a stranger. And 'im say, "Sing it this way. Put this work to it." So is always like that with the people: the people in it.'

more in keeping with the rhythms of nature: rising with the sun, people are active from early morning until the sun goes down. Such a harnessing of man's soul to the day's natural process seems to allow the creative forces a greater freedom to emerge.

So it was for Nesta Robert Marley. In the cool of first daylight or long after sunset he could be found, with or without his spar Bunny, strumming his sardine-can guitar and trying out melodies and harmonies – his only solace apart from football.

For often he would feel alienated in the city. Considered a white boy, his complexion would often bring out the worst in people: after all, why was this boy from 'country' living down in the ghetto and not uptown with all the other lightskin people? Being tested so consistently can virtually destroy someone; or, on the other hand, it can resolutely build their character. Such daily bullying ultimately created the iron will and overpowering self-confidence in Nesta.

The still air of Trench Town was barely ever disturbed by traffic noise. From those few yards that had a tenant fortunate enough to possess a radio, the favourite new songs from the United States could be heard, fading in and out as they drifted down the Caribbean from New Orleans or Miami. Nat King Cole, Billy Eckstine, Fats Domino, Brook Benton, Larry Williams, Louis Jordan and white iconoclasts like Elvis Presley and the milder Ricky Nelson all made a strong impression on Nesta; he also absorbed the Trinidadian calypso and steel band music that had been adopted by Jamaica almost as its own.

It was in Trench Town that Nesta Robert Marley was exposed to bebop and modern jazz for the first time – although to start with, 'me couldn't understand it,' he later admitted. But in 1960 he first began to take part in the evening music sessions held by Joe Higgs in his Third Street yard. Higgs was one of the area's most famous residents, having been one of Jamaica's first indigenous recording artists: as part of the Higgs and Wilson duo, he had cut a number of hit-jumping boogies, starting in 1960 with 'Manny-O' for WIRL, the abbreviation of West Indies Recordings Ltd; the producer of these tunes was the owner of the label, Edward

Seaga, who became prime minister for the Jamaica Labour Party in 1980.

Joe Higgs was as conscious in his actions as in his lyrics; these included publicly espousing the unmentionable, radical subject of Rastafari, which was growing by quantum leaps among the ghetto sufferahs, and for which he had been beaten up by the police and imprisoned during political riots in Trench Town in May 1959. This only strengthened him in his resolve. Higgs had himself learned music from his mother, who sang in a church choir. Having gained from the spiritual aspect of her teaching, Joe Higgs took particular care to play the part of both musical and moral tutor to those youth in the area with the ears to hear. The musical seminars he conducted could be rigorous affairs: a lot of emphasis would be placed on breath control and

JOE HIGGS' TRENCH TOWN MUSICAL SCHOOL WAS CRUCIAL FOR THE THREE WAILERS' UNDERSTANDING OF MUSIC; LATER HE WAS TO BRIEFLY REPLACE BUNNY ON SEVERAL AMERICAN SHOWS.

melody, and in addition to guitar lessons, he would instruct his students in the art of writing lyrics that could carry clear ideas to the people. It was not all work: sometimes entire classes would travel the short distance to the end of Marcus Garvey Drive and swim at the beach known as Hot and Cold, so called because of the effect created by an electrical power generator on the water.

It was in Higgs's yard, on one of these occasions, that Nesta had his first encounter with that natural resource with which he was to become associated in the public mind, and which allowed him to empathise with jazz. 'After a while I smoke some ganja, some herb, and get to understand it. Me try to get into de mood whar de moon is blue and see de feelin' expressed. Joe Higgs 'elped me understands that music. 'E taught me many t'ings.'

Another of the male role models who appeared consistently through the course of Nesta's life, Joe Higgs assiduously coached the fifteen-year-old and his spar Bunny in the art of harmonising: he would advise Bob to sing all the time, to strengthen his voice. At one of these sessions Bob and Bunny met Peter McIntosh, another local youth wanting to mek a try as a vocalist.

This tall, arrogant youth was older than Bob. Born on 19 October 1944 in Grange Hill, Westmoreland to Alvera Coke and James McIntosh, his father had left his mother soon after the child was born, and he was taken into the care of an aunt. The first twelve years of his life had been spent first in the pleasant coastal town of Savanna-La-Mar and then in the rough section of west Kingston called Denham Town until, in 1956, after his aunt died, he moved in with an uncle who lived in Trench Town. Lonely and isolated, there was an urgency and desperation about the boy's need to make it as a musician. Unlike Bob and Bunny, whose guitar-playing had developed only perfunctorily as they concentrated on their vocal skills, Peter McIntosh was a competent guitarist, owning his own cheap acoustic model. The boy's skill on the instrument inspired Nesta to pay serious attention to mastering the guitar.

Another older friend of Nesta's in Trench Town was Vincent Ford, also known as Jack Tartar or, more often, simply Tartar. Tartar had first come across the Marley boy when he was around thirteen and Tartar was seventeen. A close bond had developed between the two: Tartar had worked as a chef at the Boys Town school, and had then started up a little kitchen in his yard on First Street which he and Nesta would refer to as the 'casbah'; as well as the ganja that filled a crucial gap in Trench Town's desperate economy, Tartar would sell dishes like calaloo and dumplings. At times when Nesta was entirely impoverished, it would be at Tartar's that he would find free food. When Nesta made the decision to apply himself to the guitar, Tartar would stay up all night with him, turning the 'leaves' of the *Teach Yourself Guitar* book that Nesta had bought, as he strummed the chords, peering at the diagrams in the light of a flickering oil lamp. In the mornings their nostrils would be black from the lamp's fumes.

Nesta was working by now, having quit school at the minimum age of fourteen. He had had no idea of what to do for a living, and had readily accepted a suggestion of his mother's.

'I knew men who were doing welding for a livin', and I suggested that he go down to the shop and make himself an apprentice,' remembers Cedella. 'He hated it. One day he was welding some steel and a piece of metal flew off and got stuck right in the white of his eye, and he had to go to the hospital to have it taken out. It caused him terrible pain; it even hurt for him to cry.'

This rogue sliver of metal had a greater significance. From now on, Nesta told Tartar, there would be no more welding: only the guitar. Nesta convinced his mother he could make a better living by singing. By now Bunny had also made a ghetto guitar, similar to the ones Nesta constructed, from a bamboo staff, electric cable wire and a large sardine can. Then Peter Tosh, as the McIntosh boy was more widely known, brought along his battered acoustic guitar to play with them. '1961,' says Peter Tosh, 'the group came together.'

Encouraged by Joe Higgs, who also became their coach, they formed into a musical unit.

Hero-act by boys

One saved from drowning

VINCENT FORD
DIVED IN

ALPHONSO GOODSON, 17, STAR vendor, was saved from drowning yesterday morning by Vincent Ford, 14, of No. 3 First Street, Trench Town, with the assistance of Sydney Barrows, 17, of 21 Pretoria Road, and Dudley Gibbs, 15, of 11 Upper Second Street, D—————

They were to be called The Teenagers and would consist of the three youths, as well as a strong local singer called Junior Braithwaite and two girls, Beverley Kelso and Cherry Smith, who sang backing vocals. 'It was kinda difficult,' said Joe Higgs later, 'to get the group precise – and their sound – and to get the harmony structures. It took a couple years to get that perfect. I wanted each person to be a leader in his own right. I wanted them to be able to wail in their own rights.'

A close brethren of Higgs, Alvin 'Franseeco' Patterson, later known simply as Seeco, instructed The Teenagers in the philosophy of rhythm. Originally from St Ann, Seeco was another professional musician now living in Trench Town. An accomplished hand drummer, he had worked with a number of Jamaica's calypso groups. The burru style of drumming he played was an African rhythm of liberation welcoming the return of released prisoners of war; it had been co-opted into Rastafari's Nyabinghi style of inspirational chanting and drum rhythms. And it was this blend of devotion and rebellious fervour that formed the basis of Nesta's understanding of rhythm.

It was now public knowledge in Trench Town that Nesta Marley, who was beginning to be known more as Bob, was a musician of some sort. At that time Pauline Morrison was living in the area and attending Kingston Senior School. Every afternoon she would make her way home from school, usually with a large group of children from the same neighbourhood. At the end of a lane, she would invariably see Bob sitting under a broad, tall tree, accompanying himself on his makeshift guitar as he sang songs of his own composition. Fifteen or twenty schoolchildren would be gathered all around. It was a regular fixture. 'We'd come from school and see this guy singing, singing, and we'd always sit around and watch and listen to him. After him finish we clap him, and after we'd go home.'

Bob was like a bird, Pauline remembers, 'like a young hatchling just coming up'. Later, as success started to make his songs familiar, she would recognise some of the tunes from those after-school performances – he certainly played an early version of 'Simmer Down', for example. (On that long journey back from school she and her companions would often have already had another musical experience: in an entirely different neighbourhood, a young Jimmy Cliff could also be seen singing under the boughs of an ackee tree.)

Although football was almost as much a love for Bob Marley as music, he occasionally played cricket as well, on that same Gully Bank Pauline would have had to pass over. Ernest Ranglin would see him knocking a ball about as he passed and would sometimes join in for a few minutes. To Ranglin he always seemed a very well brought-up boy, extremely polite and considerate.

As a youth who knew what he wanted in life, Bob was not caught up in the negative existence of the ghetto bad boy. He did not move in those packs of adolescents who tried to imitate the exploits of the American slum gangs, typified in *West Side Story*, which they would catch at the Carib Cinema, having sneaked in the exit door.

Bob certainly wasn't some side-walk bully, although, as Pauline points out, 'If a guy come for him and trouble him, him can defend himself.' But even then he operated on several levels. On the one hand, he was affable, open, eager to assist: 'He was a very easy-going person. He was never rude or anything. Him never be aggressive. Him was always irie to me, even as a kid coming from school. And although I still get to know him and be around him, him never be rude.'

At the same time, Bob was also a loner. 'It was always the man and his guitar,' Pauline observes. 'But it was very rare you could just sit with him and be with him. Because he was a very moody person, the way I see him. Him is very moody. If people were sitting together with him, he would suddenly just get up and go somewhere else. Just to be by himself.'

At the end of the day, Bob knew, there was only one person he could rely on – himself.

THE MUSIC BUSINESS

'Judge Not', Bob Marley's first record, was released on Leslie Kong's Beverley's label. In 1970 he told The Wailers that he intended releasing an album entitled The Best Of The Wailers, featuring a number of tunes the trio had recorded for him the previous year. Bunny Livingston flew into a rage, saying that the best of The Wailers had yet to come, so the record's title would be a lie: he threatened Kong with dark consequences if the record was released. A year later Leslie Kong died of a massive heart attack.

On 6 August 1962 Jamaica was granted independence from British colonial rule: a by-product of independence for Trench Town's population was that a sewerage system was almost immediately installed. Two songs that year summed up the optimistic mood of an emergent nation: Lord Creator's 'Independent Jamaica' and 'Forward March' by Derrick Morgan. Morgan recorded for the Beverley's label, owned by a Chinese–Jamaican businessman called Leslie Kong, who ran a restaurant in downtown Kingston: Kong had started the label after Morgan and his friend Jimmy Cliff had visited him, seeking finance for the recording of a tune that Cliff had written called 'Dearest Beverley' – hence the name of the recording venture. At one stage in 1961 Morgan had seven records in the Jamaican Top Ten; one of the reasons he recorded so prolifically was that Kong made only a flat payment of ten Jamaican dollars per tune. But he also had a role as an unofficial talent scout for the Beverley's label.

On Charles Street there lived a girlfriend of Morgan's called Pat Stewart. She was acquainted with an aunt of Bob's, a 'brown woman', and one time when the youth was visiting her, Pat heard him sing. 'Bob can sing good, y'know, Derrick – why not try 'im?' she suggested.

'You really do singin', baas?' Derrick checked with him in February 1962. The answer came in the affirmative. 'Me seh well come over Beverley's nuh: mek me hear you. And 'im come up deh one day and I play the piano and 'im sing the tune "Judge Not".'

Morgan thought the song was good but not great. And he was struck by the fact that Bob seemed to dance almost better than he sang when he auditioned the tune. ''Im could DANCE!'

Leslie Kong was willing to take a chance. 'All right,' he decreed, 'me could try it now.'

'Judge Not' was recorded at Federal Studio the same month. The joyous gallop of ska – a music as fresh and unique as the nation of Jamaica itself at the time – was the backbeat to the first recorded work of the youthful, shrill-voiced Bob Marley. But the celebratory sound of 'Judge Not' could not conceal the Biblical tone that was significantly present in his first release: chiding those who pass judgement on himself and his kind, he warns that 'While you talk about me/Someone else is judging you.' Released under the name of 'Robert Marley', the song sold hardly at all and radio play was non-existent.

At that same session Bob recorded two other ska numbers, 'Terror' and 'One Cup of Coffee', although only the latter was put out as a 45, to little avail. 'One Cup of Coffee', a strange saga of separation and financial settlement, was an early indication of the visual realism that would become a key feature of Bob Marley's lyrics in years to come. For the time being, however, the few listeners the record enjoyed assumed it was the work of one 'Bobby Martell', the name listed on the label: Kong had renamed him with this kitsch moniker in much the same way as he changed James Chambers to Jimmy Cliff.

Bob recorded another pair of songs for Leslie Kong, but when he refused to pay him, the relationship ended. It was said that, after an argument over Kong's swindling him, Bob prophecied to the label owner, frightening him, that one day he would make plenty of money out of Bob, but would never have the luxury of enjoying it.

Morgan continued his association and friendship with the younger singer from Trench Town. The next year he emigrated to the United Kingdom, and Kong promoted a couple of farewell shows for him, one at the Capri Theatre in May Penn and another in Montego Bay; Derrick Morgan made sure that Bob was on the bill. Morgan noted again that Bob, perhaps through nervousness, had not balanced the energies of his performance particularly well. At the Capri Theatre show, for example, 'when Bob go on stage he was dancin' more than he was singin' . . . An 'im tired when 'im come back to the vocal, so me beg 'im and seh: "No, youth: when ya

WITHOUT THE ESTIMABLE DERRICK MORGAN, BOB MARLEY WOULD NOT HAVE GOT TO MAKE 'JUDGE NOT', HIS FIRST RECORD ON THE BEVERLEY'S LABEL.

sing two verse you dance, an' then you go back to your other verse."'

At the Montego Bay venue, Bob performed as Morgan had suggested. Yet 'One Cup of Coffee', his first song, still didn't receive the audience response that either of them had expected. In fact, the typically volatile and expressive Jamaican crowd started to boo. 'The next song, 'im just get up and seh: "Judge not, before you judge yourself!" So the audience think a him mek that song immediately offa dem! And 'im tear dung the whole place with that tune: Judge not, before you judge yourself. When 'im reach a part there the audience ray and seh: Wait, this boy a bad, 'im a jus' mek a sound offa we, same time, yeah man, an' deh so 'im hit. That was the last time I see Bob fe a long while.'

After the initial disappointment, the fact that the three records released by Beverley's hadn't sold was irrelevant. Only sixteen years old, Bob was now perfectly justified in expecting some kind of musical future for himself. To make the next step forward, he decided to make a serious go of it with his spars from Trench Town. The Teenagers became first The Wailing Rudeboys, and then The Wailing Wailers.

One of the maxims of a man called Lee 'Scratch' Perry, who worked for Coxsone Dodd's sound system, was that every man has a name for a purpose. The same can be applied to groups. And the name The Wailers, to which The Wailing Wailers was eventually abbreviated, didn't merely reflect some alley-cat screech made by the trio: whether consciously chosen or not, it also spoke volumes about the anguish and lonely hurt all three, especially Bob and Peter, had felt within their souls as youths coming up. 'The word "wail" means to cry or to moan,' said Peter Tosh later. 'We were living in this so-called ghetto. No one to help the people. We felt we were the only ones who could express their feelings through music, and because of that the people loved it. So we did it.'

Definitively ghetto sufferahs, the three

teenagers responded to music made by their American counterparts: Ray Charles, Sam Cooke and the flawless harmonising of The Impressions, led by Curtis Mayfield and Jerry Butler. The Drifters, and their lead vocalist Ben E. King, also made a strong impression on them; as did some of the tougher sounds at the pop end of R&B, particularly those coming out of Berry Gordy's studio in Detroit: tunes like 'Shop Around' by The Miracles and 'Do You Love Me?' by The Contours.

In the big picture, the future seemed to contain myriad musical possibilities. However, Bob's present-day existence could only have been described as grim. He had no real source of income, and would literally have starved on occasions, had it not been for Tartar's kitchen.

A further set of complications was on its way. Bob's mother Cedella had become pregnant by Bunny's father, giving birth to Pearl Livingston early in 1962; Bob and Bunny were thereby linked even closer by a half-sister. Bob, meanwhile, had had a passionate affair himself with a local girl, two years younger than he was, but her older brother had forbidden the girl to carry on the relationship because of Bob's white blood. The shock of being the victim of such racism, combined with Pearl taking so much of the attention that Cedella had previously given him, caused tensions within Bob himself and in the yard at 19 Second Street.

It had taken the birth of Pearl to make Cedella realise precisely how hopeless her relationship was with the baby's father. To escape from this unprofitable union and to advance her life, she decided to move to the United States, to Wilmington in Delaware, where there was yet another branch of the Malcolm family. She agonised over what to do with her son. Finally it was decided that he would stay behind and wait for her to send for him and for Pearl.

Cedella's sister Enid moved into the home on Second Street to care for her nephew and niece. When she moved back to St Ann, however, Bob lost the apartment and found himself homeless, living for a time in west Kingston's various squatter camps. It was as though, yet again, he had been abandoned. To all intents and

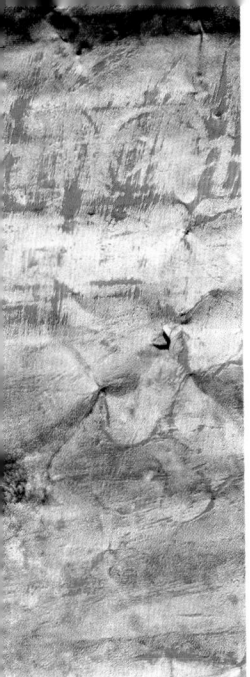

purposes he was destitute. Then Tartar took him in and gave him a corner of the kitchen in which he also slept. Bob's bed was the gambling table that Tartar set up for reasons both social and financial: Bob would have to wait until the games had finished before he could reclaim his bed.

These were very hard times indeed. Yet, in that strange way in which adversity can be turned to advantage, they also served to focus Bob's art. There was no choice, no other way out. Bunny would come round, and – less frequently – Peter and Junior Braithwaite, and they would sit around practising harmonies until they fell asleep. Falling back on himself in these endless rehearsals, Bob found his confidence and ability growing almost daily.

To provide light for their sessions, another ghetto-dweller by the name of George Headley Robinson would gather brushwood from all around the area and lug it to Tartar's yard. Some thirteen years older than Bob, 'Georgie', who made his living as a fisherman, was a devoted believer in the talents of the youth and his musical companions. He would try and instruct Bob in matters of Rastafari, constantly referring to the Bible. 'But Bob,' Georgie remarked, 'was too young to reason with me.'

'Georgie would sit there shirtless all night,' Tartar recollects, 'tending the flames as they played.' When they awoke, having fallen asleep exhausted from playing, the fire would still be burning; Georgie would immediately boil up some porridge or a kettle for some bush tea.

Then, unexpectedly, they arrived at a turning point. Alvin 'Seeco' Patterson the rhythm master was acquainted with Clement Dodd, the sound-system man who had launched his own record label. He knew of the auditions that Coxsone regularly held on Sundays at Studio One, his new one-track studio on Brentford Road, to the north of Trench Town. Shortly before Christmas 1963, prompted by Joe Higgs, Seeco took Bob and the rest of the group, including Beverley Kelso and Cherry Smith, over there.

Although Clement 'Coxsone' Dodd was not a musician himself, he had what Ernest Ranglin described as 'an extraordinary pair of ears'. He was also a wizard at conjuring up musical concepts. 'He was really the man, the man who came up with the ideas. But he couldn't play, so he would come and explain it to us. After explaining it, I always knew what the man wanted.'

One Sunday morning in 1959 Coxsone had asked bass-player Cluett 'Clue-J' Johnson and Ranglin, in a surprisingly formal manner, to meet him at the liquor store he ran in Love Lane. 'I need something to get away from this blues,' he told the two master musicians, complaining about the way Jamaican music was imitating contemporary American black music.

In the store's backyard they sat down and worked out the recipe for a new sound; they sought a formula for a music that was distinctly Jamaican but which also kept its roots in the R&B and popular jazz that beamed down into Jamaica from radio stations in the southern American states. Ska, the music that resulted from that Sunday morning session, was a shuffle-boogie rhythm of the type popularised by artists like Louis Jordan and Erskine Hawkins, the unexpected emphasis on the offbeat only stressing its addictive flavour. An apocryphal origin of the galloping sound of ska was that this was a replication of the way music on those southern stations would fade in and out. Ranglin, however, has a simpler explanation. 'We just wanted it to sound like the theme music from one of those westerns that were on TV all the time in the late 1950s.' The term 'ska' was an abbreviation of 'skavoovee', a popular catchphrase of the time, a term of approval, which Clue-J was famous for using. (Coxsone, for his part, addressed almost every man he encountered as 'Jackson', an eccentricity for which he was equally renowned.)

The next day Coxsone went to the JBC Radio studios, which could be hired for recording, and started trying out samples of this new music which was to be tested out on his sound system. The first ska record to be released, having received huge acclaim at dances, was 'Easy Snappin' by Theophilus Beckford. It featured pianist Beckford on vocals, Clue-J on bass, Ian Pearson on drums, Ken Richards on guitar, Roland Alphonso on tenor sax and trombonist Rico Rodrigues. The record was a big hit; its B side was 'Silky', with Ernest Ranglin performing his own composition.

'Easy Snappin' was also the first tune Coxsone recorded at Federal Studio. When Federal bought a two-track studio, Coxsone bought their original one-track from them and installed it in the new premises he was taking over at 13 Brentford Road. After a while, Federal then graduated to an eight-track machine, and Coxsone purchased their two-track.

It was to these new premises, which would form the base for Clement Dodd's Studio One

CLEMENT 'SIR COXSONE' DODD GRADUATED TO RECORD PRODUCTION AFTER RUNNING ONE OF JAMAICA'S MOST REVERED SOUND SYSTEMS. ON HIS STUDIO ONE LABEL HE RELEASED SOME OF THE MOST IMPORTANT JAMAICAN MUSIC OF ALL TIME.

label, that Seeco took The Wailers. Listening to them in his studio's dusty yard, beneath the mango tree that was the location for these weekly auditions, Coxsone liked their sound and several of the songs they had written. He noted that Bob Marley was particularly influenced by US groups like The Impressions, The Moonglows and The Tams. 'I was very impressed with them the first time, because I was hoping to really get a kind of group with that team feel, young voices and t'ing like that.' They were offered his standard deal: a five-year contract for exclusive recording rights and management, and a guarantee of twenty pounds a side.

The first session took place within days. The sides chosen were 'I'm Still Waiting' and 'It Hurts to Be Alone'. The first song was a beautiful Bob Marley original, even though the preamble of the vocal harmonies owed much to The Impressions. When Bob delivered his breathtakingly sweet vocal solo, his voice sounded as though it had been recorded at a different, slowed down speed from the rest of the track. 'It Hurts to Be Alone' was a Junior Braithwaite number on which he sang lead. Curiously, even though the record had been written and sung by Braithwaite, the title

could definitively sum up Bob's feelings about substantial chunks of his life. As Coxsone's house arranger, Ernest Ranglin oversaw the production of both sides.

The instrumentation was basic: Lloyd Knibbs on drums, Lloyd Brevett on bass, and Jah Jerry Haines on guitar. Bob, noted Jah Jerry, was 'a nice boy, a nice young feller: not a rough guy, a polite guy'.

For once Ranglin didn't have to spice up the song with guitar overdubs. 'You could see they had something in them. They were all very nice guys, but they seemed very young. And little, too.' Braithwaite, in particular, was very short, while both Bob and Bunny stood at not much more than five foot eight inches; by comparison Peter Tosh, at just over six foot, seemed to tower over the rest of the group.

After Coxsone had pressed up 300 copies of the two tunes, they were distributed to sound systems; the word came back that 'It Hurts to Be Alone' was going down well. As soon as Coxsone heard this, he called the group back to the studio. But there had been changes that no one had told him about. Junior Braithwaite was no longer with them: to Coxsone's surprise and initial chagrin he learned that Braithwaite was in the final stages of preparing to leave Jamaica for Chicago with his family.

If he was to continue working with the group, Coxsone insisted, The Wailers required a clearly defined lead vocalist. After some discussion, it was decided that the task should fall to Bob; Bunny and Peter were promised they would also get their share of lead vocals. Coxsone was encouraged in this decision by 'Simmer Down', a song Bob had brought to the session that served a dual purpose: a warning to the cool, disaffected rude boys not to bring down the wrath of the law upon themselves; and a frustrated response to a letter from his mother in the United States, fearful that her only son was becoming involved with bad company.

Coxsone summoned his label's finest ska musicians for the session. Again Ernest Ranglin arranged the tune, while Don Drummond, Jamaica's master of the trombone, added his deeply creative jazz parts. Drummond was the virtuoso of a group of musicians who would

very soon be working together, for a little over a year, under the name of The Skatalites. As well as Drummond, the group included Roland Alphonso and Tommy McCook, the group's leader, on tenor sax, Lester Sterling on alto sax, Johnny 'Dizzy' Moore on trumpet, Jah Jerry on guitar, Lloyd Nibbs on drums, Lloyd Brevitt on bass, Jackie Mittoo on keyboards and occasionally Leonard Dillon on trumpet. Other musicians who worked Studio One's ska sessions included Theophilus Beckford and Clue-J Johnson.

Being part of this élite team was far more financially remunerative than being one of the named artists on the record label. Coxsone paid two pounds a tune per musician, and they would frequently record twenty songs in a day. One bonanza day Jah Jerry worked on fifty songs in an epic session at Beverley's. This kind of money would have made you seem rich in the United Kingdom, let alone in impoverished Jamaica. Notwithstanding the financial imbalance between Studio One session musicians and The Wailers, Jah Jerry could not help but be struck by their extreme confidence on the 'Simmer Down' session. This was a mark, he was sure, of their regular, rigorous rehearsals.

The Wailers, noted Johnny Moore, had first come along to Studio One 'more as less as The Impressions: they were dissuaded from going along that line, and influenced to go inside themselves, however silly or simple they feared what they found there might sound like. They were simply urged to try and cultivate their own thing. And it worked. Even at that age they knew what they wanted. From the time that they realised that trying to be The Impressions was not what they should be doing, they really checked themselves and got into it. You can hear it in the music.

'At the time they were young and vibrant and you could see they were very good friends: they were very, very close to one another. They really did care about each other. I guess that's why they made a success of it as it was.

'Bob didn't necessarily seem like the leader. The thing was so closely knit, the sound, whatever they were trying to get at: that was the objective, the force of what they were trying to accomplish. Rather than worrying about you lead or me lead: everyone would put their shoulder and heave-ho. They seemed to realise that it's much easier to get things done that way.'

In rehearsal, 'Simmer Down' had seemed like some tough Jamaican variant of the protest 'message' songs that had recently become popular in the United States. In the recording studio it became positively transcendent. Popular songs with lines about the running bellies of nanny-goats? This song was not only very unusual, but also extremely commercial.

'Control your temper/Simmer down/The battle will get hotter/Simmer down,' declared Bob on what would come to be regarded as one of his greatest songs. In the style unique to Coxsone's label, the voices are buried back in the mix, fighting to get out with the same ferocity with which the trio were trying to liberate themselves from the dead-end of the ghetto.

Before the record's instant popularity had time truly to translate into sales, Bob found himself onstage as lead singer for the first time at a Kingston show. At the helm of The Wailers he steered the group through a performance that stole the event, assisted in great part by the crisp and clear sound that Count Matchouki, who had started as a DJ with Coxsone's sound system, obtained for him at the mixing desk. The audience response was overwhelming, but the other artists on the show were 'vex' – both these acts recorded for Coxsone: did they sense a conspiracy?

No matter: released just before Christmas 1963, the record was Number One in the Jamaican charts by the beginning of February 1964. The tune's subject of teenage crime established The Wailers as the musical front of the island's rebels, the rude boys. Although the three male

THE WAILERS, WITH THEIR GOLD LAME BEATLE JACKETS. FROM LEFT TO RIGHT: BOB, BUNNY LIVINGSTON AND PETER TOSH, WITH BEVERLEY KELSO SITTING.

members of the group were not, strictly speaking, rude boys themselves, this identifying with a tribal youth sect was, and still is, a useful bridge to building an audience in popular music. Yet The Wailers were never able to compete with the colossal popularity enjoyed at the same time by another three-piece male vocal trio, The Maytals, fronted by Toots Hibbert.

The subject matter of 'Simmer Down' made The Wailers stand out amongst their contemporaries. Up until now no one in Jamaican music had been expressing ghetto thinking. Even the seasoned ska musicians down at Studio One were impressed. 'The uniqueness of the sound they projected,' said Johnny Moore, 'was specifically local and really good. The lyrics were clean and really educative. The statements might be a bit serious, but the way they projected it you could absorb what they were saying. There were some good lessons, we had to admit that.'

Bob was also learning some good lessons himself. A number of the musicians he was now beginning to play with at Studio One – Johnny Moore himself, for example – were dedicated and devout Rastafarians. For years Bob's bible had rarely been out of his sight. Now he was hearing new interpretations that would make his jaw drop in disbelief. Sometimes he would wander away from Studio One after a day's sessions in a pure daze as he struggled to process the biblical information and interpolations to which he had been made privy.

Bob's soul was being nourished. Moreover, he now had sufficient funds to pay for his material needs: in addition to Coxsone having ordered gold lame collarless suits for the boys – a kind of Beatle jacket version of the famous ensemble worn by Elvis Presley on the sleeve of *Elvis Gold Discs Volume 2* – he had also put them each on a weekly wage of three pounds.

'We all used to go to church to search, and knowing that we found reality and righteousness we relaxed,' recalled Peter Tosh. 'So when you saw us in the slick suits and things, we were just in the thing that was looked on as the thing at the time. So we just adjusted ourselves materially.'

For the rest of 1964 The Wailers were rarely out of the Jamaican charts, with a string of tunes recorded at 13 Brentford Road: 'Lonesome Feelings', 'Mr Talkative', 'I Don't Need Your Love', 'Donna', 'Wings of a Dove'. Coxsone was not unhappy: 'They needed a lot of polishing but Bob had a gift, you know, he was willing just to get his steps together. He had the makings.'

Coxsone became another father figure to Bob Marley, and even, to a lesser extent, to Bunny and Peter. When he learned that Bob didn't have a home of his own, he did a deal with the youth. He would turn new artists over to Bob to find songs for them; Bob could then sit down with his guitar with them – with Delroy Wilson or Hortense Ellis, for example – and rehearse the tune. In return, Clement Dodd would let Bob Marley live at the studio, and sleep in a back room that was used for auditions or rehearsals. However, Bob was unable to put his head down until the sessions had ended, often very late into the night. And when he did, he often found his sleep was strangely disturbed, as though someone else might be in the room with him.

The Wailers had become the roughneck archetype of the three-piece harmony group, a specifically Jamaican form of high popular art. By such members of their peer group as the estimable Alton Ellis, the group was considered to be very strong indeed. 'They have a different sense of music than us, and we all love it. It wasn't so much dance-hall. Bob's sound was always different: it mesmerised me from those times. His music always have a roots sense of direction. Not even just the words – I'm talking about the sound, the melody that him sing, the feel of the rhythm. Always a bit different.'

This sense was complemented onstage. 'Bob was always this ragamuffin onstage. We – myself, people like John Holt in The Paragons – were more polished and act like the Americans. Him was a rebel: jump up and throw himself about onstage. The Wailers them just mad and free: just threw themselves in and out of the music, carefree and careless.'

Miming to their own records, The Wailers would appear all over Jamaica at dances at which the Downbeat sound system would play. This was a regular Coxsone strategy. 'That's how we got them launched. With several other of my artists, we used to tour the country parts.' Prior to this The Wailers had played live mainly at 'Vere Johns' Opportunity Hour', a variety talent show modelled on American TV programmes that would tour the island; although The Wailers would find themelves performing back-to-back with conjurors and ventriloquists, the show always had a musical bias.

The Wailers made more hits: 'I Need You'; 'Dance With Me', a rewrite of The Drifters' 'On Broadway'; 'Another Dance'; and the 'Ten Commandments of Love', an extraordinary interpretation of the Aaron Neville song. And there were more tunes that seemed like messages direct from Rude Boy Central: 'Rude Boy' itself, late in 1965; 'Rule Dem Rudie', 'Jailhouse', another paen to rude boys, containing the lines 'Can't fight against the youth now/Cause it's wrong/Can't fight against the youth now/Cause they're strong'. Small wonder that such tunes took off with Jamaica's teenagers, whatever the social origin.

In 1965 The Wailers delivered the spiritual counter-balance to such rude boy militancy. 'One Love' was a distillation of the Rastafarian sentiments Bob had absorbed in his years in Trench Town; it contained the message and philosophy of Rastafari: 'Let's join together and feel all right.'

Later on that year the group recorded 'Put It On', another anthem to self-determination. On 10 February 1966, 'Put It On' was played non-stop for over half an hour at the wedding of Bob Marley and Rita Anderson.

Alvarita Anderson had lived all her life at 18A Greenwich Park Road in Trench Town, Kingston 5. After her musician father and then her mother had moved to Europe, she had remained living there with her Aunt Viola and an uncle. She was a Sunday school teacher in the Presbyterian church, but three evenings a week she also went to the Church of God. Singing and getting the spirit like this were more than enjoyable to her. 'I thought it was amazing. The first time I went there I watched and thought, "This is sanctifying, this is holy." It came over me and I realised it was something for real that can take you away.'

Sometimes when she was out, she would see some of the local Rastafarians and feel very wary. She had been taught to be scared of them. But something about these wild men touched her heart. 'I would also feel sympathy for them. I'd think, "Oh, poor people. I don't believe they are as bad as they say." Because you'd see them and they'd say, "One Love", and you would wonder how people saying that could deal with hate. Even though I was living in Trench Town, I was exposed to certain things above the normal living: I felt that these people were innocent, because of their innocency.'

Rita, to which her name inevitably became abbreviated, had had a good high-school education. Although she had been training to be a nurse until a brief affair led to the birth of her daughter Sharon, she was wondering whether she should become a teacher.

Rita already knew of Bob as part of The Wailers. To her, when she heard them on the radio, their sound was definitively modern. For some reason, it seemed to have a profound effect on her. Then she realised why: 'It sound like angels . . . So I say to myself, I shall be meeting these people one day.'

Studio One was in the northern-most section of Trench Town. Before Bob had moved into the back of 13 Brentford Road, he, Peter and Bunny would pass through the Ghost Town area where Rita lived on their daily journey to Coxsone's recording yard. Standing at the gate, observing the world, Rita would see the trio, aware that it was these guys who were mashing up the charts with their hit tunes. But she was not necessarily impressed: she thought they looked like 'rough little guys'. An ambitious girl, her principal concern was to get away from Trench Town; and she had a musical group of her own, The Soulettes, which she had formed with her friend Marlene 'Precious' Gifford and her cousin Constantine 'Dream' Walker. They copied hit

COXSONE RECORDS

MR. TALKATIVE
THE WAILERS

TUFF GONG

ASCAP · 45 RPM

Produced by
Tuff Gong
Records
127 King St. Kgn.

KNOTTY DREAD
(Bob Marley)
BOB MARLEY
WAILERS
&
I THREES

All rights are reserved for the owner of this record any unauthorised copying is prohibited

Beverley's RECORDS

135
ORANGE
STREET

MADE IN
JAMAICA

KINGSTON
JAMAICA
W.I.

COPYING OF
THIS RECORD
IS PROHIBITED

LM 052

ONE CUP OF COFFEE
(R. MARLEY)
BOBBY MARTELL
BEVERLEY'S ALL-STARS

Supreme RECORDS

417

WHITE CHRISTMAS
(IRVING BERLIN)
BOB MARLEY & THE WAILERS

RECORDED BY JAMAICA RECORDING STUDIO 13 BRENTFORD ROAD KGN.

TUFF GONG

45 RPM.

Tuff Gong
Production
Pub. By Tuff
Gong Music.

RAT RACE
(R. MARLEY)
Bob Marley and The Wailers

Coxsone RECORDS

A Studio One
RECORDING

ONE LOVE
(C. DODD)
The Wailers

MFD. BY JAMAICA RECORD MFG. CO. LTD. 13 BRENTFORD RD, KGN. 3, JA. W.I.

EXPORT TUFF GONG

45 RPM

KINGSTON 12 SHUFFLE
U ROY & BOB MARLEY
Peter Tosh

of this record any unau

Coxsone RECORDS

C 170

SIMMER DOWN
BOB AND THE WAILERS

MANUFACTURED BY FEDERAL RECORD MFG. CO. LTD.

STUDIO 1

MADE IN JAMAICA

JAIL HOUSE
(Sourcisse)
THE WAILERS

RECORDED BY JAMAICA RECORDING STUDIO 13 BRENTFORD RD.

WINCOX Records

BRENTFORD RD.

THERE SHE GOES
THE WAILERS
THE MIGHTY VIKINGS

RECORDED BY JAMAICA RECORDING STUDIO

Coxsone RECORDS

TEENAGER IN LOVE
THE WAILERS

MANUFACTURED B
RECORD MFG. CO. LTD. JAMAICA W.I.

Beverley's RECORDS

135
ORANGE
STREET

MADE IN
JAMAICA

KINGSTON
JAMAICA
W.I.

COPYING OF
THIS RECORD
IS PROHIBITED

LM 021

JUDGE NOT!
(R. MARLEY)
ROBERT MARLEY
BEVERLEY'S ALL-STARS

COXSONE RECORDS

509

RUDE BOY
(BOB MARLEY)
THE WAILERS

MANUFACTURED B
RECORD MFG. CO. LTD.

Supreme RECORDS

416

LET THE LORD BE SEEN IN YOU
(R. KING)
Bob Marley & The Spiritual Sisters

RECORDED BY JAMAICA RECORDING STUDIO 13 BRENTFORD ROAD KGN.

WAIL Bob **SOUL**
TRADE MARK

Bob Marley
and The
Wailing Wailers

18a Greenwich
Park Road,
Kingston 5

N   M

BUS DEM SHUT

UPSETTER RECORDS

Peter Tosh
DREAMLAND
(BUNNY)
THE WAILERS

PRODUCED
AND DIRECTED
PERRY

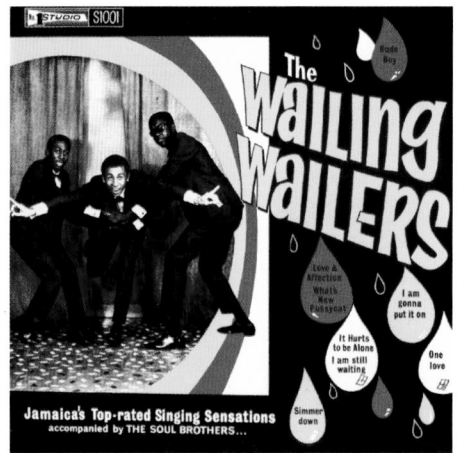

tunes off the radio, often Motown material by the early Supremes, Martha and The Vandellas, or Mary Wells.

When a friend took Rita up to Studio One one time, all three of The Wailers were there. They adopted a distinctly distant air until Rita reminded Peter that she was the girl who they would see standing on Greenwich Park Road. When she also revealed that she was a singer, an audition was arranged for The Soulettes at which they impressed Coxsone; the girls were passed on to Bob for management and to find material for them.

If anything, Rita now realised, it was shyness that had been behind the offhand manner exhibited by The Wailers, and especially by Bob, towards her: their hit records had not gone to their heads, as she had initially suspected. Now she saw that staying on top of the current music and being consistent with hits one after another was not easy. She was also surprised, given that they had had a number of big songs by now, at how little they were making.

Bob's responsibility towards Coxsone's new artists increased his workload, as Rita saw from his work with The Soulettes. He rewrote 'I Love You Baby' for them, and it became the trio's first release. Most of the songwriting for The Soulettes, Rita noticed, took place in the studio at the time they were recording. Bob's skills as a lyricist impressed her, especially his willingness to use himself as a model. 'Through using himself as an example, he was able to express what was happening in people's lives, especially when it came to identifying with the street people, the common people.'

Bob's approach to the acts under his care was like a Jamaican version of the Motown charm school. Rigour was the keynote. He would insist on a disciplined approach to

PETER, BOB AND RITA

work. But he carried such an air of discipline himself that it was impossible for The Soulettes not to be in the same studio without it rubbing off on them. A respectable, responsible public image should be presented at all times, he insisted – especially when Coxsone was around!

Such a stance made Rita and the two other girls initially very wary of their unsmiling tutor. 'He was very firm about what we were about: if you come to the studio, you don't come to play; you're here to work. As long as Bob was there, that discipline was established.'

Then Rita found that if she did as he suggested, chinks of light quickly appeared in the armour. 'You have to be prepared to meet him. Then when you do, you find that behind all of that he is the nicest person, like an angel.'

She also had her own sense of reserve. 'When I met these guys I was not sure if this was where I wanted to be. They knew my upcoming – how I was brought up – and they could see how I was grown up different from the regular girl you could hit on easily. But then because them being The Wailers, I was proud to be among them. But I was also wary: what if my mother finds out?'

Rita had been looking after her child full-time when she became involved with The Soulettes. The Wailers, however, had no idea that she was a mother. 'One day I was in the studio and my breasts got real hard with milk, and it started to come through my brassiere. Bob looked at me and said, "Oh, you have a baby!" Because I hadn't told anybody. I said, "Of course!" The other two said, "You didn't tell us!" Then we all started to get closer. They were nice guys, and I began to feel strong from having them as my friends. I got more firmly into myself. This was when they started to tell me about Rastafari. How being a pretty black girl you mustn't do this, mustn't wear that, mustn't eat pork . . . All these things.'

To Rita's surprise, one day Bunny told her that Bob claimed to be in love with her. From then on he would occasionally bring her short love letters from Bob. At first Rita was not convinced – Bob had a rival. 'It didn't happen so fast. It took a time for me to decide whether it was Bob or Peter. Because I was liking Peter more, because he was more friendly and would chat and laugh, and Bob was too serious – Peter was more jovial. But Bob was for the discipline, which impressed me very much.'

It was some months before a sexual relationship began between Bob and Rita. Eventually they made love for the first time in Bob's old home, Tartar's kitchen, Tartar having discreetly absented himself for the evening. From now on, when they saw each other at night, Bob and Rita frequently returned to Tartar's: sometimes Tartar would take Rita home to Greenwich Park Road on the crossbar of his bicycle; sometimes he would lend the bike to Bob to carry her back. Bob told Rita that Bunny's father, Mr Toddy, had offered to let him live at his home, but that he always felt like an outsider whenever he visited there. He was turning into a man, and the people there would still treat him as a boy.

There was also a larger problem connected with Bob's residence at Studio One. That sense of unease he had often felt in the room he'd been given had intensified, until it had become thoroughly specific: he believed, he told Rita, there was a duppy in the room, as though somebody was physically trying to hold him down. Bwai, he would say, he can't sleep in the night because the thing just keep coming back to haunt him.

Rita decided to spend the night with him there, sharing his bed of an old door balanced on some building bricks . . . and experienced precisely the same sensation. 'I felt as though someone came into the room and held me down. You'd try to get out of this grip and feel as though you were going into a trance: you couldn't speak; you couldn't talk; you couldn't see anything – you just felt the sensation. I wondered if it was something I'd smoked, but Bob said it happened to him every night.'

Realising that Bob couldn't stay there any longer, Rita made a suggestion: Bob must come and stay with her at 18A Greenwich Park Road. All she had was a little room she shared with her cousin and baby Sharon, but at least Bob would be safe there from this duppy. The next night Bob climbed into Rita's room through the window. As soon as he was tucked up in bed with her, her cousin and baby Sharon, the girls began to giggle. Rita's Auntie Viola came into the room and turned on the light. Outraged at what she saw, she made Bob and her niece leave the house the same way that Bob had sneaked in: through the window. The couple passed a night under the stars.

The next morning when Rita threatened to leave the house for good if Bob wasn't allowed to stay there, Auntie Viola relented. Realising her niece was serious about this relationship, she took the line of least resistance: she agreed to build a shack by the side of the house in which the couple would be able to live.

MUSICAL INDEPENDENCE

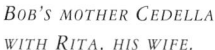

What Rita did not know was that Bob's mother had remarried in the United States. Ever since she had arrived in Wilmington, Delaware, Cedella Booker, as she was now known, had intended to bring Bob up there. Now at last she had her green-card, and had written to her son, telling him he should come and live with her, even if only for a short time.

Bob was uncertain. His career as a musician was going well. Why should he risk losing it? But he soon came to the conclusion that the only thing he would be losing was his reputation. He had his wages of three pounds a week from Coxsone, but otherwise he was still broke, and was beginning to feel resentful about this. Anyway, before he had become so involved with Rita he had already made up his mind to move up to the States for a short time; he knew the experience would be important for his life.

Now he had another decision to make. For the first time since he had fallen for the girl in Trench Town, Bob was truly in love. His life had been full of loss, with the pattern of people taken from him. This time it seemed as though it was he who could be throwing away an important relationship: he believed that if he didn't formalise his relationship with Rita he would lose her to someone else while he was away. There seemed only one solution: marry Rita.

A sensitive soul, which was why Bob had chosen her as his girlfriend, Rita was not oblivious to the deep loneliness this young man had constantly encountered in his life. She had seen the times when he would lose confidence in himself. 'Who is me? A fockin' blood-cla'at white man pickney?' 'God is your father,' Rita would remind him. 'The therapy of the Bible was what I had to use, and how colour is nothing,' she recalls. 'This father was just sent physically to bring you, but your real father is watching over you and he will never disown you,' she would say.

Rita loved Bob deeply. Yet when he asked her

ROBERT NESTA MARLEY WITH HIS BRIDE ALVARITA CONSTANTIA ANDERSON AT THEIR WEDDING ON 10 FEBRUARY 1966; IT WAS FOUR DAYS SINCE BOB'S TWENTY-FIRST BIRTHDAY.

to marry him, there was also an element of compassion in her decision to accept. 'Bob had a lot of hurt. He was very sensitive – just born that way, and he just had to adapt to it. When I went off with Bob, it wasn't just love-love-love, in terms of falling in love and being head-over-heels in love with him. It was out of real sorrow for this guy. I'm saying to myself: "Shit, we have it bad, but this guy's having it worse, and I don't see why he should be having it this way."'

Not that Rita herself wasn't about to take on her share of pain: the very next day after Bob married her, on 10 February 1966, four days after his twenty-first birthday, he left Jamaica for Wilmington, Delaware – just as his father had left his mother the day after they were married.

Cedella had already heard rumours that her son was planning to marry, but had received no confirmation of this. When she picked Bob up at the airport in Philadelphia for the forty-mile drive

BOB'S MOTHER CEDELLA WITH RITA, HIS WIFE.

RIGHT: RITA MARLEY.

back to Wilmington, he told her that it had already taken place. 'He was madly, madly, madly in love with that girl . . . All his heart, his mind, his soul. He'd say to me, "Mama, if you would ever see her, you would love her. She is just a plain girl, and she walk and roll." I asked someone what that means – and it's kind of knock-kneed. He loved those things about her.' Cedella noticed that local girls might call up for her son, but he would hand the phone to his mother, refusing to speak to them.

In Kingston, meanwhile, Rita continued with her own musical career. Bob's departure had confused her. 'Is this what they call marriage?' she would ask herself. But Tartar gave her strength and motivation while she waited for his return. 'He'll come back soon,' he would reassure her.

AS THE SIXTIES PROGRESSED THE WAILERS, WITH BOB INFLUENCED BY WHAT HE SAW ON HIS TRIPS TO THE UNITED STATES, BEGAN TO ADOPT AN INCREASINGLY MILITANT BLACK POWER IMAGE.

Besides, Bob had left his new bride with an important task.

On 21 April 1966, just over two months after Bob's departure, an event of extraordinary significance was to occur for all followers of Rastafari. His Imperial Majesty Haile Selassie I, Emperor of Ethiopia, was due to arrive at Kingston airport. Bob had written to Rita: 'If possible, go and see for yourself.' She had required no urging: this could give her the proof she needed.

For Bob's part, having grown up among the rebellious thinkers of Trench Town and Studio One, his feelings about the philosophy of

Rastafari were already extremely positive. He believed in it sufficiently to lecture non-believers about its worth – Rita had benefited from his instruction. But he was still questing to penetrate to the heart of this mystery; he needed further guidance.

From her vantage point on Windward Road, which leads in from Palisadoes airport, Rita Marley had what was perhaps the most profound of many remarkable, God-given experiences she would enjoy in her life.

Seated in Governor-General Clifford Campbell's purring official limousine, Haile Selassie was driven into Kingston. Rita eased her way to the front of the crowd on this section of the Windward Road and stood in the warm, light rain, waiting for the car to come nearer. Rita was anxious. She had made a secret pact: if, somehow, she saw the sign she was looking for, she would accept the divine status of Haile Selassie.

As the Daimler limousine drew parallel with her, Rita's thoughts were not positive. 'How is it they are saying that this man is so great,' she wondered, 'when he looks so short, with his army hat over his head in such a way I can't even see his eyes.

'Then I said to myself, "What am I even thinking about? Jesus is a spirit."' At that exact moment Haile Selassie raised his face: he looked directly into Rita's eyes and waved. 'And I looked into his hand and there was the nail-print. It was a mark, and I could only identify that mark with the scriptures of history, saying, "When you see him, you will know him by the nail-print in his hands." So when I saw this, I said to myself that this could be true, this could be the man of whom it was said: before the year 2,000 Christ will be a man walking on this earth.'

Later, Rita learned of other momentous events that had taken place that day. How, for example, a flock of seven white doves had ascended into a thick blanket of cloud to guide His Majesty's royal plane down; how, as the doves emerged from the overcast sky, the sun had shone clearly through the chink in the clouds. Rita heard of how tears had come to the eyes of His Imperial Majesty when he stepped out of the door of his plane. Wasn't this even further proof? Didn't the

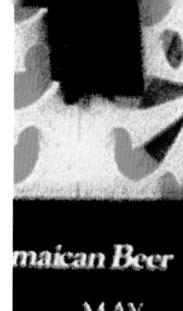
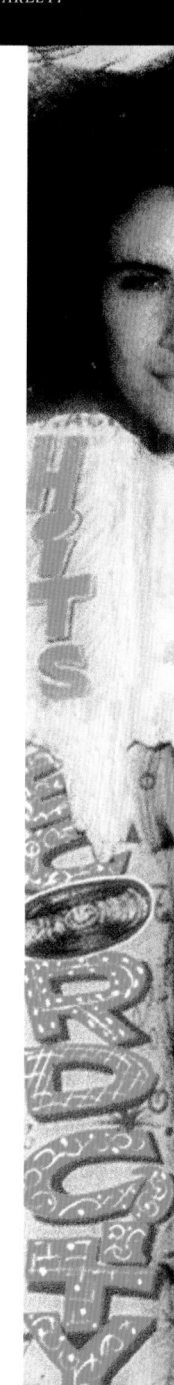

FROM LEFT TO RIGHT: CARLTON BARRETT, WIRE LINDO, SEECO PATTERSON AND BOB MARLEY.

shortest chapter in the Bible contain just one line: Jesus wept when he saw Israel people.

Rita wrote to Bob and told him that what she had seen had far surpassed all her expectations; that this thing seemed to be true.

What she had seen had shaken her to the foundation of her soul. She spent long days wondering about it. 'Then I stopped processing my hair, changed my diet, started to see my brother as a brother. I find I slide from that Christian thinking into recognising Haile Selassie, into recognising Africa, into recognising the Rasta philosophy of God and living their life-style, one that suits me more than this other one which seems so hypocritical. You realise it is the same as Christianity, but with maybe a little more freedom.'

Mortimer Planner was living in Trench Town at this time. With a warm glow in his heart, he observed the effect that the Emperor's visit had had on many of Jamaica's citizens. People were wandering about the streets of the capital, visibly perplexed by these matters of profound spiritual and theological importance. So many people were asking themselves the same questions that Rita Marley had puzzled over: was this really the man the Rastafarians claimed him to be? The more that His Majesty remained in their midst, Planner noted, the more people started having different considerations about their lives and about the world.

In 1939, as an early convert to Rastafari, Planner had moved to Trench Town. Born in Kingston in 1920, he was one of the founder members of Kingston's first Rastafarian encampment in the Dungle. His devout studies of all matters connected with the faith, combined with his brilliant intellect, established Planner, or 'Planno', as he simply became known, as one of the elders of Rastafari.

He was part of the natural mystic within the orthodox Nyabinghi school, the branch of Rastafari that keeps the sovereignty of ancient, sacred African rhythms through hand-drumming. Planner had played drums all his life. Carrying these rhythms to recording studios, he would harmonise with whatever the other musicians had to offer.

After the construction of the government

yards, he had become a tenant at 5 Fifth Street. Planner was consulted on all matters of serious import by the 'clean, poor people' of Trench Town, as he called them; acknowledging the true nature of his neighbours was essential in attempting to arrive at any solution. 'They were not particularly law-abiding,' he noted. 'That was how the society have the people. That was one part of the people's predicament.'

When the deputation was gathered to pay homage to His Majesty in Ethiopia in 1961, Mortimer Planner was chosen as one of the members of this small, honoured group. Planner loved Ethiopia. In the unpolluted atmosphere of Addis Ababa he breathed in the clean air and gazed in awe at the city's tall eucalyptus trees. Most inspiring of all was his visit to His Imperial Majesty Haile Selassie I.

So it was Mortimer Planner, his Kodak Brownie camera dangling around his neck as though he were a tourist, who had ascended the steps of His Majesty's plane when it landed in Kingston to extend a welcome from the brotherhood of Rastafari. The mystic breeze that blew from this moment was to dominate the rest of his life. Gradually it showed him, he believed, how to teach the world. Specifically, however, Planner paid heed to Haile Selassie's parting words of advice: international co-operation will quicken progress. Planner prayed that the people of the world could become receptive to such a simple truth.

Like his brethren, Mortimer Planner believed that democracy had run its course: the time of theocracy was now coming. Planner had no doubt of the role that Rastafari would play in the time of change and world crisis leading up to the year 2,000. He had read it all in Revelations.

Rita flew to Delaware in August 1966. She and Bob fell into each other's arms: this absence had been difficult for both of them. She found that, much to his mother's chagrin, her husband's hair bore the first hints of an Afro. Rita had much to tell him. For example, that after seven or eight years of the same mutated boogie beat of ska dominating the music of Jamaica, it had begun to change: the bass-line was starting to break up, coming in shorter, more pronounced

patterns of notes than it had for ska.

Rock steady was the new form; literally a steadier form of the beat, its origins probably had a very simple explanation: that the unusually hot summer of 1966 had made the faster dance movements of ska impossible. Languid and sensuous, rock steady sounded like trouble. It was little surprise that the rude boys had taken it up as their music – cooler than cool, hotter than hot. Several records vied for the title of the first rock-steady tune, among them Roy Shirley's 'Hold Them', Derrick Morgan's 'Tougher Than

'Planner was someone we would listen to. He was a community elder, someone who everyone would respect for what he stood for in the Rastafarian faith. And he used to sell herbs – that was his trade. And he would talk about Rastafari.

'He was respected in that sense of communicating with the people and being able to tell us what was happening in Africa. And he was a great reader, and a good psychologist; he had a lot of head: to survive in that type of community he had to be something of a psychologist.

'He had been into Rastafari for a long time. When we knew him, he was established into organisations like the World Federation and Rasta groups that went to Ethiopia and visited His Majesty. He had a great past in terms of what he used to do.

'Planner grew up that way: in the ghetto as a bad boy and come up tough and then found himself. Not bad in terms of doing wrong things. But growing up in that kind of community he had no chance but to be tough.'

Tough' and Alton Ellis's 'Girl I've Got a Date'. The latter tune was produced by Duke Reid; whatever truth lay behind the various claims of having had the first rock-steady disc out of the traps, one fact was certain: Duke Reid had seized the moment in a way that his great rival, Coxsone Dodd, had not.

Although Coxsone was to enjoy The Wailers' 'Rocking Steady' – which contained these Bob

Marley lyrics: 'When first I heard Rock steady/It thrilled me to the bone '– his studio had temporarily lost momentum (although within a year a trio of producers – Bunny Lee, Lee 'Scratch' Perry and Osbourne 'King Tubby' Ruddock – were to have brought about a third change, into reggae music). Anyway, The Wailers were about to quit the Coxsone stable for good.

What hit a sharper nerve in Bob Marley than these changes in Jamaican music were Rita's stories about the visit of His Imperial Majesty. He could not fail to notice the changes that had clearly descended upon his wife. His time in the United States, where he had taken waitering jobs, driven a fork-lift truck and worked on the assembly-line in a Chrysler plant, had been a crucial period of self-reflection. One chapter was over now, he knew.

When he returned to Kingston two months later, it was with two quite specific purposes: as far as his musical career was concerned, Bob Marley had resolved to set up his own record company and become a self-financing musical artist – to this end, he had been both storing away new songs and stashing away every cent that came his way (although this hoard only amounted to some seven hundred American dollars). His other main intention was to pursue his quest for knowledge about Rastafari. Little did he know that the two would become irrevocably interlinked.

Bob had already encountered Mortimer Planner in his day-to-day runnings in Trench Town. Now he was impelled to actively seek out this shaman of the ghetto. In his nervous request to Planner to provide him with instruction in the great truths of Rastafari, the singer's natural humility prevailed.

'Him learn so much from the experiences of people who suffer,' was Planner's explanation for the readiness with which Bob absorbed his teaching. 'Bob was taught in a Rasta university. And him understood well. Him a bright student.'

As Bob's 'mentor and tutor', as he described himself, Mortimer Planner guided that profound but unformed sense within the musician. 'It had for long been coming to the conscious thought within his soul: Serve Rastafari! Understand how you have to hear it and see it and feel it to come free. How you have to let it pilot you and open your eyes and see within your life how you want to live.'

Planner's teaching took many forms. He would explain to Bob the links between Egyptology and the Coptic church, for example. But he would also describe the symbolism at the heart of various international systems in intricate detail: such mysteries as the reason for the image of the Egyptian pyramid on the dollar note; or the true significance of the English Crown, and its relation to the Church of England and to that of Rome.

This was crucial, the Rastaman sage believed, in helping Bob to come to terms with who he was: the personification of a hybrid of the United States and Britain. 'His mother is a green-card American, and his father was British. So Bob come out a British–American. And him have to move far from there to be the successful universal figure that him end up to be.'

Something had shifted within Bob's unconscious, at the very deepest level. It was as though he doubted the validity of the paeans to rude-boy culture formerly sung by The Wailers. Rastafari, he began to instruct the ratchet-knife wielders of Trench Town, was the only course. At this time, Planner observed, Bob had a strong influence in shaping the youth out of their rude-boy image.

Rita, did Bob talk much about the fact that his father wasn't around?

'Not regularly, no. There was nothing to talk about, really. How can you talk about someone you never know.'

But these large-scale changes within Bob were not without considerable struggle. Early in 1967 he appeared to undergo something of a minor nervous breakdown. Bob Marley was unable or unwilling to speak to anyone other than Rita or Planner. If others attempted to speak to him, he would reply only through Rita or Planner.

Not surprisingly, this was the cause of considerable discussion in Trench Town. Everyone had a point of view: some believed Bob to be seriously mentally ill; others felt that downright despair was behind this behaviour;

then there were those who perceived him to be suffering from a depressive malaise; while a more radical faction, with whom Planner aligned himself, believed that this withdrawal was motivated by a need for psychic self-protection that might ultimately lead to extended mental powers.

Whatever the cause, this syndrome vanished as quickly as it had arrived. As well as becoming Bob's spiritual coach, Mortimer Planner began to take on the role of his business manager: in a country where there is virtually no music business tradition or infrastructure, the task of management very often befalls the artist's closest friend. Planner backed Bob to the best of his abilities, although this help often consisted of little more than moral support.

Bob had revealed to the other Wailers that he intended to set up his own operation. The shack that Auntie Viola had built at the side of 18A Greenwich Park Road would become by day the Wail 'N' Soul 'M record store, in honour of its first two acts, The Wailers and The Soulettes; this was also to be the name of The Wailers' label. To this effect Bob installed a counter window in their little home, to which it reverted by night. A first single was released, 'Bend Down Low', recorded at Studio One but produced by Bob and released on his own label; 'Mellow Mood', the B side, was one of Bob's finest songs ever.

However, 1967 was hardly more than a few months old before the grim financial reality of running his own label and shop began to tell on Bob. He needed a way out. So, with Rita and her daughter Sharon, Bob moved back to St Ann, to farm some of the land Omeriah Malcolm had bequeathed to his mother after he passed away in 1963, the same week that she had moved to the United States. But Bob and his family needed some help, and to that end he made a great personal decision: with Rita beside him he went to uptown Kingston, to the offices of Marley and Co., his late father's family firm. (His father had died in 1955, not long after Bob's mother had failed legally to secure some money from him.) To the embarrassment of his father's two brothers whom he found there, Bob introduced

Rita: 'It was different for me, because I'd never been exposed to the country. I'd been in Kingston all my life. It was different: I had to carry water, collect wood to make the fire, and I had to sleep on a little, small bed on the dirt because they didn't have flooring. But it was all out of love – I had decided to do so, and it didn't matter. I was going into the faith of Rastafari and I was seeking to find an independent sort of self.

'Because Bob was already exposed to this lifestyle, it was a thrill for him to see me just living it. It was something he had decided he would do eventually – just be a farmer and stay in the country and live. So this was always his feeling: his need to go back into the open country, and just be himself.

'We did a lot of writing and singing there, sharing a lot of special times, special moments. I was getting to know the other side of him more so than just being in the studio.

'We did things like "Chances Are", and a lot of his songs – sometimes Bob only write one verse today, and then when he gets into the studio he finds the chorus and the other verses. He'd try out stuff on me. Listen to this one, listen to that one. And look up into the sky and the air – a lot of inspiration coming from there.'

himself and asked if he could borrow a tractor to plough his land in St Ann. 'But their attitude,' recalls Rita, 'was "Why you come to us? Yes, Norval might be your father, but he didn't leave anything here for you." And so we left very disappointed, very upset. That had been the only hope: let's go and check these people and see if we can get some help. Because we didn't have nothing, we didn't have anything.'

Towards the end of the year Bob returned to Kingston and worked with The Wailers on three more singles for the Wail 'N' Soul 'M label. 'Thank You Lord' expressed the optimism that Bob and Rita felt, despite the financially hard times; the tune was backed by the B side, 'Nice Time', an expression of his joy at returning to Jamaica, and the nickname of Cedella, their first child, to whom Rita had given birth in Kingston Public Hospital shortly after they had returned to Trench Town. There was also 'Hypocrites' with its B side of 'Pound Get a Blow', and a tune called 'Pyaka', which was produced by Mortimer

Planner and sold well: a 'pyaka', a word with African origins, is a hawkish person, and the song was a social comment on the current situation in Jamaica at the time, as well as on the group's deteriorating relationship with Coxsone Dodd. The sound was rougher and tougher than the Studio One material had been; the feel was looser, freed-up, though that was partially the effect of the slower rhythm of rock steady.

The shop and label brought independence, but they were hard work. Every time The Wailers came out with a new wax, the three members would personally take it round Kingston's record shops to feel the vibe. But it was Rita who took the copies round by hand, selling them into the stores. Everyone in the record retail business knew about Rita the Rastawoman who sold records, aware that every time she walked into their premises she would be bringing a new tune from The Wailers. Sometimes when she had a heavy load to deliver she would ask Bob to give her a hand.

In 1968 Bob managed to scrape the cash together to buy a second-hand Hillman Minx car. One day when he was out with Mortimer Planner, he let the revered elder drive. Surely the man who was important enough to greet His Imperial Majesty could steer Bob's car through Kingston, even if he didn't have a full driving licence? When they were stopped by the police and this offence was discovered, the pair were imprisoned overnight. As soon as he was released, Bob left Kingston and returned to the country. Shortly before the family left the city, Rita had given birth to their second child, David as his name read on his birth certificate, 'Ziggy' as everyone called him.

Bob had got the cash for the car as a consequence of a deal that Planner had struck for him with Danny Sims, an American who was resident in Jamaica. Danny Sims had run Sapphire's, the first downtown black supper club in Manhattan. Sims, who promoted concerts throughout the Caribbean, ended up managing Johnny Nash, a handsome Texan-born singer with a sweet, powerful voice who had had a number of big-selling records in the United

States. In 1966 Sims had moved to Jamaica after discovering he could record American music far more cheaply in Kingston. Nash moved there with him, and some of his songs began to develop a Jamaican feel; he was probably the first international artist to co-opt Jamaican rhythms into his tunes, exemplified by the rock-steady feel of a big international hit he had with an interpretation of 'Cupid', the Sam Cooke tune.

Many of the musicians Nash met in Jamaica were Rastafarians. To find out more about their religion, Nash accompanied Neville Willoughby, a top radio disc jockey, to west Kingston to a Grounation, a ceremony at which the Nyabinghi rituals of drumming and chanting were taking place. Mortimer Planner and Bob and Rita Marley were also there at the Grounation. Nash couldn't believe the number of beautiful commercial songs, his own compositions, that Bob sang.

Rita on Ziggy: 'This was his first son, so there was much excitement: what shall we call him? I wanted David, because of how he was born at home in Trench Town. I said, "This little boy must be David." And I also saw Bob as a great writer: sometimes I would even call him King David. His appearance sometimes is very royal when you look at him – and that was before fame, success and money. And I also thought it was a good name to make a great son: because he was born so humble in a little house in Trench Town, on newspaper. We couldn't afford much. Auntie was the midwife: Bob was there helping to clean up blood. It was a special baby to us, a special thing in our life, even though Cedella was there already. But having a boy is important.

'And Bob said, "Well, this is Ziggy, man," because his foot was all turned. "This is Ziggy, Ziggy." And I said, "What is this Ziggy?" And Bob said, "It's football!" – a name for, what they call it, dribbling. They used to call out to Bob, "Ziggy, Bob, Ziggy!" He was good at that, taking the ball and moving it up and down. And so Bob said, "This is Ziggy, this is Ziggy!" That's how Ziggy got that name.'

Immediately he told Danny Sims about them.

When Sims got in touch with Bob, the musician sent Planner along to negotiate. After Planner and Sims had had 'a few lickle rough talks', the American ended up addressing the dread as 'chief', and an agreement was struck. Sims would apply himself to breaking Bob as both a songwriter and an artist in his own right; he would receive adequate royalties for his songwriting and a publishing deal with Sims's company, Cayman Music; in addition, The Wailers would each be put on a retainer of fifty US dollars a week.

Five days after Bob had signed with Danny Sims he received a message from a man called Dickie Jobson who had ridden down on his bicycle to Trench Town to try and find him. Could Bob please come and check him, was the message: he might be able to help in some way.

Bob came up to see Dickie, who told him he had a close friend in the music business called Chris Blackwell, who ran Island Records. Dickie had heard Bob's recent music and had been very impressed: would Bob like to meet his friend?

Unfortunately, Bob replied, he had just signed a deal with Danny Sims. But maybe another time.

Planner observed Sims's efforts with Bob and The Wailers with interest. Soon he came to a positive conclusion: that Sims loved Bob and had only his best interests at heart. During the course of their relationship with Sims, which fizzled out in 1972, The Wailers recorded over eighty songs for the American, some of which they had already released. There was a rock-steady update of 'Put It On', for example, and a new 'Nice Time' on which the great South African musician Hugh Masakela played trumpet. There were also fresh gems like the first try-out of a song called 'Soul Rebel'. But what was most notable was the way in which Sims did not acknowledge the deep-seated new spiritual belief in Rastafari in the music, espoused by Bob and the other two Wailers. According to Mortimer Planner, Danny Sims consciously steered Bob away from writing about Rastafari. Such subject matter, he believed, would hardly help Bob crack the American market, Sims's

From St Ann's Bay came Burning Spear, a vocal trio who had taken the favoured Jamaican form of the three-piece harmony group to its most extreme roots. The group's leader was Winston Rodney, who by the early seventies would himself personally take on the Burning Spear title. His gravelly vocals sounded as though they contained every piece of truth the island of Jamaica had ever known.

As a youth, Spear was digging Bob. 'Bob was Jamaican number one star. Bob was the man. There was no other man. We have a lot of singers who were even in the business before Bob. But Bob ended up being the man.'

For whatever reason, one morning late in January 1969, Spear found himself in the innermost reaches of St Ann, close to the area of Rhoden Hall. As he stepped out along a rough road, Spear came across Bob travelling in the opposite direction on a donkey. Bob was headed for his cultivation, the land he was farming: his donkey was garlanded in plants. Getting off his donkey, Bob sat down on the grass verge with Spear and rolled a

spliff. And for many hours the two men reasoned upon the matter of Rastafari and its roots, the culture, His Majesty, the music . . .

'Then I remember saying to him, "Jah B," – I call him Jah B – "'Ow can I get started in this business?" And Jah B would turn to I and say, "Check Studio One. Tell Mr Dodd I sent you."

'And we were talking like a Sunday, when we meet in the hills, and on the Monday I was back out of the hills and thinking about it. Until the time came when I checked Studio One. That was a Sunday, too, and they were doing an audition thing, listening to young singers. And I was one of the ones who they select my song. My first song was called "Door Peep".

'So the whole thing for Burning Spear started because Bob told I to check Studio One. That was the first time we had really exchanged talk, and we could look at each other and talk and laugh. That was one of my biggest musical experiences. Before I even get started. Dealing with the main man.'

principal target.

All the same, Danny Sims was the first international record figure to recognise and respect Bob's talents, long before others did. Bob, moreover, respected Sims's connections, and the fact that they could get his records played.

Sims did not have an exclusive deal with The Wailers and they were free to record for whoever they liked in Jamaica. Accordingly, early in 1969 Bob found himself travelling back into Kingston and pulling his car up in front of the offices of Leslie Kong, the producer with whom he had made his very first records.

The previous year Kong had produced 'Do the Reggay' by The Maytals, which established the new beat that had followed on from rock steady. Kong was hot and had recently had an international hit with Desmond Dekker's 'Israelites'. But the sessions from The Wailers would not come anywhere near to emulating this success. Many of the songs, however, were strong and substantial and would be seen as classics in years to come – 'Caution', 'Cheer Up' and 'Do It Twice' were among the numbers written by Bob. Peter Tosh, meanwhile, sang a fiery lead on the protest hymn 'Go Tell It On the Mountain' and his own hectoring 'Soon Come'.

But none of these records sold. Commercially, this was a lean time for The Wailers. If it hadn't been for Danny Sims and his retainer, things would have been far worse although it still was not easy. Bob and his family had moved back to Trench Town, to First Street now. The mood in the area was more settled, although the police might occasionally move in in the middle of the night and mash up some unfortunate suspect's dwelling.

The reputation of the area was still such that outsiders had been afraid of walking Trench Town's streets and lanes to buy discs at 18A Greenwich Park Road. Bob now had another tiny record shop, the Soul Shack, which was mainly Rita's province. On the corner of Beeston and Orange Streets, it was at least in the downtown commercial area, though it was hardly the pulse-beat of a recording empire. 'But when we got the shop downtown it was a thrill, even though there was more work to be done by getting up to go down and locking up and coming home,' recalled Rita. 'You'd have to meet obligations to pay for the records to be pressed. You don't see any improvement in your living conditions in Trench Town, and you're not getting any airplay.'

So much had been going on that Bob needed some time to think: his drive for self-determination had been interlinked with his espousal of Rastafari, but its success so far was clearly very relative.

Bob decided to go up to the United States once more and stay with his mother. This time, Cedella Booker met a son whose outlook seemed radically altered. She had been prepared for the worst: Bob had already written to her, telling her of his interest in Rastafarianism. But how could her boy become involved with such people?

Both mother and son avoided the issue, Bob only hedging around it through the subject of diet. Nowadays, he said, he did not eat meat. For breakfast porridge or plantain were fine. But

Rita Marley: 'Danny spent a lot of money and time in working with us. Keeping us in the studio day after day and night after night at Federal Studios. It was owned by Ken Khouri. And before that there had been times when we would have to stay outside the gate, waiting to be seen by Khouri just to get an audition. And we'd be told, No, no, no, no, no: next week, next month. So getting in there with Johnny Nash and Danny Sims was like a feeling of victory. And later we became the owners of it. So life is something else.'

what do he eat for the rest of his meals? wondered his mother. Fish tea, vegetables, them kinda t'ing – but strictly no meat.

'So I try to cook to please him – give him what he wants. But then him always cautious about the pots I use to cook his food. Because him ask if I cook bacon in that, because pork is bad. My husband is an American – he likes to eat bacon and eggs. And Bob start to tell him how dangerous them things is, and so mi no want to cook it no more. And I tell my husband he have to cook it himself.'

Bob had not travelled alone: his family had come with him. Rita wanted an environment other than Trench Town for the children to grow up in: 'Everyone was getting big, and I said that I couldn't wait around for records to sell. This was my decision, not Bob's.' Cedella and Ziggy started to go to American schools, Rita was employed as a nurse, and Stephen, with whom Rita had been pregnant when they had flown up to the States, was born there in Wilmington. Bob, meanwhile, found himself working on the assembly-line at the Chrysler plant again.

This was at the peak of the Vietnam war, however, and immigrant workers from the Caribbean were deemed likely cannon fodder. In October Bob Marley received his call-up papers. His response? To board the next flight to Kingston.

BOB AND RITA AND THEIR CHILDREN: (FROM LEFT) BOB'S STEP-DAUGHTER SHARON, ZIGGY, AND CEDELLA; SEATED IN THE PUSH-CHAIR IS STEVEN.

ZIGGY STANDS IN FRONT OF THE PAINTING OF THE YOUNG MARLEY FAMILY.

*JULIAN, ZIGGY, STEVIE AND
CEDELLA MARLEY (FROM TOP
CLOCKWISE).*

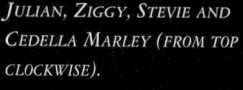

Bob's mother, Mrs Booker, with Rita Marley, Cedella, Julian, Ziggy and Steven.

Tyrone Downie and Diane Jobson, the Tuff Gong inhouse lawyer and close friend.

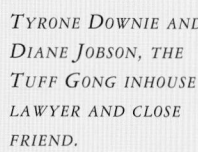

RIGHT: THE WAILERS:
(LEFT TO RIGHT) EARL
'WIRE' LINDO, ASTON
'FAMILY MAN' BARRETT,
BOB, PETER TOSH,
CARLTON BARRETT AND
BUNNY LIVINGSTON.

y o u t '

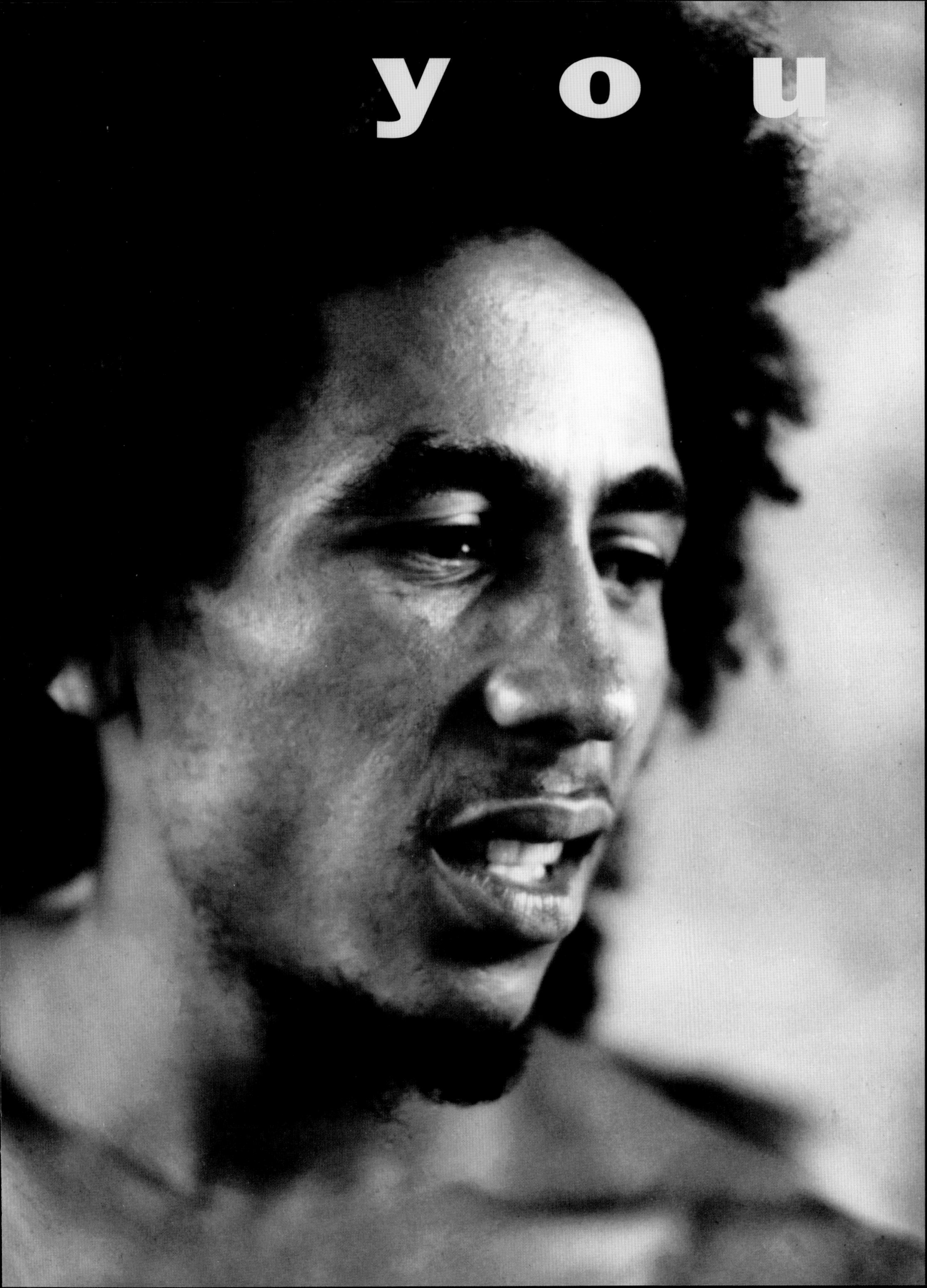

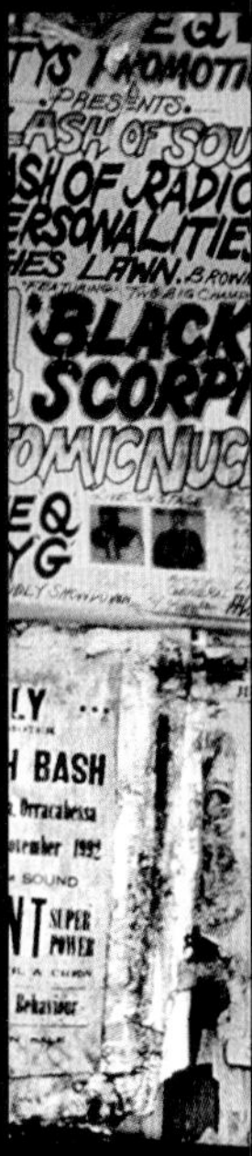

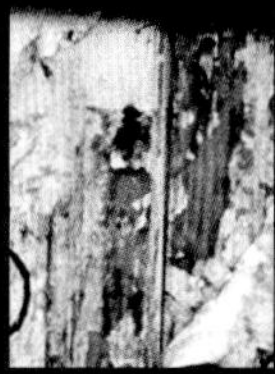

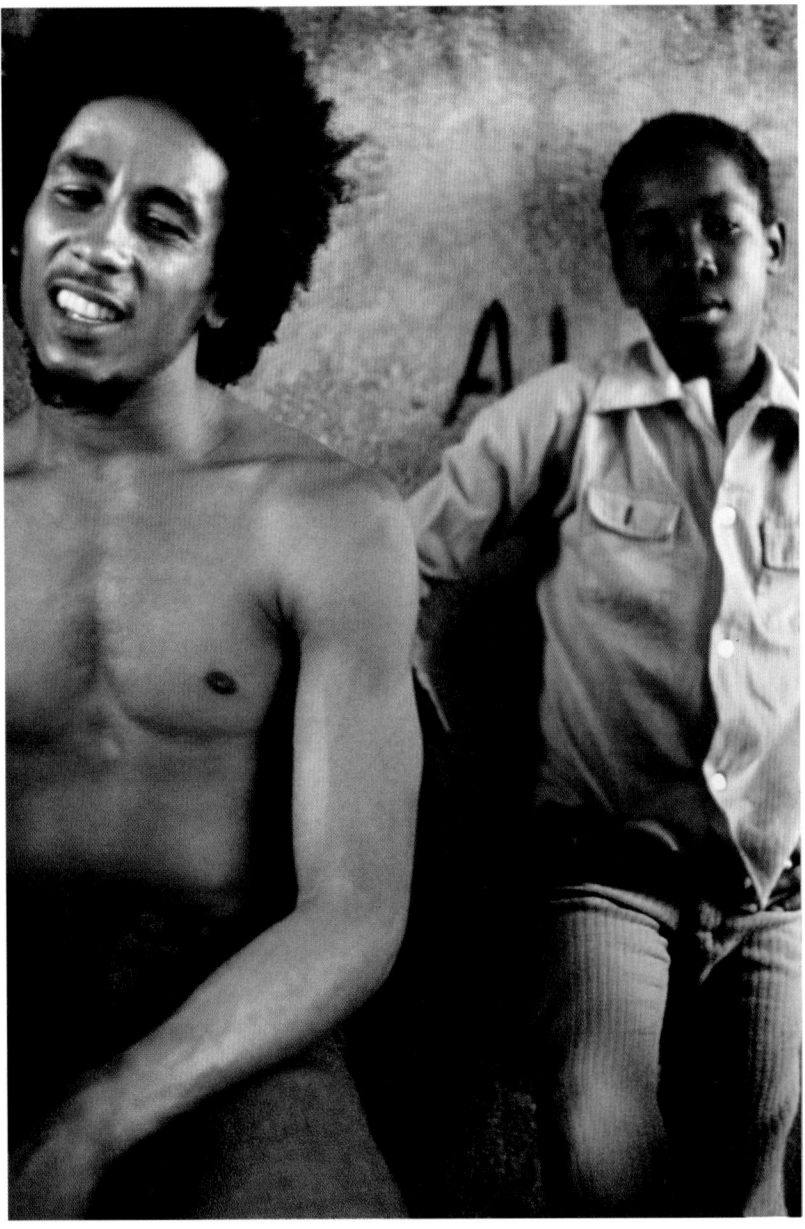

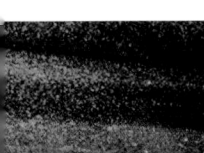

SCRATCH

LEE 'SCRATCH' PERRY, ALSO KNOWN AS 'LITTLE' AND 'THE UPSETTER', IS ONE OF THE GREATEST ARTISTS — IN ANY FIELD — THAT THE CARIBBEAN HAS PRODUCED; HIS ECCENTIRC BEHAVIOUR WAS SIMPLY ONE PART OF AN ARTISTIC SCHEME THAT REVOLUTIONISED JAMAICAN MUSIC.

Lee 'Scratch' Perry, who was born in Kingston in 1939, had graduated from being a 'selecter' on the Downbeat sound system and a 'fetcher' at 13 Brentford Road to a far more formidable figure. On Charles Street he had his own shop, Upsetter Records, where he sold the records he produced. Before Bob left Jamaica on his second trip to Wilmington, he was already in the habit of coming to check this extrovert figure; their mutual flight from Coxsone had created a bond between them.

Some had attributed the birth of reggae to Scratch alone – ultimately he would reveal himself to be one of the finest artists the Caribbean has produced in any field – after he started dabbling with a musical pace that made you feel, he said, as though you were stepping in glue. He had had an international hit with 'Return of Django' by The Upsetters, his house band, which consisted of a group formerly known as The Hippy Boys.

The Hippy Boys had been formed by Aston 'Family Man' Barrett. Family Man, whose nickname came from the prodigious number of children he had fathered, had been unruly and unfocused as a youth, and had subsequently been sent to a Jamaica Youth Corps camp in Manchester for eighteen months. Now, living in the cool mountain climate of the region, he felt the force of music for the first time.

Picking up the art of metal-work at the camp, Family Man worked as a welder,

locksmith and bike mechanic when he returned to Kingston. But where this new skill really benefited him was in giving him the ability to make his first bass guitar. Why the bass? 'I loved all the instruments. But the bass is the backbone of the thing. I love bass and I love music and I listen to it and feel I could take it to another stage, a higher stage. And I've worked on that over the years. When I am playing the bass it is like I am playing a bass harmony. I try to harmonise with the melody from the artist. So I come up with some kind of line they would call melodic.'

Choosing to become a bass-player was a blessed decision. For when Family Man, also known as 'Fams', linked up with Lee Perry, the producer decided to make the bass the lead instrument of this new form of reggae in which he was now working. Family Man worked as a rhythm team with his younger brother, Carlton, or 'Carly' as he was called. Born in 1950, Carly had built his first set of drums out of some empty paint tins, and had initially been influenced by Lloyd Nibbs, the great drummer from The Skatalites. The combination of Family Man's sonorous, authoritative bass and Carly's driving, percussive drums made them the toughest rhythm team in Jamaica.

Together they had formed The Hippy Boys. On guitar was Alva 'Reggie' Lewis, on keyboards Glen Adams and singing lead vocals was Max Romeo. With a friend of Family Man's called Tony Scott, they made a number of records: a song written by Scott called 'What Am I to Do?', an instrumental with the title 'Dr No Go' and a version of The Staples Singers' 'I Will Take You There', which transmogrified into Harry J's 'Liquidator'. Before this, Family Man had worked on his own, making his first recording, a tune called 'Watch The Sound', with The Uniques, the vocal trio comprising Slim Smith, Lloyd Charmers and Jim Riley. This was followed by a brief spell with Bunny 'Striker' Lee, and through him Family Man met Striker's good friend, Lee Perry.

Family Man and The Hippy Boys worked with both Scratch and Bunny Lee: the two producers would book the same studio, and run their sessions back-to-back, using the same musicians. 'It's two different kinds of flavours, two different kinds of producers,' said Family Man. 'Lee Perry is more like an artist – he is a singer and a musician. Bunny Lee just listens to it and knows. Scratch is more likely to be involved in the percussion sections and arrangements too – although him don't play instruments, he was a musical genius.'

The first thing The Hippy Boys recorded for Scratch was a cover version of an instrumental by The Meters, called 'Sophisticated Sissy'. With a Jamaican musical flavour added to it, the song was retitled 'Medical Operation'. The Hippy Boys were renamed The Upsetters, after another of Lee Perry's several nicknames. As The Upsetters they had a big hit with 'Return Of Django', named after the Sergio Corbucci spaghetti western – its comic-strip ultra-violence made it a huge favourite with those downtown roughnecks who enjoyed firing off revolver shots at the screen of Kingston's Ambassador Cinema. The tune crossed over to the UK, making the Top Five there in 1969, and The Upsetters toured Britain on the back of it.

Family Man knew that there had long been a connection between Scratch and The Wailers. Both the Barrett brothers were following the path of Rastafari by this time, and were aware that the three-piece group from Trench Town were dealing with a spiritual message. 'So we have a special respect and love for The Wailers, and the whole concept of them. It was good energy coming from the beginning.'

When Bob returned from Wilmington, Scratch and The Wailers linked up. For Family Man, who had loved the Wailers since he had first heard 'Simmer Down', it seemed like a miracle that he should be playing with them. The recordings that resulted were the finest work done by both parties. 'Though it may never be known who influenced whom,' says Steve Barrow, 'the recordings they made together constitute a significant turning-point for the participants and for Jamaican music.'

In the back of his shop, Scratch Perry worked with the three members of The Wailers, rehearsing them and reconstructing them. In particular, he persuaded them to drop their doo-

wop harmonising and to follow the innate feel of the sound within their own heads, literally to find their own voices. The first song that The Wailers, Scratch and The Upsetters recorded together, at Randy's Studio in the downtown section known as Parade, was 'My Cup', quickly followed by 'Duppy Conqueror', in which The Wailers threatened to mash down any bad forces that came along to test them, with their spiritual strength and power. 'Small Axe' and 'Soul Rebel' followed.

Then Glen Adams came up with the majority of the lyrics for a song called 'Mr Brown', a spooky story illustrating the manner in which slight rumours can whip up into a hurricane

PERRY'S BLACK ARK
STUDIO WAS HARDLY
WHAT WESTERN ROCK
MUSICIANS WOULD
EXPECT. THE MAIN DOOR
WOULD BE LEFT OPEN AND
OTHER MUSICIANS OR
BRETHREN MIGHT WELL
WANDER INTO THE STUDIO
IN THE MIDDLE OF A TAKE;
TOWARDS THE END OF THE
SEVENTIES, SCRATCH
ADORNED THE ENTIRE
STUDIO AND ITS ENVIRONS
WITH TINY BLACK
CROSSES.

*ASTON 'FAMILY MAN'
BARRETT WAITED FOR BOB
IN JAMAICA UNTIL HE
RECEIVED A MESSAGE,
ASKING HIM TO JOIN THE
SKIPPER IN LONDON. A
CHANGE WAS ABOUT TO
OCCUR.*

artists to whom Bob had been listening to over and over again, was only too evident. Numerous singles emerged from these sessions, and the songs were packaged by Scratch into two LPs, *Soul Rebels* and *Soul Revolution*.

These sessions with Scratch Perry had been of immense significance for the more introverted Bob Marley. They had put The Wailers back on a creative course that was at the cutting-edge of reggae; the rhythm section that would become an integral part of The Wailers had been unearthed; Family Man would prove an invaluable in-house arranger and second lieutenant; and in Lee 'Scratch' Perry Bob Marley had discovered a foil with whom he would work

force in Jamaica: this tale originated with a story that a crow, that somehow came to be called Mr Brown, had been seen riding through Kingston on a coffin on its way to a cemetery; then the same Mr Brown was claimed to have been seen in a courtroom, dressed in a shirt and necktie. It was as though the power of obeah had been unleashed, and people became afraid to leave their yards at night. The story's developments were even covered in the *Daily Gleaner*. The subject-matter made it an appropriate tale for working with Scratch, who was fond of such magical twists and turns.

Eventually, after several sessions, enough material was recorded for two albums. It was psychedelic reggae, and the inspirational influence of Jimi Hendrix and Sly Stone, two

Rita: 'Lee Perry had the ears as to what the street people were listening to. Any kinky thing happening, he would immediately know: "Mr Brown ride through town in a coffin." He and Bob would get together and laugh about it and say, "What is this? What is going on there?" And then the two of them get together and b-a-n-g: it's a song, it's a hit, what's happening in the street.

'They had a chemistry. And that was lacking from The Wailers for a time: from Bunny and Peter . . . The chemistry after a time started to diminish, and Bob felt that something was lacking: he knew he wasn't able to be as creative as when he started out to be.

'So this is where Perry came in as a relief. If it was not happening with these two brothers, then there was someone else he could get some expression from. Scratch would be able to get things out of Bob in a jovial way, and go into the studio and make it a chemistry: put it on tape and make it work.

'But then Peter and Bunny thought Scratch was a madman, and a battyman. There was a problem there. This was why Bob and Scratch became more of a team than the other two.'

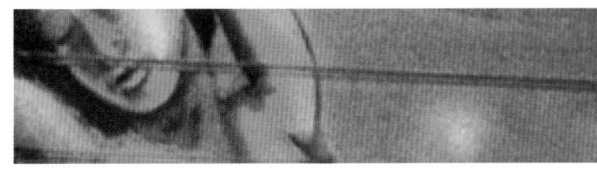

From time to time there could be disruptions in the reasonably harmonious relationship between Bob and Scratch, often over the issue of money, as Bunny Lee remembers: 'Bob and Peter and Bunny beat up Scratch one day. When John Holt's tune "Stick By Me" reached Number One, they did have "Duppy Conqueror" out. And they ran into John down by Duke Reid, and him did tell them he could buy a good car from 'Stick By Me'. Him ask Bob what kind of car them car is. And same time Scratch drive in and them jump upon Scratch. They mash up Scratch bad. 'E end up in the hospital. John teased them, "Hey, only a Rastaman dare sing about duppy."'

story that, after years in prison, Bob was back and on top.

'Duppy Conqueror' was the first tune from these sessions that was put out as a 45, at the end of 1970. It began a string of Jamaican hits which also sold well wherever there was a strong Jamaican community in the United States, Britain and Canada. 'Mr Brown', 'Kaya' and 'Small Axe' were all big sellers in 1971, and 'Keep On Moving' hit in 1972.

In 1971 The Wailers also recorded 'Mr Chatterbox' for Bunny Lee.

Despite Bob's friendship with Scratch, the beating the group had given him outside Treasure Isle was symptomatic of The Wailers' frustration at not receiving what they figured was due to them.

Around this time he became close friends with a man called Alan Cole, known to some by his nickname 'Skill'. Cole, a tall, well-built youth, five or so years younger than Bob, was the island's superstar of soccer, a midfield player of formidable talent who had been the youngest footballer ever on the Jamaican national side. They had met on the football pitch; the game was still Bob's only love outside of music. At the

for almost the rest of his career.

Although there was often an indefinable tension to their relationship, Bob respected Scratch as a musical genius; he was awed by the street suss through which this non-musician heard musical possibilities that would escape a trained player. Scratch's flair as a natural shuckster was also evident in the street-level PR he performed for the group: to explain away the erratic course Bob's career had taken in recent years, and the time he had spent in the States and in Nine Miles, Scratch came up with the

beginning of the 1970s, before Cole left Jamaica to play football for the Brazilian team Recife, he became the manager of The Wailers for a time. Aware of Bob's frustration at his inability to make reasonable money, he formed the Tuff Gong record label, founding it with ten dollars of his own money; he gave thirty-three per cent of the company to Bunny, the same percentage to Peter, and thirty-four per cent to Bob. The record label's name was taken from one of Bob's street nicknames.

The first Tuff Gong release, in the summer of 1971, was a tune called 'Trench Town Rock'. It was a song about suffering, about the life lived in Trench Town, and the elevating effect of music on the ghetto sufferah. Bob, Rita and The Wailers would sit out at night making music: 'and when it hit you feel no pain.'

'We were classed as ghetto people, but we knew that our time would come, because we were sowing good seed,' said Rita.

The group's time did come, almost immediately this record was released. A Number One tune, it stayed at the top of the charts for much of the summer. The Wailers were finally on top of the hit parade, their rightful position – and on their own label.

Suddenly, there was more activity. Danny Sims asked Bob if he would fly to Stockholm. Johnny Nash was in the Swedish capital, where he was starring in a film called *Love Is Not a Game* that was being made there. Could Bob

Bunny Lee: 'Niney [the producer] did have him out a record "Blood and Fire" which was selling well. Then Niney was saying that Bob and myself did break into him place and is stealing him records and is selling it. And Bob punch him. But is just Niney, because Niney and Rita and Bob is good friends. So we make the tune. We just go around to Randy's and rig up the tune quickly. Because it is one of them old-time tunes him did sing for Coxsone called "Mr Talkative". But we change it: at the front of the record it has Bob and myself talking, like we is talking about a session. And Bob seh: "See: the singer come." "Oo? Niney? Well, a Mr Talkative dat. Bwai gone." And Bob gone.'

Did it sell ?
'Yes, it did all right.'

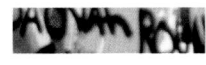

write some songs for the soundtrack?

Creatively, the trip was productive – although the movie flopped in Sweden and never opened anywhere else. Bob provided Johnny Nash with a mixture of old and new material: 'Stir It Up', which he had initially written for Rita during his first absence in the United States; 'Cornerstone', which had already been recorded with Scratch Perry; and 'This Train', which dated back to The Wailers days with Studio One. There was also the sexy 'Guava Jelly', which Johnny Nash, Barbara Streisand and the great Jamaican singer Owen Gray would record, 'Cornerstone', 'Comma Comma', 'Dewdrops' and 'I'm Hurting Inside', another Bob Marley song describing his internal pain.

Bob, however, was in a state worse than misery in Sweden. By a curious twist of fate, there was a close family witness to the torment he was suffering: Leroy Anderson, Rita's father, was a saxophone-player who had left Jamaica in 1959, playing in Britain with a number of calypso groups; then a tour of Scandinavia had culminated in Leroy's settling in Stockholm with a Finnish girlfriend who bore him two daughters.

Between musical engagements, Leroy would drive the streets of Stockholm in his Mercedes taxi. One summer night, he met an old drummer friend. There's a guy in town called Bob Marley, he told Leroy. Leroy had never met his daughter Rita's husband, but he certainly knew of their marriage. The drummer even had an address where he believed Bob was living.

Leroy found Bob living in a villa a little way out of the city. The others in the party – Danny Sims, Johnny Nash and an American keyboard player called Rabbit Bundrick – seemed to be living the high life in their rented accommodation. Bob, however, had a room in the basement, and seemed to be under great internal stress. Somehow he had become mentally 'spooked', as Leroy noted, and was having hallucinations.

Bob was relieved to see his father-in-law, not

least because he finally got to eat some authentic Jamaican cooking – a welcome break from the chintzy smörgasbords he was offered everywhere in Stockholm. But a little later it came as no surprise to Leroy when he learned that Bob had simply upped sticks and flown to England.

In Jamaica, just prior to the Swedish trip, Family Man and his brother Carlton had met up with Bob and Bunny. An agreement had been struck that they would work together both as a recording and a live unit from now on. No sooner had the deal been made, than Bob had left the island.

In the meantime, Family Man had been hired to form a new group to play at the Green Miss, a club that was opening on the edge of Vineyard Town in east Kingston. The group was called The Youth Professionals and featured Carl Dawkins on vocals, Tinleg the drummer, and a young pianist, still a schoolboy, who Family Man had heard of called Tyrone Downie. ('I got him into some session first, on the piano. Him did have a nice touch. So I show him a few tricks, too.') Then Family Man was offered a better paid job, turning over the bass-playing position in The Young Professionals to another new young guy, Robbie Shakespeare.

The gig Family Man Barrett had opted for instead was in the house band of a Norwegian liner that ran between Miami, Jamaica and Haiti; by the poolside Family Man would play soca and count the cash he was saving. Every week the ship would dock in Ocho Rios and the bass-player would desperately attempt to contact his brother, Carly. 'Bob come yet?' he would demand. For three months the reply came in the negative.

Then there was an unexpected twist. Danny Sims, Carlton Barrett told his brother, was arranging for plane tickets to carry Peter, Bunny and the Barretts up to London. The idea was that they would play support dates to Johnny Nash, currently in the British charts with 'I Can See Clearly Now', on a UK tour. As it turned out, the musicians only played one such show, on the outskirts of London. All the same, they rehearsed for several weeks in the same

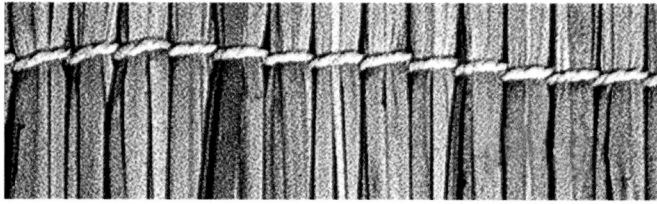

complex in north London in which Nash was practising his set.

At first Danny Sims let the group stay at a house he owned in the bustling section of Queensway, close to Hyde Park and not far from the West Indian communities of Notting Hill and Shepherd's Bush, and then booked them into a small hotel nearby. But the group wanted to stay in a house together. So Sims found them one in the blank suburban wasteland of Neasden, another area with a large West Indian population, close to the North Circular Road.

Soon a serious problem occurred, one that could have had severely negative effects on the group's future in the United Kingdom: the group were all arrested on suspicion of smuggling ganja.

Using the group's Neasden address, a friend of Bob's from Trench Town had sent him a large quantity of herb, wrapped up in a bundle of *Daily Gleaners*. As soon as the weed arrived in London, it was detected by customs. The next thing The Wailers knew was that their front door was being broken down in the early hours of the morning. All of them were taken down to the local police station and locked up in the cells. Although the house was only being used as an

accommodation address for the weed, things looked extremely bad for the group members: even if it did not result in imprisonment, deportation looked almost certain – and it would have been virtually impossible to get readmission into Britain. In the end, however, the man employed as the house cook, a relative of Bunny Lee's, agreed to take the rap.

This was the final straw. Bob was tired of the stop-start nature of his career. Sweden had been miserable; the support tour with Johnny Nash had failed to materialise – although Bob had played guitar in a backing group for Nash on some dates in English secondary schools; CBS had singularly failed to promote 'Reggae On Broadway', a Bob Marley solo single; and now life as it was lived in Trench Town had come home to roost in suburban north London, almost landing the Tuff Gong in jail.

Bob made a decision. There seemed to be, as far as he could make out, only one avenue of escape. He arranged for Brent Clarke, a record company promotions man of Jamaican origin who did work for Sims, to effect an introduction to Chris Blackwell, the white Jamaican founder of Britain's most successful independent record company, Island Records.

ISLAND

Chris Blackwell had founded Island Records in 1958 in Jamaica, producing his records himself. His initial release was an LP by Lance Hayward, a blind Bermudan jazz pianist. His first big hit didn't come until the following year, when Laurel Aitken's 'Boogie In My Bones' became a major smash-hit in Jamaica. In 1962 he had decided to move to London, having made licensing agreements with the leading Jamaican producers. Blackwell's releases were aimed at Britain's Jamaican immigrant community: ironically, one of the first records he put out was a tune from Leslie Kong, 'Judge Not' by Robert Marley: the surname was misspelled as 'Morley' on the British release.

Unlike most white Jamaicans, Chris Blackwell had discovered the truth about the love in the heart of Rastafari; as a teenager in Jamaica he had been on a boat that ran aground in shallow waters; after a long and exhausting swim to the shore, he collapsed on a beach where he was picked up and carried to a Rastafarian encampment; its inhabitants cared for his wounds, and fed him with both ital food and rhetoric from the Rastafarian philosophy.

In 1964 Millie Small, an act he was managing, had a huge worldwide hit with 'My Boy Lollipop'. After that Chris Blackwell was drawn into the world of pop and rock: he managed The Spencer Davis Group, which featured Steve Winwood, and launched Island as a rock label on the back of Winwood's group Traffic. Soon Island became the most sought-after label for groups specialising in the 'underground' rock of the late 1960s.

By 1969, Blackwell was working again with

CHRIS BLACKWELL, WHO HAD A FAR GREATER UNDERSTANDING OF RASTAFARI THAN MOST WHITE JAMAICANS.

Jamaican music, in particular with the reggae artist Jimmy Cliff; Blackwell had first issued records by Cliff in the UK after Leslie Kong had changed the singer's name from Jimmy Chambers for releases on his Beverley's label. In 1971 Blackwell's childhood friend Perry Henzell cast Jimmy Cliff as the lead in *The Harder They Come,* based on the life of Ivan Rhyging, a Robin Hood of the ghetto who had come to a tragic end in a shoot-out with police in 1948. Adding an extra element to the Rhyging story by turning the gunman into a ghetto youth desperate to mek a try in the cut-throat Kingston music business, Henzell created a rough-hewn classic that became a staple of the late-night cinema, then in vogue.

The Harder They Come had one of the best soundtrack albums ever released. As a primer for hip white kids wanting to find out about a new music, it was invaluable. Among British whites, reggae seemed about to make a complete volte-face: from having been the unfashionable music favoured by skinhead football thugs, it was suddenly becoming *de rigueur* at fashionable London dinner parties that ended with joints of Congolese bush. In the sexy rebel image sported by Jimmy Cliff in the movie, it seemed as though Chris Blackwell had found what he'd been looking for: a way to take reggae into the rock album market. And he would spearhead it, he had decided, with Cliff.

Then Jimmy Cliff announced that he was going to leave Island. He could have made more money with a major label, he told Blackwell, criticising the amount of time the boss had spent on rock music. To no avail a distressed Blackwell told him he believed his understanding of the rock market was crucial in trying to break reggae.

But a week later Bob Marley walked into his office. 'He came in right at the time when there was this idea in my head that a rebel-type character could really emerge. And that I could break such an artist. I was dealing with rock music, which was really rebel music. I felt that would really be the way to break Jamaican music. But you needed somebody who could be that image. When Bob walked in, he really was that image, the real one that Jimmy had created

in the movie.'

Although Blackwell had released Marley's first single, he had hardly kept track of his career. All he knew was that he had been warned about The Wailers, that these guys were 'trouble'. 'But in my experience when people are described like that, it usually just means that they know what they want.'

Blackwell cut a deal with the group who came to him as Bob Marley and The Wailers, as Bob had been billed on 'Reggae On Broadway'. He would give them £4,000 to return to Jamaica and make an LP. When he received the final tapes they would get another £4,000. He also agreed to give to the Tuff Gong label the rights to Wailers material in the Caribbean, which was to provide a useful source of cash in the coming years. (A deal also had to be struck with Danny Sims: for another £4,000 Blackwell bought Bob out of his contract with CBS.) 'Everyone told me I was mad: they said I'd never see the money again.' Blackwell ignored these naysayers, instead giving advice as to how the three singers should pursue their career. The idea of a vocal trio with backing musicians was dated, he told them: they should take their favourite musicians and forge themselves into a tight road band, capable of touring and presenting several layers of identity in addition to Bob Marley's.

On their return to Jamaica, the group immediately went into Kingston's Harry J's studio. By the end of the year, after further sessions at Dynamic and Randy's studios, the album, which was to be called *Catch a Fire*, was completed. Chris Blackwell set about marketing the record.

The decision was made that *Catch a Fire* should be the first reggae album sold as though it was by a rock act. In line with this, rock guitar and keyboards were also added to the LP at Island's Basing Street studio in London's Notting Hill.

Then the cover was worked on, an outsize cardboard replica of a Zippo cigarette lighter. It hinged upwards and the record was removed from the top of the sleeve; in fact, it often stuck within the packaging, but the desired effect was created all the same.

Danny Sims, eager to sell singles via

American radio air-play, had had no time whatsoever for Rastafarian subject-matter. Chris Blackwell, on the other hand, positively welcomed it. As well as feeling sympathetic to the philosophy of the religion, he understood its strength as a marketing tool. The British music press had always been more important in selling albums in the United Kingdom than the limited radio air-play that was then available.

'So what Bob Marley believed in and how he lived his life was something that had tremendous appeal for the media. The press had been dealing with the greatest time in the emergence of rock 'n' roll and it was starting to quieten down. Now here was this Third World superstar who had a different point of view, an individual against the system, who also had an incredible look: this was the first time you had seen anyone looking like that, other than Jimi Hendrix. And Bob had that power about him and incredible lyrics.'

When *Catch a Fire* was released in Britain in December 1972, it was pitched at the very hippest sections of the media. The group instantly became a critical success, although a commercial breakthrough was still some way off.

To build on the media interest generated by the release of *Catch a Fire*, Chris Blackwell deemed that a British tour should take place in the late spring of 1973. The task of setting up this first British tour by The Wailers fell to Mick Cater. Cater was employed by the Island Artists management division of Island Records, working out of the company's Notting Hill premises.

Before *Catch a Fire* had been released, Chris Blackwell had come into Cater's office and played the tapes of the album to him and his colleagues. 'And we all sneered. As far as we were concerned, at that time the only people who were interested in reggae were skinheads.'

Asked to book a tour, Cater nevertheless went into overdrive. Following Blackwell's suggestion that the group should be treated as though they were a hip rock act, he sent a copy

5.   The remaining terms and conditions of this agreement are
those set out in the Conditions.

     Would you please countersign this Agreement where marked to
indicate your agreement to the terms and conditions herein set out.

Yours faithfully,

for and on behalf of
ISLAND RECORDS LIMITED

Agreed and confirmed:

Bob Marley
Bob Marley

Neville Livingston
Neville Livingston

Peter M°Intosh
Peter Mackintosh

m e k

a   try

THESE PICTURES, TAKEN IN 1974 AT BOB'S RENTED APARTMENT IN CARLOS PLACE, LONDON, SHOW THE GONG IN TYPICAL SONGWRITING MODE. THE SHOT ON THE RIGHT WAS CHOSEN AS THE IMAGE FOR THE FRONT OF SONGS OF FREEDOM, THE BOB MARLEY BOX SET.

of *Catch a Fire* to the social secretary at every university and polytechnic in Britain. Before long he had set up a string of thirty-one dates, fifteen of which were in Jamaican reggae clubs. There was a distinct contrast to the principal London dates, however. The Wailers were slotted in for four nights at The Speakeasy, a long fashionable, somewhat élitist club catering largely to musicians and the music business.

Such was the buzz created by *Catch a Fire* that this set of London shows was a complete sell-out. More than that, the first night at The Speakeasy turned into the hippest cultural event that London had experienced that year. Bianca Jagger, Bryan Ferry, Brian Eno and assorted members of Traffic were all in an audience that comprised London's top taste-makers. Moreover, for once this crowd waited patiently in its seats; the fact that The Wailers were so resolutely unpunctual in arriving onstage at their appointed hour seemed to be part of the attraction: this Jamaican soon-come way of thinking was deemed to be definitively cool.

When The Wailers appeared, the contrast between the affluent audience and the group, with their shuffling demeanour, could not have been more pronounced. Crammed on to the tiny stage of The Speakeasy, the group had both a humility about them and a power in their performance. Such an approach was literally stunning. The strangely quiet, almost hushed performances of The Wailers at The Speakeasy on those nights in May 1973 were life-changing experiences. It was as though there was a spirit hovering over the group.

The group now performing under the name of The Wailers still comprised the trio from Trench Town, along with the Barrett brothers on bass and drums and Wire Lindo on organ – the same musicians who had played on *Catch a Fire*. When the idea of the tour had first been mooted, Bob and Peter and Bunny knew they had to stick with the team that had made the record. 'We don't want to carry some other guys to go onstage and make ourselves look foolish,' considered Bob. 'So we have to get the original guys that play.' Bob had come to Scratch and said that Chris Blackwell had worked up a tour. 'So we want to get those musicians, if it's all right. Scratch say, why not? And them start there,' Pauline Morrison remembers.

This UK tour was not, in fact, the live début of this line-up. In 1970 Scratch Perry had promoted a show in the Jamaican capital to bring attention to the *Soul Revolution* LP he had produced for the group.

The venue chosen by Scratch had been the Sombrero night-club on Molynes Road, off Waltham Park Road, in uptown Kingston. Not unlike the Speakeasy date, this was a show that attracted Jamaica's coolest audience, including a good mixture of other musicians and producers. In front of a crowd of around three hundred, The Wailers played for two hours, selecting material from their work with Scratch and from the earlier Studio One days. The event was a big hit, and was followed up by a date in Negril.

For The Wailers the shows were a confirmation of the new level they had reached through working with Lee Perry, a final shaking-off of the lean period that had come before Perry's time. Excited by the reception they had received from so many of their ranking peer group, it seemed as though the blocks to their collective career had finally fallen away. This was further confirmed by another show played by the same team: in Kingston at the opening of Skateland, a skating rink at Halfway Tree. But

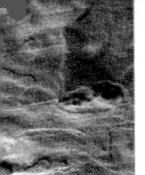

time had to pass before they could again be reunited onstage.

Arriving in Britain, the group met Mick Cater, whose task hadn't ended with simply booking the dates: Chris Blackwell had asked him to travel with The Wailers on the tour. Cater still wasn't convinced: he didn't want to go to the first date, at Lancaster University, at all. 'I travelled in the van with the group, and couldn't understand a thing they were saying. I was also exhausted by the time I got there, because they wouldn't have the heater off.'

Mick Cater eventually made it to every single show the group played on their first UK tour. As well as the profound experience of being with The Wailers and hearing their music, he also remembered eating thirty-one curries with them – it was the only food they would eat on the road in Britain. By the time the last of those curries had been consumed, The Wailers had become a crack on-the-road outfit, as tightly sprung as a ratchet knife.

When the group began to perform, however, Cater rapidly changed his opinion: 'They were playing support act to a disco. I watched the show and was amazed. From then on I wouldn't let anyone else work with them.'

At that time Phil Cooper was the Island Records promotions manager for the north of England; it was natural that he would also make his way to that Lancaster show. Previous acts with whom Cooper had regularly worked had included Mott The Hoople, Free, Traffic, Cat Stevens and Roxy Music. The Wailers were different in every way possible, not only in their attitude. 'They were musically different, and visually different. Their presentation was hardly the European approach to rock 'n' roll. Instead what came off them was the warmth of sunshine and friendliness, and they had lyrics that had an unbelievable meaning. Bob believed in every word he sang. All the lyrics were very specifically from his life. Back then, people didn't necessarily understand this, how everything related to a particular time and moment.'

Cooper went backstage after that Lancaster University show and met The Wailers for the first time. 'They were very friendly, but also almost shy. They'd arrived somewhere to perform and were really confused about where they were and why they were there. Bob didn't have locks when I first met him: only mini-locks.'

As Mick Cater perceived it, 'At first the United Kingdom was as confused by The Wailers as The Wailers were by the United Kingdom.'

After the show was over, Cooper had to drive Seeco, still acting as roadie before he graduated to percussionist, to the local hospital. He was vomiting severely and his body was wracked with aches and pains. Seeco quickly recovered from the illness, but it was an omen of the sicknesses, with their dire consequences, that would plague Peter Tosh on the next UK tour.

By the time they had returned to London for the shows at The Speakeasy, Cater was a complete convert to the music and performances of The Wailers. He was also beginning to note the differences in personalities between the three Wailers proper: 'It took a very long time for Bob to trust me. Peter and Bunny were integral to the group, but Bob had such charisma. He was the best live act there's ever been, both with Peter and Bunny and later without them. A complete powerhouse onstage, but off, nothing like that, just very quiet. There was the private Bob, and the public Bob.'

At the soundcheck for the first Speakeasy show, a Jamaican-born London schoolboy slipped through the stage-door, clutching his precious camera. Dennis Morris, who was then only fourteen, had read about The Wailers in the British music press: 'They seemed to be a very underground thing; even reggae itself was really this new thing in Britain.'

Hesitantly, Dennis introduced himself to the Jamaican trio. 'They seemed really pleased to meet me. They'd never met a young black English person; but I'd never met a young Jamaican rebel. I found myself talking mainly with Peter and Bob – Bunny was a little blackheart man. Peter was strutting, a wide boy, full of himself. But Bob was very positive of where he was going, very direct, with a lot more humour than Peter. Bob was softer, lighter, with that twinkle in his eyes.

'They told me that they were going on the

'I don't
come to
bow. I
come to
conquer.'

cat

c h a   f i r e

road. The next morning I left to go to school and met up with them. My parents didn't know I was going to disappear. They just knew I was crazy about cameras, and was always saving up for them.'

Dennis Morris travelled to Blackpool and Birmingham with The Wailers. Birmingham, with its large West Indian community, provided an audience sympathetic to The Wailers' material. But in the north-western seaside town of Blackpool they played a venue whose attractions alternated between chart acts and ballroom dancing; the group drew a crowd of no more than a hundred people and it was almost exclusively white. Dennis Morris was none the less struck by the way in which one woman jumped onstage and began dancing with Bob. 'It was the white audience in Britain who took Bob up first, really. The Rastas got into him later. Chris Blackwell had put him into that crossover market, and white people were the first to pick up on it. Later, of course, Bob had a huge black audience. But they seemed to misinterpret what Bob was personally saying about Rasta, and read it as just being a black thing, a black power thing almost. But to me Bob always insisted, 'It's the system we're against – it's not a black and white thing.'

As well as playing the élite Speakeasy club, The Wailers played another date in London on that first tour: the Greyhound pub, in Fulham Palace Road, Hammersmith. A steaming, smoky joint, it had established itself as a venue for groups who had climbed a couple of rungs up the long career ladder.

At The Greyhound, The Wailers played to a house that could not have been fuller. In the audience was a young drama student; this man had an evening job in another pub and had already had to ask his boss if he could take an hour off to watch the edition of the BBC's *Old Grey Whistle Test* which was the first television performance by The Wailers in Britain. His name was David Rodigan and he was later to become renowned and respected as the UK's most knowledgeable reggae radio DJ. By 1973, Bob Marley was already a hero figure for Rodigan: 'I just thought that he was the man who'd followed on from Prince Buster, and he simply was reggae. From "Put It On" onwards, his songs had absolutely captivated me.'

After watching Bob onstage at the Greyhound, Rodigan had tried and failed to get backstage to meet his hero. Leaving the venue and walking down Fulham Palace Road with his girlfriend, however, he saw a cloud of smoke billowing out of a shop doorway. 'It was Bob, behind a huge spliff, with Wire Lindo. So I went up to him and told him how important his music was to me. He smiled at me and said, "One Love. Thanks." And I watched as he climbed into a car that had pulled up, and he waved and called goodbye.'

After the Speakeasy dates Benjamin Foot was made tour manager for The Wailers. 'I had the advantage of having been brought up in Jamaica, so I spoke the patois.' His father, Sir Hugh Foot, had been Governor-General of the island; and Chris Blackwell had been briefly employed as Sir Hugh's ADC in his late teens. Today Benjamin Foot works for the Save the

In 1980, when Bob was on his way back from playing at the Zimbabwe Independence celebrations, he stopped in London for a few days and agreed to appear on Rodigan's Saturday night reggae show on Capital Radio; Rodigan's entire programme was to be given over to a history of Bob Marley's music. 'I took him into a room at Capital,' recalls Rodigan, 'and I asked him if he minded not talking about politics and religion, but just talking about music. And Bob beamed and said, "At last." You know, Bob Marley was so amazing, so remarkable. He really was the original blueprint.'

Children fund in Addis Ababa, an appropriately poetic destination.

'I was always worried,' Foot says, 'that they were going to be miserable, or even angry, when we went to play in these grotty venues that they were booked into. England was tough-going the first time around – in the provinces people didn't know what was going on. The Wailers had to play on such tiny stages, too. But they were extremely professional and never objected at all.

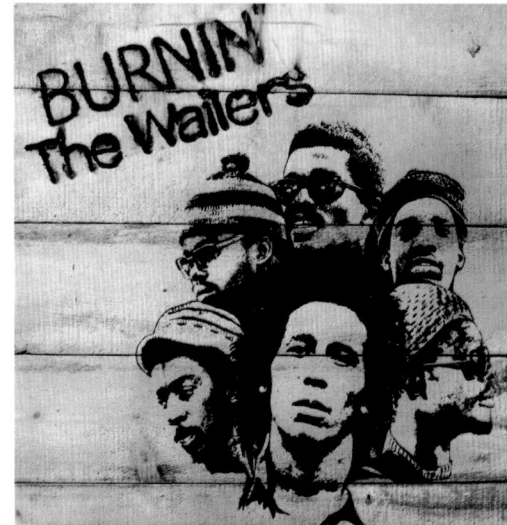

They were very positive towards me, always very keen that things should run smoothly. Peter and Bunny were certainly more difficult to please than Bob. There was some tension, but when they got up and played it always disappeared.

'Those early days with Peter and Bunny were unique: you had the three writers and therefore a spread of songs. You had the harmonies of Bunny's high voice and Peter's low voice; and it was those harmonies that really made it.'

As Foot worked more and more closely with Bob Marley, he began to note certain tensions within the musician. 'One has to be careful about a legend,' he considers, 'but I felt that Bob wasn't secure in himself at this time. I think he was perturbed that one of his parents was white, and he wanted to prove himself very much as being a black Rasta. He would behave in this way that

was very tough and hard, which wasn't really him at all.

'On his own, we got on very well. But when he had his court around him, he'd behave in this very tough way with me. It was a pose, though, it wasn't the real man. Bob's particular problem, I always felt, was that he was an up-and-coming black star, based on this entire Rasta philosophy; and he didn't quite feel the part.'

Foot was also tour manager with The Wailers on their early tours of the United States. Joe Higgs, who had instructed The Wailers in how to sing harmony parts back in Trench Town, substituted for Bunny on the first set of dates. Bunny had refused to travel on an 'iron bird'.

The American dates began in July 1973, at a tiny jazz club in Boston called Paul's Mall. It was those Boston shows, Benjamin Foot believes, that first broke The Wailers in the United States. 'They played a week of three sets a night in Boston – it would terrify me having to go and get them out for a third set at 1.00 a.m. All the same, it did them an incredible amount of good. Because that was where they really broke: after that they had an underground following in the States.'

The next venue on this tour was Max's Kansas City in Manhattan, New York: the group had a week-long residency supporting a young singer from New Jersey called Bruce Springsteen. In August The Wailers crossed to the west coast and played the Matrix Club in San Francisco.

Returning to Jamaica, The Wailers quickly recorded *Burnin'*, their second album for Island. For *Catch a Fire* Bob had gone up to London on his own to supervise the overdubbing of certain guitar parts; this time, all The Wailers went. When Chris Blackwell showed them the two studios, they opted for the smaller one, down in the basement of the building. It reminded Family Man of Treasure Isle. 'We say, "This is the one: feel the beat." You can really feel the bottom.'

Two months later the group were again playing live in the States. *Burnin'* had just been released and The Wailers had a support slot on a Sly and the Family Stone tour. What one would imagine to be an ideal series of concerts turned

Bob on Joe Higgs: 'Him, y'know, is one heavy music man, Joe Higgs. I feel like him need a little more time fe love, him want a little more love. Joe good but him want a little bit more time fe get him things together. Joe Higgs helped me to understand that [jazz] music. He taught me many things.'

into the complete reverse. After four dates they were bumped from the tour and left stranded in Las Vegas. 'Sly was really worried at the effect they were having on his audiences,' Benjie Foot noticed. (Family Man had also been aware that Sly's audiences were intrigued by The Wailers. 'I was always quick to go to the exit doors to hear what the audiences were saying as they were leaving the theatre. They always talking about the "opening group". "What kind of music is that?" they are saying.')

Family Man: 'The first place we break the reggae was in Boston, at a basement club they call Paul's Mall, a jazz club. There is a jazz workshop next door, and every time the jazz guys take a five from there, they say, "You guys have everybody from the vibrations you are playing." After a while we went back there and played again, because we were shaking the roof down.'

What was to become a legendary radio broadcast started out as a partial substitute for the group losing their tour: driving up to San Francisco The Wailers played their entire set live on KSAN, concluding with a version of the song 'Lively Up Yourself', which they had recorded for Scratch Perry and which Bob was considering including on their next album. The show earned the accolade of becoming widely available as a bootleg.

In the middle of November 1973 The Wailers, with Bunny once again part of the group, returned to England for their second tour that year. The weather was bitterly cold, and for the first dates the group had been booked into a series of shows in colleges in the grimmest industrial cities in the north of England. In the end, they played only a total of four dates out of the twenty-six that had been booked.

After an almost mournful performance at Leeds Polytechnic, the group set out to drive the 200 miles back to London. Mick Cater had by now become wary of long journeys with the group in their cramped mini-bus: 'The bibles would come out and the arguments would become very heated.' But on this occasion matters became far more serious. Cater was a great admirer of the increasingly moody Peter Tosh: with a black carved fist in red, gold and green emblazoned on his stage sweatshirt, he

resembled a biblical figure – an effect which was further reinforced when Tosh kicked off live sets with the portentous lines from 'Rastaman Chant': 'Hear the words of the Rastaman . . .' Now Cater saw a very different side of him. 'Peter went mad. In the middle of the motorway on the way back from Leeds, he threw a very strange tantrum. He had flu. But I remember thinking that there was more to it than just being ill: he really seemed to have gone mad.'

The next show was in Northampton, on 30 November. Thick snow was falling as they arrived at the venue. Bunny and Peter, who had been arguing violently with Bob, interpreted this as a clear sign that the tour was doomed, which Bunny announced in the exaggeratedly precise BBC English he reserved for only important issues. By abandoning the dates and boarding a flight back to Jamaica, they turned this perception into a self-fulfilling prophecy.

Rita, was Bob dispirited with all the problems of touring with Peter and Bunny?

'In a sense he was. But I don't think he would allow anyone to crumble his ambitions. Like he said in one interview, he couldn't sit at home idle and think of how when Ziggy and his children grew up they would ask why he didn't go to work to send them to school. So he was pushed because he felt he had a responsibility more than the other two guys. I was always there with that wife talk – that something had to be done for the children.'

WHO GAVE you the order
To shoot us DOWN
JAH JAH JAH PROTECT US
He'd NEVER LEAVE US ALONE
So ALL ye wicked People
WHO want To see us DOWN
Good bye

it WAS the Devil Deciples
WHO attack us IN the NIGHT
They WILL MAKE WAR AGAINST The LAMB
Mo the Lamb WILL OVER COME
SO WHEN you WAKE UP IN The MORNI
the INNOCENT blood WILL be oN you CONCIENC

THE APPEARANCE OF THE
WAILERS ON BBC2'S
WEEKLY OLD GREY
WHISTLE TEST ROCK SHOW
BROKE FURTHER GROUND
IN THEIR PROMOTION OF
CATCH A FIRE. THEIR
PERFORMANCE AND
CURIOUS APPEARANCE WAS
THE TALK OF MUSICAL
COGNOSCENTI FOR WEEKS
TO COME. HERE THEY
REHEARSE FOR THE TV
PROGRAMME AT THE
ISLAND REHEARSAL
STUDIO.

natu

r a l   m y s t i c

THE WAILERS: FORWARDS

'Me really used to work hard, y'know, but if you in a group and you get tense . . . me no want say this but me little bit tense with The Wailers we have first time, Bunny and Peter. Is like them don't want understand me can't just play music fe Jamaica alone. Can't learn that way. Me get the most of my learning when me travel and talk to other people.'

Bob, why was your last tour of England cancelled?
'Yeah . . . Well, the thing was, some of the members of the group can't stand the cold.'

None of the musicians involved would ever tour Europe or the United States in winter again. The official reason offered by the Island Records office for the cancellation of the tour was that 'it snowed'. Although their fans were disappointed, this explanation had the advantage of making The Wailers seem even weirder than they were already imagined to be; though at this time no one knew that the trio from Trench Town was virtually over. 'I never try to come between Bob, Peter and Bunny,' says Family Man, 'because I have a special respect for the man there, my favourite spiritual group singing about God and t'ing and Rastafari. One time I hear them say we finish with the tour. I think, "Finish with it? I think the tour just get started. Must be something I don't know about." The power of this thing with Rastafari and God . . . Well, I just accept that and go through. They have that saying, "Everything happen for a wise purpose."

'Now Bob have to get busy, not only as a singer, but also as a businessman. He see that if you have a product you have to go there to promote it.'

Bob and Bunny continued to maintain a good relationship. Bunny simply wasn't prepared to make the sacrifices that life on the road as a new group entails. Bob was ready for this: he knew that it would not always be so uncomfortable. Peter, meanwhile, was being told by those around him that he was as powerful a performer as Bob, and could easily make it on his own. All three members of the group had outgrown each other; they needed space to work. What they didn't need was the carry-go-bring-come people who gathered around them, distorting how each felt about the other, and causing tension.

Back in Jamaica Bob Marley busied himself with writing or improving new material. Among the tunes he was working on was one which he had played to Benjamin Foot when he had arrived in London for the Burnin' tour. Appearing at Foot's home in west London early in the morning, direct from the overnight flight from Jamaica, Marley picked out a tune for him on his acoustic guitar that he said he had written on the plane. 'It seemed to me to be a rather ordinary, semi-folk song. Which probably goes to show why I'm not still in the music business,'

says Foot. The song was called 'No Woman, No Cry'. It contained a line referring back to Bob's time at Tartar's yard in Trench Town: 'Georgie will make the fire light.' As a mark of respect, the composing rights were given to Tartar – Vincent Ford – hence the songwriting credit that the song has.

One day Bob drove down to Trench Town to visit a girl he was seeing. Georgie Robinson heard he was in the area and had gone up to Boys Town to play football. Finally, Bob came over to Tartar's yard to see both his long-time friends.

'Wha' 'appen, ol' Georgie?'
'Nothin' much.'

Bob leaned on the wall of the yard and asked Tartar to fetch him his old acoustic guitar. Then he started to perform 'No Woman, No Cry'. The song, with its deeply personal reminiscence of their impoverished life in the yards of Trench Town, moved Georgie to the edge of tears.

Another new song had been written in

As the original three-man line-up of The Wailers ground to a halt, Bunny Livingston began increasingly to be known as Bunny Wailer. Although his music would never achieve the mainstream popularity enjoyed by Bob or even Peter Tosh, it was of a consistently high standard, beginning with the excellent Blackheart Man album in 1976.

Despite their popularity, Bob and the Wailers received almost zero air-play from Jamaica's two radio stations. This was for one very simple reason. The large Jamaican record companies had longstanding 'arrangements' with the disc jockeys and programme directors that ensured independent labels like Tuff Gong barely got a look-in. Although he was no longer working as Bob's manager, his spar Skill Cole, the man who had helped set up Tuff Gong, was incensed by this.

One day he decided he'd had enough: 'We go up there and have to beat boy. We go and fight a system where they just have money power. We are on the street; we are street boy. We beat programme director, disc jockey. We no afraid of no guy. Puncture the man car supposed to get puncture. Box a bwai supposed to get box if he won't play them tune. Konk them up in them head and kick them batty. They was fighting us because we was Rastas.

'Bob Marley was the singer: he was a quiet little brethren. Can't do nothing more than be quiet and give you the best lyrics and the best music. So mi just deal with things the right and proper way.'

Jamaica as a consequence of Bob's being held up in a police night-time car check. Simply entitled 'Road Block', it was one of the hits of the evening when it was first played before a packed audience at Kingston's Carib Theatre. Playing support to Marvin Gaye for this yard show, the group included all three original members of The Wailers, as well as the Barrett brothers and the young keyboard player Tyrone Downie.

There were two dates with Gaye, the Carib Theatre show being followed by a larger one at the National Heroes stadium. The concerts were benefits for the Trench Town Comprehensive Sports Centre, which the highly conscious Marvin Gaye had been eager to perform. However, he had only recently returned to live work, and was below form on the Carib show. The Wailers, moreover, were performing in Jamaica for the first time since they had

Family Man, what did you think when you first heard 'No Woman, No Cry'?
'It was good, like a semi-chant with a little ballad feel. And not only did it play a tempo, but it played a riff within the tempos, to give that soulful feeling. We used a rhythm box to set the feeling.'

Did you think of it as a hit?
'It was good stuff. And when we play it we see the response from the audience. On the first live album it seemed to be the only music that seemed to be mixed to the standard of the time. The rest of it sound too tinny, like live stuff.'

recorded the Island albums and had toured hard, promoting them. They mashed Marvin down at the Carib, although the second date was a more even match. (Throughout his career, even up to his penultimate dates with The Commodores in New York, Bob was accomplished at appearing as the opening act and irrevocably stealing the show, as Sly Stone had already learned and Fleetwood Mac would later discover.)

Yet it still seemed almost miraculous that Bob, Peter and Bunny managed to make it on to the same stage together. Although they would briefly perform together again, with the Jackson Five and then with Stevie Wonder, to all intents and purposes the hit-making trio from Trench

Town was a thing of the past. From now on there would be a new group: Bob Marley and The Wailers.

(Bob's time in Trench Town was almost over, too. Tony Spaulding, the Minister for Housing, had arranged for the Marley family to move to a new government housing development in Bull Bay, on the coast about ten miles out of Kingston, near a large Rasta community. In 1972 Bob had appeared on the PNP 'bandwagon', a lorry-load of musicians that travelled around Jamaica at election time. The new house was something of a repayment. In turn, however, Bob would later be asked for another favour which would almost cost him his life.)

Working as tour manager for Marvin Gaye was a man called Don Taylor, a garrulous Jamaican based in the United States whose previous experience in the music business had included managing Little Anthony and the Imperials. Trekking up to 56 Hope Road the next morning, Taylor woke Bob and pitched him a plan for becoming his manager. Impressed with his initiative, Bob decided to try him out.

'One good thing I have to say about Don Taylor,' says Chris Blackwell, 'is that he was the person who Bob could turn to and work with. He was able to get him on the road and bring to life what wouldn't have happened if Bob had not toured. Bob's success came from people seeing him and saying, "Fuck: I can't believe this guy!" and then going and buying the record.

'I realised I was in big trouble if I couldn't get Bob to tour, and there was nobody I had who could handle his management. And Bob had no use for the guys around in Jamaica. Don Taylor came in and hustled it together. In that respect he is undoubtedly a key man in Bob's success – no doubt of it. It wouldn't have happened if Bob hadn't gone out touring, and Don got that together for him.'

By this stage, Chris Blackwell had invested over half a million dollars in Bob Marley, a colossal figure for that time. 'I was always sure he was going to make it. Except at this time before Don Taylor turned up when I suddenly felt I was never going to get him out in front of the public.

'When *Natty Dread* was finished and the record sounded fantastic I was really worried. Because if we couldn't get him to tour, what were we going to do with it? I was gearing it up. And I was also paying him royalties he hadn't earned. People read they are the greatest thing since sliced bread, but they haven't got any money actually coming in. So I would advance royalties to Bob that he hadn't really earned.'

By October 1974, Bob's new LP, which had at first been titled *Knotty Dread*, was completed. In London, where he had gone for the final mixing and overdubbing of the record, Bob was introduced to an American guitarist called Al Anderson, who had overdubbed some parts on to 'Lively Up Yourself' and 'No Woman, No Cry'.

Bob invited Anderson to accompany him to Jamaica when he returned to the island. He was concerned about precisely who he should be playing with in the future. Clearly, the differences between himself and Peter Tosh and Bunny Wailer were insurmountable. The chance of any further collaboration with Peter Tosh had been irrevocably severed when Chris Blackwell declined to issue a solo album by the self-styled Stepping Razor; such a release, claimed the Island owner, would conflict with his marketing strategies for Bob Marley. Tosh departed in a huff to form his own label, Intel-Diplo HIM (Intelligent Diplomat for His Imperial Majesty), and released a flurry of militant, powerful singles. Bunny's reluctance to tour, meanwhile, meant it was impossible to rely on him for the worldwide strategy that Bob was envisaging for his music. To add to the complications, Wire Lindo, the keyboard player on two overseas tours, had announced he was quitting the group to work with the American musician Taj Mahal.

DON TAYLOR (LEFT) WITH AL ANDERSON, THE AMERICAN GUITARIST WHO JOINED THE WAILERS. LIKE MANY JAMAICANS, TAYLOR CAME FROM A BACKGROUND OF EXTRAORDINARY POVERTY. AS A YOUTH HE MADE HIS LIVING DIVING FOR COINS THROWN BY TOURISTS ON SHIPS IN KINGSTON HARBOUR, AND WAS SAID TO BE THE FIRST OF THOSE YOUTHS TO OWN A SUIT. AS MANAGER OF BOB MARLEY AND THE WAILERS, TAYLOR GOT THE SHOW MOVING AT A CRUCIAL TIME WHEN IT MIGHT OTHERWISE HAVE STALLED.

When Bunny 'Wailer'
Livingston signed to Island
Records he insisted that his
contract include a clause
which would release him
from all obligations to the
label should Chris Blackwell
pass on. When Blackwell
hesitantly agreed, Bunny
was pleased. 'That means I
can leave the label
whenever I want,' he
grinned mysteriously.

PETER TOSH

PETER TOSH AND MARLENE, HIS COMMON-LAW WIFE.

Peter Tosh was an extremely talented man, but, at the same time, he was very bitter. Arrogant, unreasonable, inflexible, he was in many ways almost the personification of Bob Marley's shadow. What bound them together more than anything was that they both naturally rebelled against what Tosh described as the 'shit-stem'.

Tosh was no stranger to tragedy. His legendary prickliness intensified after he wrote off his car on the new bridge being built on the Spanish Town Road in 1973: his then girlfriend was killed and Tosh suffered severe fractures of the skull. Although there were those who would always be suspicious of Marlene Brown, his later common-law wife, many understood her as being a tower of strength to this erratic, enormously talented man, whose pain could match Bob's.

Yet his accusation that Bob's success was only because he had white blood was inexcusable.

Rita Marley: 'That's the opposite of what it took him to get there. And if so be the case, there really had to be something at the end to pay off the sacrifice during the early years of coming up.

'Because there is still a God. And he looks out for all of us. Like the song says, "When the rain falls, it don't fall on one man's house". So the sacrifices Bob had to make in his teenage years for being half-white allowed him to become famous or successful. And he deserves it, because he bore a sacrifice.'

Chris Blackwell: 'Peter was always difficult. I found Bunny easier than him, because Bunny was consistently no: he didn't want to tour overseas, he didn't want to do this, do that, didn't want to have anything to do with Babylon. Peter was yes and then no, yes and then no. And that was more difficult. So really I hardly worked with Peter at all after Burnin'. But I did continue to work with Bunny.'

*PETER TOSH CAME TO A
TRAGIC END IN
SEPTEMBER 1987; HE WAS
GUNNED DOWN IN A
ROBBERY AT HIS KINGSTON
HOME BY AN OLD
ACQUAINTANCE.*

PRIVATE LIVES

The move to Bull Bay emphasised the conditions in which the Marley family had been living in Trench Town. Whereas their last house in the ghetto had been built from wood and zinc, with an outside shower, Bull Bay was built of concrete and had two bathrooms. 'It was kind of strict at home: you came home, you did your homework and you went to bed,' Cedella remembers, adding that 'Bob was around'.

This was significant. While the family had been in the United States, staying with Bob's mother in Delaware, he had been free to immerse himself exclusively in his music. At the same time, he also began to indulge in a number of extra-marital relationships, which from now on would become a theme of his life. In all he had eleven children, only three of whom were born within his relationship with Rita. Five of the children, in fact, were born within seven years of his marriage to Rita. First, as early as 1970, there was Robbie, to a woman called Pat Williams. Then, in 1972, there were two more babies: Rohan, to a Jamaican girl called Janet, and Karen to a black English girl also called Janet. In 1977 Anita Bellnais, the Caribbean women's table tennis champion, gave birth to a son Kimane Marley. And Bob's son Julian was born to a black English mother.

Of course, Bob had many girlfriends who didn't bear him children; the incident on which the song 'Road Block' was based occurred as Bob was driving across the island with Esther Anderson, his then main squeeze. Although Bob was usually around the house in Bull Bay, he would spend nights with Esther in Kingston.

The presence of the 'extra-marital' children born to

Bob meant it was impossible to hide the relationships from Rita. So Bob's wife would pluckily play the part of Earth Mother – a role for which she was certainly suited – to all Bob's children, often taking the babies born to other women into the family home for periods of time and bringing them up with the legitimate members of the family. It was not easy for her. 'It is something you learn to live with over a period of time. I think Bob had such a lack of love when he was growing up. He seemed to be trying to prove to himself whether someone loved him and how much they loved him. There came a time when I had to say to him, "If that's what you want, then I'll have to learn to live with it." But there were certain things I would have to draw a line at.'

Ziggy never felt there was anything odd about the other children who used to hang around the house. Living up to his name, he loved playing football with his father, running on the beach, and then eating ice-cream with him.

This was far preferable for himself and Cedella to the life they had led in Wilmington. At George Gray Elementary School they had experienced prejudice for the first time when other black children taunted them for being Jamaican and not American. When their auntie had come down to the school and cussed a whole load of bumbacla'at, the other children, who couldn't understand her Jamaican accent, had thought she was a witch.

First educated in Jamaica at Melrose School, close to Marcus Garvey Drive ('They gave us nasty food to eat, like government bun and milk'), Bob and Rita's children were then sent to a private primary school called Vaz; Ziggy, who had been locksed since the age of two ('Daddy wouldn't let him have it cut, and it was just this big, huge thing,' Cedella recalls), was made to have his hair cut.

When their parents went on tour, the children were left in the care of Aunt Viola, who had discovered Bob and Rita in bed together. To all intents and purposes, the children were quite happy for their parents to go away. Not only would they come back with all manner of presents, but their strictness at home was burdensome, although Aunt Viola was just as much a martinet. Cedella would be made to take endless showers: more light-skinned than her brothers, who spent more time in the sun, Viola insisted that dirt showed up on her more.

After Bull Bay, Bob bought his first house, on Washington Drive. From there the family moved to a larger home, in the suburb of Barbican, where they had their first telephone.

By this time, however, he was living almost full-time at 56 Hope Road. Cindy Breakspeare, who had been Miss World of 1976, had borne Bob a further son. By the last tour Bob, who once admitted that women were his only vice, was travelling with Pascaline, a daughter of the President of Gabon. Even after he passed on, however, she remained in some way part of the family, giving invaluable assistance to Bob's mother in the years following her son's death.

Not long before he died, Bob bought Rita a large house in the exclusive Jack's Hill region of Kingston, in the foothills of the Blue Mountains. Their next-door neighbours were the Marleys of Marley and Co. (Ironically, when the recession of the early 1990s hit Bob's father's relatives, Rita purchased their house and gave it to her daughter Cedella.)

*BOB HAS HIS LOCKS
TENDED TO IN HIS SUITE
AT THE ESSEX HOUSE
HOTEL DURING HIS LAST
EVER TRIP TO NEW YORK.
HIS WEAKNESS FOR WOMEN
WAS LEGENDARY; HE ONCE
ADMITTED THAT THEY
WERE HIS ONLY VICE.*

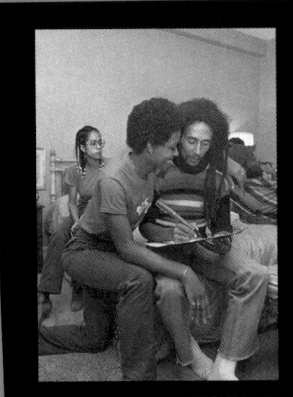 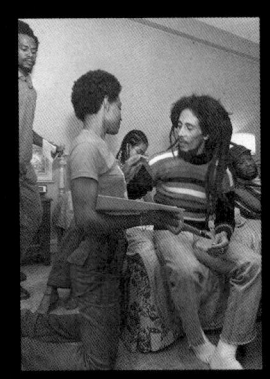   

Even without the tragedy that accompanied it, Bob's stay at the Essex House in New York would have been memorable. Separated for the first time from the rest of the group, a mood of semi-decadence prevailed over the entourage: for his part Bob tucked himself away in his bedroom for much of the time.

Bob Marley and The Wailers

It was crisis time. So Bob sat down with Family Man and his brother Carly, all that was left of the group that had made and toured *Catch a Fire* and *Burnin'*, to talk things through. 'We have time to sort ourselves out and to close together,' says Family Man. 'Mi sit down in an armchair with Bob and say we can work it still: when we go up to UK as Upsetters in '69, nothing wrong if one man short. And Bob laugh and say 'im going to book some studio time at Harry J's. 'Im say 'im going for two horn men. And 'im want mi to bring two rhythm men. I say, All right, I know who I'm going to bring. I went for Gladstone Anderson, who play piano, and Winston Wright to play organ.

'That was when we began to start the new series – *Natty Dread*. That is where everything get serious. No problem going forward, no matter what it is.'

Rehearsals for the new album, conducted with the customary seriousness and diligence, took place at Island House, 56 Hope Road, Chris Blackwell's headquarters in Jamaica, close to the residence of the Prime Minister. At the rear of the property was a small garage-like storage room. Together Bob and Family Man soundproofed the small building, taking care to use the most natural materials. Afterwards, Family Man ceremoniously planted a bamboo tree in front of the building, with a seedling he had brought from his farm in the hills by Mount James.

Despite the soundproofing, the rehearsals inevitably drew complaints from buildings all around. Only the Indian embassy, situated right behind the rehearsal building, never made a murmur of complaint: clearly, they knew how to enjoy themselves! Miss Gough, an old English lady living on the premises, occasionally mentioned that the music was very loud. More often than not, she simply smiled in appreciation at the musicians.

Soon afterwards, as a token of goodwill, Chris Blackwell sold 56 Hope Road to Bob Marley at an extremely favorable price.

At the end of 1974 Bob went out to stay with Lee Perry for a few days, at his home in Cardiff Crescent in the Washington Gardens section of Kingston. 'We were all of us talking, talking, and Bob said, "Bwai, mi not know what fe do,"' remembers Perry's girlfriend Pauline Morrison, who as a girl had seen Bob singing under the tree in Trench Town on her way home from school.

'So I said to him how American artists would all have a very identifiable set of people to work with. And if you have three girls with you, you will look representative of the way people are performing in foreign. Bob laugh and say, "Which three girls?"

'I say to him, "You have Marcia Griffiths, you have Judy Mowatt, and you have Rita, your wife." He said to me, "Them girls, deh?" Mi say, "Of course, because those are the three girls mi really see now could go fe back up a man like you."

''Im say, "OK, mi see how it go."'

Marcia Griffiths was the diva of reggae, having had a stream of Studio One hits in the 1960s before scoring a massive international success, 'Young, Gifted and Black', with her boyfriend Bob Andy, also a seminal figure in Jamaican music.

Judy Mowatt, meanwhile, had joined a singing trio called The Gaylettes in 1967. When the group split she continued as a solo act. She and Rita Marley first sang together when Marcia needed some harmony vocals on a song she was recording at Studio One with Bob Andy. The trio settled on the name the I-Threes.

The evening that Judy and Rita had first worked with Marcia at Studio One, Marcia had

CARLTON BARRETT, FAMILY MAN'S BROTHER, WHO WAS SHOT DEAD IN APRIL 1987 IN A CONSPIRACY HATCHED BY HIS WIFE AND HER LOVER.

I-THREES

In 1972 Judy Mowatt had been asked to perform in a show at Kingston's Ward Theatre in which The Wailers were also playing. Rehearsing the Elvis Presley song 'Suspicious Minds', Judy heard someone harmonising at least two octaves higher than herself. Looking around to see who it was, certain that it was another woman, she was amazed to discover that it was Bob Marley.

'I knew that he was a great songwriter, and he was a man for whom I had great respect. So I said to him, "I want you to write me a song." And he said to me, "No, man, I have a reservoir of songs down at Trench Town." He said I should come down to Trench Town and I could get any amount of songs I wanted.'

From this time Judy began regularly to visit Bob's home in the ghetto, becoming friends with Rita, whom she had already met. 'As a Rastawoman, she displayed a lot of qualities that I always wanted to emulate. She seemed the perfect mother, and she was also very knowledgeable about the faith.' Brought up as a Christian, it had not been hard for Judy to accept Rastafari. Initially she had difficulty in accepting that Haile Selassie was Christ incarnate, but as a Bible student she found it written in Revelations 5 that Christ shall return in a new name: King of Kings, Lord of Lords, Conquering Lion of the Tribe of Judah. 'Then I discovered that His Majesty had that title and I realized His Majesty not only had that title, but His Imperial Majesty is the 225th king to be seated on

King David's throne. So he's from the direct lineage of King David. And we learn that Christ shall come through that David lineage.'

Judy and Rita would sit and reason as they waited for Bob to return each evening from his games of soccer. Bob would often be playing with Alan Cole, who eventually became Judy's 'kingsman' – she had three children with him.

Sitting on the doorstep of his yard, Bob would play the guitar and teach them new songs. Judy was particularly impressed with a tune Bob had called 'Down In the Valley', written about Lulumba, head of the breakaway Congolese state Kalanga. Although the song was thoroughly rehearsed in these evening sessions, Bob never recorded it. When Judy made her *Black Woman* solo album in 1979 she made sure she included the song on it.

Bob Marley was clearly far more than simply a musical leader to Judy Mowatt. 'He was like my father, my brother, my friend . . . everything. He was someone you could talk to: he had this fatherly aura; he was a young man, but he had a lot of authority. He had a lot of discipline – he was a very disciplined person. When we were on tour, Bob would be first on the bus, so we have to be on time, and often we are trailing after him.

'He is also a man with a lot of love and respect for all people. Bob cared for humanity. Bob said, "My life means nothing to me. My life is for the people." And he demonstrated that throughout his life.'

*THE FEMALE VOCALISTS.
THE I-THREES. LEFT TO
RIGHT: JUDY MOWATT,
RITA MARLEY AND
MARCIA GRIFFITHS.*

j   a   h

i v e

been due to perform at a club in New Kingston called House of Chen: she asked them to sing harmony vocals with her on a song by The Supremes called 'Remember Me'. The audience was enraptured, and Bob got to hear about it.

The performance had taken place close to the day when it was reported in the local press that Haile Selassie had died – on 27 August 1975. This, remembers Judy Mowatt, was a very sad, cold day in Jamaica. Some immediately lost their faith. But many more clung on, knowing that this was a false message the Bible had predicted.

Bob on Al Anderson: 'I met Al in England while he was doing some overdub guitar. We talk a little and it's nice, ya know? So I ask him to come and play with the group. Him think about it for some time and then him decide he would do it. Boy, him great! Fuckin' good, mon.'

Why did you choose an American to play lead guitar?
'We really not deal with people in categories like if you come from Jamaica you have the right. Regardless of where you are on earth you have the right. I can't deal with the passport thing. To me him prove himself not an outsider because if him can play with us then him no outsider.'

'We were not afraid. We knew that it was not true. We knew that He had the power to disappear.'

Soon after Rita's daughter Sharon ran up to Bob: 'Is it true? Jah is dead?' Bob denied it. A few days later he recorded 'Jah Live', one of his most beautiful songs, in answer to Sharon's question. As soon as the recording was completed it was rush-released as a single in Jamaica.

'So Bob wrote this song, "Jah Live",' recalls Judy Mowatt, 'and went into the studio and he invited us to do the back-up singing. Immediately after he started to do the album *Natty Dread* and we were asked to do the back-up vocals on that. And when he did the first tour away from Bunny and Peter we were asked to tour with him. We felt highly privileged to be asked to work with such a great performer. I was excited. I saw it as divine intervention. Because Bob is a messenger of the Lord, and God has chosen me to work with that messenger. I felt really elated.'

Early in 1975, Bob aired this new line-up, in a show supporting the Jackson Five. By early spring, the group now working under the name of Bob Marley and The Wailers had expanded even further. As ever, the Barrett brothers were there holding down the rhythm section. Al Anderson, meanwhile, had joined as guitarist; Seeco Patterson, Bob's brethren from Trench Town, became the group's percussionist; Tyrone Downie played piano and synthesizer, leaving the Caribs, the resident group at the Kingston Sheraton Hotel; and Wire Lindo returned to the fold on organ.

Natty Dread had been released to great critical acclaim. Credited for the first time to Bob Marley and The Wailers, the record also registered far higher sales figures than either of The Wailers' two previous Island albums. To continue the record's promotion, an American tour was set up.

TYRONE DOWNIE, THE KEYBOARD PLAYER WHO FAMILY MAN TALENT-SPOTTED WHEN TYRONE WAS STILL AT SCHOOL. LATER HE WAS TO TAKE OVER FROM THE BASS-PLAYER AS THE MAIN ARRANGER WITHIN THE WAILERS.

During this US tour, Bob paid a visit to his mother in Delaware for a couple of days. This time Bob had clearly decided to instruct her fully in Rastafari.

'Bob tell me that His Majesty is the Almighty God – it not Jesus no more. And me with my little thin sense doesn't even understand what's going on. Me say, "How you know that? He is a man." 'Im seh, "Yes, he is a man." I turn to him and I say, "I think he is a great man. But I don't think he is God." And 'im seh, "'Oo yuh t'ink is God?"

'I never 'ave no answer: because I was looking that God is a white man like the picture I have on the wall.

''Im said when we reason, "You know,

momma, why is so hard for you to believe me when I say His Majesty is God? Because from the time you are a little girl growing up, you hear them talking about Jesus Christ: you go to church and you're into it.

"But today 'im come in a new name: no Jesus Christ no more. And 'im said 'is name shall be terrible amongst the heathen – which is the unbelievers. If you wasn't my mother, him seh, me wouldn't even bother to talk to you. But anyway, you is a Rasta from the day you is born. And as time goes on you will see. And as time goes on mi see everything just like how him never have to tell me no heap o' nothing no more."

'Bob and I sat and talked until it was three o'clock in the morning, and it never happened again. It happened that we spent hours together, but not in that intense manner.

'Whatever it was, it was given to me that night, and I fully received it, and my blessing is there going on now.'

Bob played another short residency in Boston at Paul's Mall, followed by a brief foray into the English market (two London shows, one in Birmingham and one in Manchester), as well as – for the first time ever – some European dates. For the two dates in June at London's Lyceum Ballroom, Mick Cater had personally sold every ticket in less than a day, the venue not having a box office of its own. ('We could have sold out five nights,' reflected Cater later.) *Natty Dread* had not only appealed to a hip white audience, but for the first time British resident Jamaicans had gone for Bob's music *en masse*. As a consequence, on the first night, the Metropolitan Police's notorious Special Patrol Group was sent into action to clear the streets around the venue of over 3,000 people, mainly Jamaicans, who were trying to get in to see Bob Marley without tickets. Two fire doors were demolished, and Tyrone Downie found himself

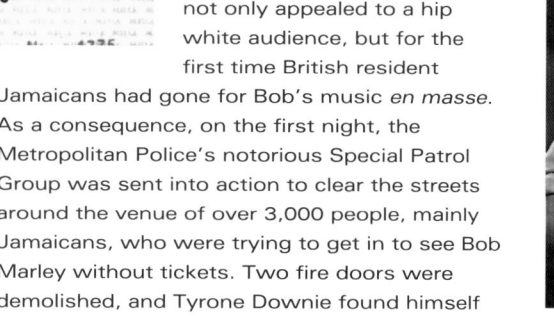

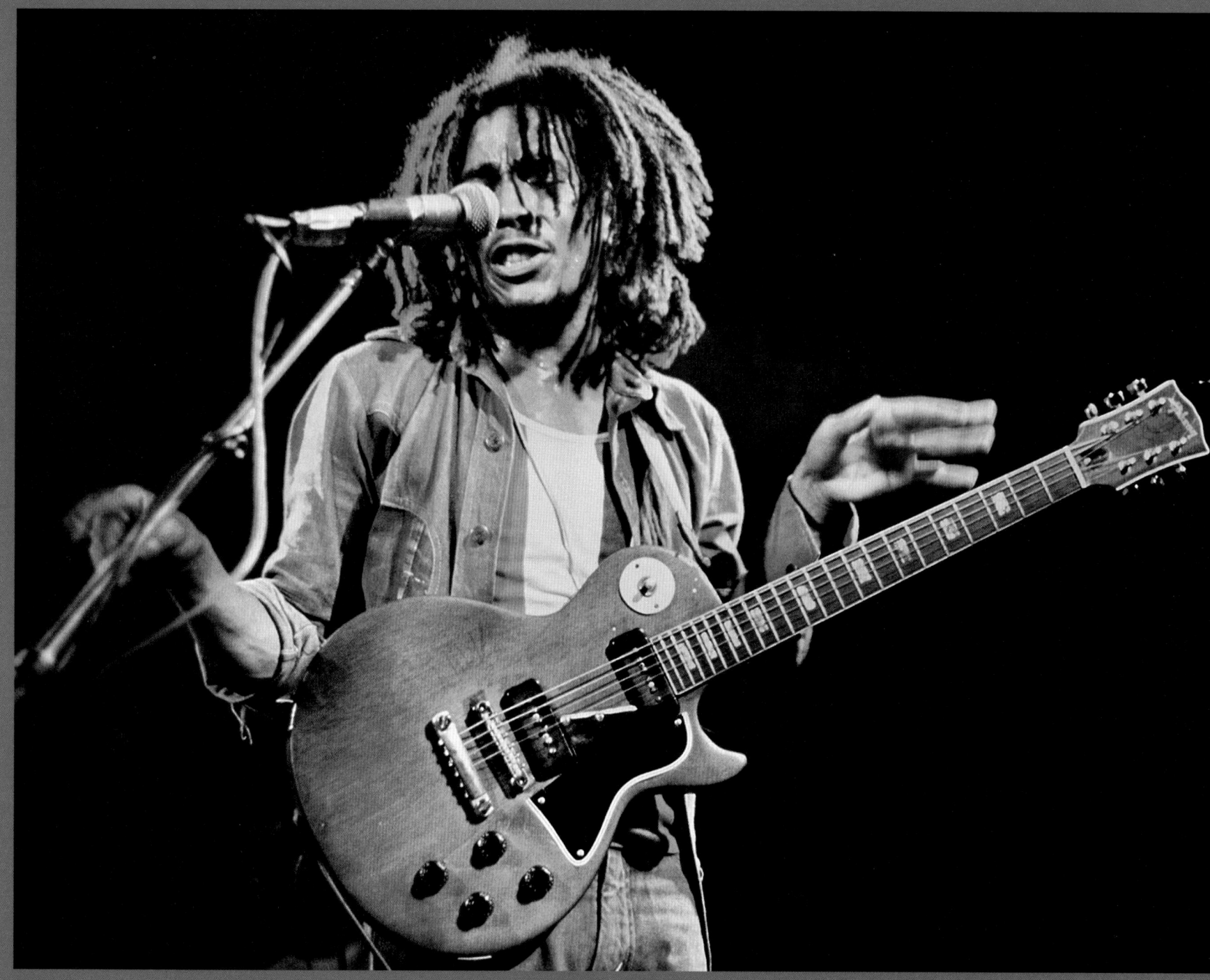

locked out of the venue, almost missing the beginning of the performance.

The shows proved to be as extraordinary as the build-up predicted. Bob Marley and The Wailers tore the Lyceum apart. The road crew had struggled to get good sound and power – a notorious problem at this venue, but particularly so in this case as the shows were being recorded for a possible live album – and their painstaking efforts were enhanced a thousand-fold by the electrifying performances produced by Bob and his group. Quite simply, they were fantastic.

Bob held the audience as though they were part of his collective soul. He could have told them to go out into the street and to burn and to loot and they would have obeyed him. 'From that gig,' Dennis Morris recalls, 'every person who was there decided they were a Rasta, and it snowballed. The whole movement just spread.'

SOUL SHAKE DOWN

SUN IS GOING DOWN → doesn't include these

IDENTEFECATION xx INCLUDES !

Gum sion (she got) xx V pro/acousta.

WE'VE COME ALONG WAY) 6

GUAVA JELLY

ONLY RIVER 1. GUAVA JELLY

Get STONED 2. THIS TRAIN

FUSSIN AN FICHTIN S. CORNERSTONE

TWILIGHT TIME 4. COMA COMA

TOO MUCH LOVE 5. FAR CRYING OUT LOUD

BABY BABY COME HOME 6. STIR IT UP

SATURDAY NIGHT (X.X.X) 7. CRY TO ME

PUSH IN TIME 8. I'M HURTIN' INSIDE

9. POUR SUGAR on ME

TIME CHART	RECORDING BOTH DIRECTIONS							
	150 FT.	300 FT.	600 FT.	900 FT.	1200 FT.	1800 FT.	2400 FT.	3600 FT.
1⅞ IPS	30 min.	1 hr.	2 hrs.	3 hrs.	4 hrs.	6 hrs.	8 hrs.	12 hrs.
3¾ IPS	15 min.	30 min.	60 min.	1½ hrs.	2 hrs.	3 hrs.	4 hrs.	6 hrs.
7½ IPS	7½ min.	15 min.	30 min.	45 min.	1 hr.	1½ hrs.	2 hrs.	3 hrs.

ion,

DYNAMIC SOUNDS RECORDING CO. LTD.,

15 BELL ROAD

KINGSTON 11

ENGINEER............STUDIO......JOB NO........DATE.........4T 2T
CLIENT............ARTIST................REEL NO....OF.....M....S

WAILERS.

	MASTER NO.	TITLE	TAKE NO.	TIME	COMMENTS
	X 1	IT MUST BE TRUE LOVE	15.4.10		MAYTALS
	X. 2	IT MUST BE TRUE LOVE	15.4.10		MAYTALS
5.5.70	VOICED 3	SOUL SHAKE DOWN PARTY	29.4.10		WAILERS
	4	SOUL SHAKE DOWN PARTY	29.4.10		WAILERS
5.5. ~~~~~~	5	SOUL SHAKE DOWN PARTY	29.4.70		WAILERS
	6	STOP THAT TRAIN	29.4.70		WAILERS,
	7	Stop the TRAIN	29.4.10		WAILERS
5.5.70	VOICED 8	Stop the TRAIN	29.4.10		WAILERS
19.5.10	VOICED 9	CHEER UP ✓	~~29.4.10~~		WAILERS
19.5.10	VOICED 10	CHEER UP	29.4.70		WAILERS

FS = Fal s start   IT = Incomplete Take   HL = Heads leader

TL = Tails leader

*RASTAMAN VIBRAT

1) TRENCH TOWN

KINKY   REGGAE
SHERRIFF

ROAD BLOCK

CON CRETE

JUNGLE

2) BELLY FULL

INGS

NO

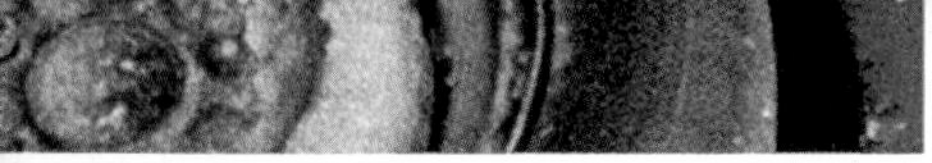

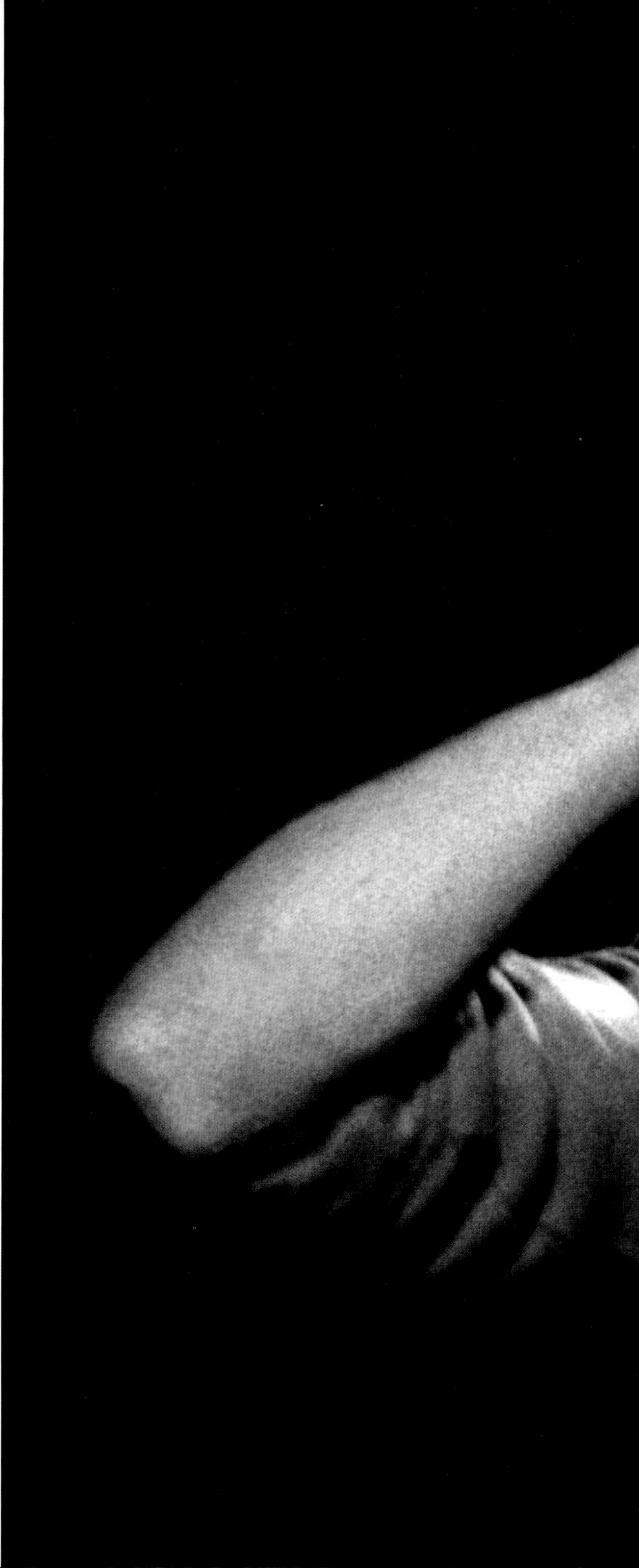

jelly

ON THE ROAD

On the long road treks between European and American shows, Bob was always first on to the group bus each morning. Hunkering down on his bunk, he would pull out a worn pocket-size cash book and jot down the previous evening's earnings. As the rest of the group settled down for the journey, spliffs would be rolled, bibles produced, and reasonings would commence on arcane interpretations of biblical symbolism, various members of the group pacing back and forth along the central aisle of the bus as they lectured their brethren. On the road, Bob Marley and The Wailers were a compact, tight unit, with no superfluous personnel. Family Man and Carlton Barrett were the only musicians who could be counted as being permanent members of the group: all the rest – even loyal spars from 'back a yard' like Wire Lindo – blew in and out of the line-up.

But what about such Babylonian problems as drugs laws? Police and customs border patrols

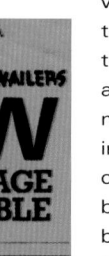

were a hazard on European tours as the group crossed the various frontiers back and forth; Holland's liberal marijuana legislation inevitably entailed a thorough cleaning-out of the bus before they left the country's border, the vehicle travelling for the last half hour with every possible window and door open. The group was especially wary of driving into Germany: the German border police often carried out body searches on various Wailers. At one show in Düsseldorf Bob was questioned for twenty minutes by police while he palmed a spliff.

Bob and The Wailers brought the ghetto on the road with them. Wherever they went they'd take over the top floors of hotels, the sites of the most luxurious suites. Down the stair-wells and lift-shafts the sweet, musty, aroma of ganja would drift until it had permeated the entire building.

Gillie, Bob's spar and cook, would set up shop in the floor's housekeeping kitchen, where for the first time ever, the stove would be crammed with boiling pots of ground provisions,

rice and peas, and fish tea. The group members would rarely go out after the shows: it was back to the hotel and up to the suites for ital food. Bob and The Wailers would keep very much to themselves, although every black model within fifty miles was likely to be there too.

'Wherever he was staying,' recalls the writer Vivien Goldman, 'Bob would pick up his battered Ovation guitar and start to strum, singing fragments of songs he was developing – like the song "Guiltiness", for example, which I remember later listening to and thinking, "Oh, didn't I hear that in that nice suite overlooking the park in Munich?"'

Bob Marley and The Wailers were initially far more popular in Europe than in the United States or even in Britain. Everywhere, however, the tours experienced a familiar pattern. 'On the first tour,' remembers Mick Cater, 'there would be, say, 1,500 people in the venue. On the next dates there would be 5,000 to 10,000 in the audience. And the next time round Bob would be playing huge outdoor venues.'

In Sweden Bob Marley was a huge star. On every tour he would play one of Stockholm's major venues, set outdoors in a fairground. The first occasion he played there, in 1977, he drew a respectable audience of 7,000. By 1980, the last time he toured there, the gates had to be closed for the first time ever when over 30,000 people jammed in.

'Two weeks after the end of each tour,' recalls Mick Cater, 'I'd give Don Taylor a breakdown of the final financial settlement. And about another two weeks later Bob would show up with someone else – always a different person – to see the same figures. One time, he came with Diane Jobson, his Jamaican lawyer. Bob was unquestionably the boss, and he'd play people off against each other, just to see what happened.'

At the end of the 1980 European tour Bob called Mick Cater to his apartment in Harrington Gardens in South Kensington. He told him that he wanted the tour profits, which came to over a million pounds, in cash. It took Cater a week to get this amount from his bank. When he had the money, he took it over to Harrington Gardens.

BOB AND THE WAILERS DRIVE THROUGH EUROPE ON THE 1977 'EXODUS' TOUR. BEFORE THE FIRST DATE, IN PARIS, BOB SUFFERED AN INJURY TO HIS RIGHT FOOT DURING A GAME OF SOCCER.

Artist: WAILERS   after organ sustained chord   Title: LIVEN UP YOU[R]

1 KEEP! Low! ORGAN.	2 ✗ VOCAL o/D ①	3 ORGAN.	4 DRUMS.	5 ✓ DRUMS	6 B/D	7 BASS.
9 R GUITAR.	10 PIANO.	11 LEAD GUITAR	12 TAMB'N o/D.	13 ✓ VOCAL o/D ③	14 GUITAR o/D ① (AL)	15 RIFF GUITAR o/D (AL)
17 o/D BACKING	18 o/D BACKING.	19 o/D BACKING VOCALS.	20	21	22	23

Title: SO JAM S[O]

		4 PERC o/D	5 R GUITAR. + D. MACH.	6 REEBOP. CONGA o/D.	7 B/D.
[OR]GAN.					
o/D LEAD VOX	12 BACKING VOCALS o/D.	13 GUITAR. o/D SLIGHTLY DISTORTED.	14 GUITAR. o/D (AL)	15 UPRIGHT PIANO o/D RABBIT.	
	20	21	22	23	

Title: BELLY FULL

		4 CONGA.	5 RHYTHM. GUITAR.	6 SNARE	7 B/D.
[OR]GAN.					
9 BASS D/I	10 TENOR SAX	11 TENOR SAX.	12 o/D GUITAR (AL) 1	13 LEAD VOX	14 BACKING VOCALS.	15 o/D GUITAR. (AL) 2
17	18	19	20	21	22	23

TRACK ① is duff   re-transfer 2[4]
numbers before any
or check 24T bad.

Client: ISLAND   Subject: WAILERS

RECORDING AT HARRY J'S

The first four LPs Bob Marley made for Chris Blackwell - *Catch a Fire, Burnin', Natty Dread* and *Rastaman Vibration* - were all recorded at Kingston's Harry J's studio. Equally good for bottom, top and mid-range sounds, it also had one of Jamaica's top engineers, Sylvan Morris, who had started out with Coxsone at Studio One, and moved to work with Harry Johnson at the time of *Natty Dread*. Morris was capable of empathising with the artists he was working with and bringing out the true feeling of the music in a way that was unparalleled in Jamaica. 'Some engineer who work for you, you don't even see them dancing,' said Family Man. 'Well, Sylvan Morris is not like that.'

Despite his lack of locks, Morris was an ardent believer in Rastafari. He actively encouraged Bob to bring his Rastafarian brethren to the studio, aware that they were essential in helping the Tuff Gong to attain the right mood. If it required Gillie in the studio's kitchen blending June plum juice or Bob's beloved Irish Moss, then surely this could only add to the recording's effectiveness? At the same time, Morris was also tough enough to stand up to any artistic arrogance he might encounter. 'I also determined when the artist I was recording was singing, whether they needed to change a lyric or not - even with Bob Marley. I would always make sure they did it without any excuses.'

Natty Dread was the first record on which Morris worked with Bob Marley. 'His approach was very

disciplined. They used to do a whole lot of rehearsals, and when they came by the studio, they would lay down four tracks: bass, guitar, drums, piano. Always just four tracks. But even from the laying down of the basic rhythm, you could hear that certain vibration. On all of the rhythms you could hear that basic discipline, and I think it was really because of the rehearsals. Bob was a stickler for rehearsals.

'Family Man was the individual who you'd call the organiser. They relied on him to do a lot of the arranging. Because he was also very disciplined: for him the thing had to be right. So they relied on him a lot. It was a total effort. But Family Man was the main guy that Bob relied on.'

Morris also noted the way that Bob introduced the I-Threes to the recording. 'Again, the main theme is always discipline. Bob Marley was a very disciplined man. And he commanded discipline within his music. So they had to conform. So this was probably one of the reasons why they became so good, the I-Threes.'

'Bob had this air about him that he would just say something and it had to be right. They always know that, and because they know that, the discipline is there in the sound. And because all these girls were so professional. They were stars in their own right. They were just real good and they knew what they were doing. They weren't people you would have to train; they were just perfect soloists.'

By the time *Rastaman Vibration* was recorded, they were working with a larger, riper sound. 'Maybe something in the scene was changing. I didn't look on it that way at that time. I just deal with music as such. But certainly the consciousness had started to settle within the whole scene: where the Rasta thing was sort of blossoming. So the lyrical content was starting to be expressed as well: the maturing within the Rasta scene. I think now they started to establish themselves in the Rasta cult to the fullness.'

Morris particularly recalled the recording of the tune 'War'; Alan Cole had urged Bob to record the song: he had bought a pamphlet containing the words of His Imperial Majesty that became the lyrics. 'It hit me very strong with that particular tune. Because of Haile Selassie's statement within it. It was the first time I was hearing statements like that. By this time the whole scene was a passionate scene: "I'm a Rastaman, this is me, I'm going to put out as much as I can in terms of how I feel." They handled everything in that vein. Religiously so. My personal remembrance of Bob is that he wasn't a very laughing character. If he smiled, he would smile very briefly. He always seemed to be so disciplined. If someone made a joke he would just laugh briefly.'

Do you think he was a happy person?

'Yes. I would say that. Because he was probably getting what he wanted musically. His message in music, he was getting what he wanted. So I think he was happy.'

'After a while, when they went away and did Kaya, I definitely think they started to change their sound then. Very commercial. As a matter of fact, I remember getting a vision [dream]: I was in the States and saw when they were going to release that album. We were all in the vision: Chris Blackwell, everyone. I remember all of us seemed to like the album. But I made a statement: "What happened to the drive?" Which, in truth, was something that I heard in life.

'When they first started, whenever they came into the studio and laid the rhythms, there was that pulsating, disciplined vibration, which probably I heard and other people perhaps didn't. The earlier albums seemed to have more drive.'

No Woman

N o   C r y

*WITH JUNIOR MARVIN
HANDLING MUCH OF THE
LEAD GUITAR, BOB HAD
MORE FREEDOM TO MOVE
ABOUT THE STAGE. HIS
REPUTATION AS A LIVE
PERFORMER GREW
IMMEDIATELY. BUT EVEN
IN 1963 DERRICK
MORGAN HAD ALREADY
NOTED BOB'S EXTRA-
ORDINARY APPEARANCE
WHEN HE ENTERED THE
CONCERT ARENA.*

The H.I.M. Haile Selassie I backdrop was used first on the 'Rastaman Vibration' tour and from then on whenever Bob played live. The original canvas was painted in 1976 by Neville Garrick, Bob's art and lighting director. Today it is attached to the wall of the Bob Marley Museum in Kingston, Jamaica.

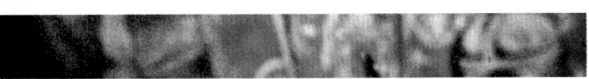

Bob looked at it, counted it. 'Then he said. "OK, put it back in the bank."

Bob was ruthlessly professional on the road; after every show he would listen to a tape of the performance. 'He ran the group with a rod of iron,' says Mick Cater, 'and if they caused problems they ran the risk of getting a slap. I remember on one show, Junior Marvin was really show-boating, showing off, and he got slapped afterwards.'

Bob Marley split the money from live work right down the middle between himself and the rest of the group – fifty per cent to him, fifty per cent to The Wailers, who for a time became moderately rich people, certainly by Jamaican standards.

Promoted from UK northern promotions man to head the Island Records international division, Phil Cooper had the task of spreading the word on Bob Marley. Not an easy undertaking at first: 'Everybody had heard of ska and blue beat, but they hadn't received major attention. To start with it was an uphill struggle with the people who distributed Island overseas. But I just used to grit my teeth and keep banging my head on their doors.

'It was easier with DJs and journalists, although you still had to go and seek out the right ones, the ones who understood. Because Bob and The Wailers became a major success with students in the UK, they crossed over to the right audiences in Europe. Right from the start they'd pack out the Paradiso in Amsterdam, for example. If you were a journalist who had any suss, you'd be into them.

'It was funny, really: in every major city Bob played you'd have these press conferences with about ten journalists there and none of them would understand a word: everything Bob said would be in patois. But they couldn't believe they had this access and opportunity and they'd go away and write what they thought he'd said.'

Cooper was also responsible for arranging Bob's overseas interviews, everywhere except for the UK and USA. 'Whenever I turned up Bob would turn to Don Taylor and say, "Promoter-man is here". I'd take him round the European radio stations. It was a chore for him, but he'd always have a smile on his face, because he knew it was important for getting his message across.'

Persuading tour managers like the redoubtable Tommy Cowan, himself a former Jamaican star, that Bob's routine must be broken for a press interview was a harder battle. It meant that Bob had to be woken even earlier than usual.

When *Rastaman Vibration* was released in May 1976, the album rocketed into the British Top Ten. Suddenly, Bob Marley and The Wailers were internationally serious contenders. The success of the record simply confirmed what had been abundantly clear since those dates in London at The Speakeasy promoting *Catch a Fire*: that Bob Marley was an unparalleled artist, working in a precise and unique musical field. Many of the more reactionary rock fans, especially those who associated reggae with skinhead violence, had initially scorned the buzz that built around the first Wailers Island releases. Now they were being converted.

The success of the new album was even more marked in the United States. '*Rastaman Vibration* came out after we'd done a big marketing

> 'I live a long time before me see any money, but my work here is not to become a "star" or anything like that, and my life no go toward material vanity. I find myself doing this music t'ing and me have to do it. Really, I am just a man of the heart.'

> **Chris Blackwell: 'The one person I would say I met who Bob was wary of, or had a lot of respect for, was Scratch. Bob was like a master in the studio, but not as far as Scratch was concerned. Scratch would push him a lot more. I think Bob's best tracks are the ones that Lee Perry produced. He was always important. But certainly when I was working with Bob, he and Bob never really got on that well.**
>
> **'Scratch produced some tracks on *Rastaman Vibration* – the good ones, the groove ones, but Bob didn't give him any credit. I don't know if it was a rivalry or what. There was some unease about the relationship.'**

High Times magazine: Who sets the system?
Marley: 'De system been set! Manley come, comes ta someone. Dat someone, dere was someone before dat, someone comin' from where it was comin' from in England. It comin' down from England now. I don't know how financial dem set up, how much money Jamaica borrow from England, or what kinda plan Jamaica an' England 'ave, but I know Jamaica owes money to certain people. And if de politician run for politics an jus wanna run for politics and don't unnerstan de runnings an' all de t'ings a' gonna face him, den he gonna run away from de system, an' if ya run from de system, de people kill you! Y'unerstan'?

'Dat is when ya dare to go up 'gainst God, fight 'gainst God. If ya come to do somet'ing, ya do it. But if ya come to do something an' ya don't do it, ya fighting 'gainst God. And all de people ya trick all de while. So where's system getting from?

I don' know de business deal dem have, but dey can't just look upon Jamaica an' say, All right Jamaica, we give ya some a dis and some a dat. All right Jamaica, we're withdrawin' from ya, or whatever. Because either you swing wit' capitalism, or ya go wit' de other 'ism' – socialism. Tell 'em bout some more 'isms'. See, ya govern by dis 'ism' or dat 'ism'. We gotta trim it in right dere; no middle way. Even if ya go upon dis 'ism', him don' wanna lose friendship wit' America. Let me tell ya something – de same situation dat put de people in gonna catch 'em. Devil trick devil. I find now people want Africa. But if America help Africa, I don't even want dat neither. But what de people want is Africa.'

campaign,' says Chris Blackwell. 'There was a lot of press on Bob. It was breaking out in *Rolling Stone* – a moment when there was some real interest. There was some good momentum in America. It went to Number Eight in the charts. It sold well.'

A major American and European tour was set up to promote the album, beginning in June 1976. Like much of Bob's live work, the *Rastaman Vibration* dates started in Miami, just an airline's jump away from Jamaica. 'Coming rootically all the way from Trench Town, Jamaica, the proverbial, the prophetic, Bob Marley!' was the onstage introduction by Tony G, Bob's effervescent road manager.

The tour then swung up to the Tower Theater, Philadelphia, for a show with great personal meaning for Bob: his mother had driven the hour-long journey from Wilmington to see her son perform for the first time ever. She was almost beside herself with excitement. 'When I sit and view him onstage, it's as though I'm looking at a different person. It's not Bob I'm seeing now, I'm seeing somebody else. The glory that I see in this man here made me sweat – and when they turn on the light it look like blood running down.

RASTAMAN VIBRATION'S MOCK CANVAS SLEEVE CONTAINED SOME USEFUL ADVICE: 'THIS ALBUM JACKET IS GREAT FOR CLEANING HERB.'

'And mi look and see he is singing from the depths of his heart. And when he is putting his sounds and his words out, the personality is a different one, because he was under such a glorious sensation of the spirit that you could see it just flowing. And it make me feel so good, such a thrill.

'When I see all the crowd of people, I say, "Is this God? Is this me?" I couldn't believe it. But I know God is glorious, he is great, and everything he does is well done. Rastafari lives. Just give thanks.'

Bob Marley and The Wailers then moved on to Boston and afterwards to New York, where the group played the Beacon Theater. In New York Bob was interviewed by *High Times* magazine, who supplied him with fresh buds of Thai grass. 'Do you think herb will be legalised?' the interviewer asked him. 'I don' know if dis government will,' Bob replied, 'but I know Christ's government will.'

After playing Chicago, Bob and the group moved on to Los Angeles. On Sunset Boulevard, where they played to a rapturous audience at the hip Roxy Club, there was an enormous billboard advertising *Rastaman Vibration*, along the street from one for the Rolling Stones' *Black and Blue* album, which had been defaced by feminists. The Tuff Gong empathised with the pace and warmth of Los Angeles, and the group did a mini-tour of southern California, taking in dates in Santa Monica, San Diego, Long Beach and Santa Barbara.

'Mi really love "No Woman, No Cry" because it mean so much to me, so much feeling mi get from it. Really love it.'

The tour then crossed the Atlantic for four dates in France and Germany; as yet, progress in Europe was somewhat slow: at a German open-air festival, Bob followed 'progressive' rockers Jethro Tull onstage, only to find that almost all the audience had gone home.

But the Bob Marley and The Wailers shows in London at Hammersmith Odeon were like a summation of their success up to that point. Both 'No Woman, No Cry' and the live album, recorded at the London Lyceum date, had been big hits in Britain: the single had almost instantly achieved icon-like status, elevating Bob to a hitherto unknown stature. The *Live! Bob Marley and The Wailers* album, meanwhile, had greatly enhanced Bob's reputation, justifying Chris Blackwell's wise decision to rush-release the record. (At first it had been available only on import in the United States, thereby increasing its desirability.)

All the same, when Don Taylor, Bob's new manager, was setting up British dates, it soon

'The first thing you must know about me is that I always stand what I stand for. Good? The second thing you must know about yourself listening to me is that words are tricky. So when you know what me a stand for, when me explain a thing to you, you must never try to look 'pon it in a different way from what me a stand for.'

became apparent that there were some who had not yet been caught by the Marley infection. One established London promoter had suggested that Bob was not capable of selling out more than one night at the 4,000-seater Hammersmith Odeon.

Mick Cater knew better. He booked Bob Marley and The Wailers into the venue for five successive nights. Such a run was almost unprecedented at Hammersmith Odeon, and suggested the superstar status – Bob was already being billed as 'the first Third World superstar' – he was very soon to achieve. 'Rather like the Rolling Stones,' observes Cater, 'Bob never really sold colossal amounts of records. But he sold concert tickets by the barrow-load.'

Cater advised Hammersmith Odeon management that they would need to hire extra security for when the advance tickets went on sale. The venue's management ignored his suggestion, and were surprised when 1,000 people turned up on the morning that tickets were released.

Pandemonium reigned around the shows themselves. Tensions were high between the black community and 'Babylon', in the form of white officialdom. Three months later there would be running street battles two miles away from Hammersmith between black youth and the police at the Notting Hill carnival. Since the Lyceum shows, many of London's blacks had begun growing their locks. They had a new attitude towards Bob: 'He's ours.'

The stage of Hammersmith Odeon was stacked with the kind of speakers that graced the Trench Town sound systems. Nobody sat in their allocated seats, and when Bob and the group came onstage the event simply went off. It was just like Bob had always known it was going to be: he was rocking . . .

But there was a downside. In the opening ten minutes of the first night eighty people were mugged in the stalls, as sticksmen prowled the show. At the end of the evening twenty boxes were filled with handbags that had been looted and dumped on the floor of the auditorium.

Sometimes this out-on-the-edge stuff lost its threatening element and simply became bizarre. On the third night a guy stood on the front door: 'Tickets!' he shouted, holding his hand out and taking dozens from innocent white liberals before he disappeared to sell them again round the corner from the venue.

BOB GOT SHOT

There had always been political overtones about the 'Smile Jamaica' concert, scheduled for 5 December 1976 at Kingston's National Heroes Park. At first Chris Blackwell had advised against the show, which had originally been scheduled to take place in the grounds of Jamaica House: what Bob told him about the proposed show suggested it was to be billed as a PNP event.

Bob Marley went back to Michael Manley, and was assured that this was the last thing the Prime Minister wanted. Bob was being invited by the government of Jamaica and would therefore be performing for the entire nation: the 'Smile Jamaica' poster was to contain the words, 'Concert presented by Bob Marley in association with the Cultural Department of the Government of Jamaica'.

To some extent, Bob had had his arm twisted. He was repaying a debt to Tony Spaulding, the PNP Minister of Housing, who had set Bob's family up in their new home in Bull Bay. Moreover, a week after press releases about the concert went out, Manley called an election: there was no way that JLP supporters would not now see this concert as a case of Bob performing for Manley.

There were, noted Judy Mowatt, 'some eerie feelings in the air'. (On the Jamaican radio airwaves, however, everything sounded 'irie': massive play was being given to 'Smile Jamaica', a musical celebration of the island's virtues that Bob and The Wailers had recorded after the concert was announced.)

The night before the tune had been recorded, however, Judy Mowatt had had a 'vision'. She dreamed she was being shown a headline in a newspaper: 'Bob Got Shot' it read, 'For A Song'.

Troubled, Judy went to Harry J's later that day for a session to record this new tune, 'Smile Jamaica'. Now she noticed something about the song that hadn't been apparent previously: that it contained a line that ran, 'Under heavy manners'. This phrase was the PNP's principle political slogan. Bob had been off the island until recently, on the Rastaman Vibration tour, and seemed unaware of the political implications of these words. Clearly, realised Judy, they would mark Bob out as a PNP supporter. Anxiously, she told Marcia Griffiths, relating the content of her dream. 'Go and tell him now,' Marcia urged.

In the Harry J control room Bob was surrounded by his Twelve Tribes brethren. The air was thick and grey with herb smoke as they listened to various playbacks. All the same, Judy told Bob she must talk to him. 'Yeah, mon,' he said, and went out on the steps with her. She explained how the 'Under heavy manners' line would label him as a PNP supporter. Bob agreed.

Returning to the studio control room, he spoke to his brethren: 'Gentlemen, wha' yuh think, 'pon the line "Under heavy manners?"' And everyone said, 'Bwai, mi not think about it.' Then one say, 'Bwai, it nuh right, because they use it fe them slogan.'

Now everyone was taking it upon themselves to advise against using the words – though none of them had bothered to mention it earlier, Judy could not help observing.

Early on the morning of Friday, 3 December, Bob, Seeco Patterson, Gillie and Neville Garrick, his art director, drove out to jog a mile or so along the beach at Bull Bay; 'a lickle eye-opener', as Bob referred to these regular morning expeditions. 'Man, I had some weird dream last night,' a puzzled Bob told Neville, 'I couldn't make out if it were gunfire or firecrackers, but it sound like I'm in a war.' Almost immediately, one of those out-of-the-blue incidents that so characterize Jamaica occurred: police arrested Garrick at gunpoint as he was rolling a spliff in his car when they stopped to buy some milk, and took him to the Matilda's Corner police station. Bob followed him down there, and, using his influence, took him back with him to 56 Hope Road.

The night before, Judy Mowatt had a further another troubling dream. In it she saw a rooster and three chickens. Someone shot at the rooster

'It was a night I and I was rehearsing at 56 Hope Road, and cool out there, y'know. And then gunshot start to fire and t'ing, y'know. But after a while we hear it was like some politically motivated type o' t'ing. But it was really a good experience for I and I, y'know. Nobody died.'

BOB AT 56 HOPE ROAD,
ENGAGED IN ONE OF HIS
FAVOURITE HOBBIES.

and the bullet hit one of the chickens, whose intestines spilled from its side. This dream scared Judy: 'I looked at Bob as representing the rooster, and we were the back-up chickens.'

Going to 56 Hope Road to rehearse for the 'Smile Jamaica' concert she told Marcia and Rita about this dream. Marcia admitted she had also had premonitions, and decided to go home. But Rita and Judy stayed on and rehearsed. Later that evening Rita was due to take part in rehearsals for a pantomime, *Queenie's Daughter*, at the Ward Theatre; they agreed to leave at the same time, Rita to the theatre and Judy to her Bull Bay home.

The rehearsal was held in the downstairs room. Judy, who was seven months pregnant, continued to feel edgy: at the end of each song they ran through, she found herself wandering over to the doorway and looking out.

'Subconsciously I knew something was going to happen.'

When the rehearsal was over, she asked Bob if he could drive her home. But Bob said he was waiting for someone, and he asked Neville to drive Judy in his BMW instead. Neville was not particularly pleased. Notwithstanding his experience with the police that morning, he was looking forward to the arrival of Up-Sweet, who would be bringing herb fit for connoisseurs with him. Neville knew that by the time he got back from Bull Bay, the best herb would have gone.

Later Judy realised that she and Neville (accompanied for the ride by Sticko, a former 'sticksman' employed as gateman) had left in the nick of time. 'Because if they saw Bob's BMW leaving, they would have shot it up with Neville and myself.' As they drove out Judy passed her cousin, who was also pregnant, walking through

'Until the philosophy which hold one race superior and another inferior is finally discredited and abandoned . . . WAR! So that is prophecy, and everyone know that that is truth. And it came out of the mouth of Rastafari.'

the gate. Afterwards her cousin told her she had only walked a few yards up Hope Road when she heard shooting: she kept on walking.

Leaving the rehearsal room, Bob had wandered over to the kitchen. Peeling a grapefruit, he looked up as Don Taylor came into the room. Bob's manager walked straight into the line of fire of a gunman who had appeared in the doorway, and was firing shots indiscriminately in Bob's direction. Taylor took four shots in the groin – the gunman was firing from one of the lower steps leading into the kitchen – and a bullet that missed him ricocheted off a wall, grazed Bob's chest and lodged in his left arm.

Rita, meanwhile, was sitting in her yellow Volkswagen Beetle, starting up the engine. Five shots were fired at her through the vehicle's rear window. Another blasted through the door, and a final bullet went through the front windscreen. Although at least one bullet hit her in the head, the glass appeared to take the impact so that it did not penetrate.

Still up in the rehearsal room, Family Man heard the shots. Realising this was a 'serious business', he ran down the passage-way into the bathroom and jumped into the metal tub. He was followed by the three horn players, Glen Da Costa, Dave Madden and Vin Gordon, who bundled in on top of him, and Tyrone Downie. Suddenly Bob jumped on top of them all. As he tried to hide himself as low down in the bath as he could get, he somehow knocked a tap and water began to pour over Family Man's head.

At this stage, however, Family Man was not aware that Bob had been hit. Only when they all stood up, Family Man somewhat damper than when he'd dived in, did he notice that Bob was squeezing and rubbing his left arm.

That evening Chris Blackwell had gone out to Scratch Perry's yard off Washington Boulevard. Scratch played Blackwell an extraordinary tune – lazy, sticky, languorous – called 'Dreadlocks In Moonlight'. He said he had written it for Bob to record, but the Island boss told him that he loved the demo vocal Scratch had put on it, and that he should release it himself on Island. How long would it take him to mix it? About half an hour, came Scratch's optimistic reply. Blackwell

decided to wait. Perry, who didn't have a phone, eventually finished the mix some two and a half hours later.

Chris Blackwell had been scheduled to meet a film director at 56 Hope Road to discuss filming the 'Smile Jamaica' concert. By the time he arrived at the building once known as Island House, the shooting had already taken place. And Blackwell discovered that had Scratch's tune not been so good, he would have been there at exactly the time that the bullets were flying.

The cops came to Bull Bay that evening, looking for Bob's children, Cedella, Sharon, Ziggy and Steve. The experience was frightening to the extreme. Their father had been whisked away from hospital after his wounds, which were proved to be superficial, had been bandaged up. He had then been driven up the meandering roads to Chris Blackwell's Strawberry Hill home in the Blue Mountains. A police guard was mounted around the premises.

The children were being taken up there, but the police didn't bother explaining this to them. All the kids knew was that their parents had been shot. And although they had heard that their father was well, Cedella had been told that her mother had been shot in the head. 'So I said, "She's dead, right?" Because if somebody gets shot in the head you don't expect them to live. There was a lot of panic: we were looking at each other and wondering where we were going. After that we just got really militant. We never trusted anybody again. I didn't like any of my dad's friends anymore. You come to discover that sometimes the bad men are the nicest people. But they are nice people who would kill at the blink of an eye. I wouldn't wish anybody to go through having their parents shot.'

Rita Marley, who had passed out when the bullet sliced her skull, was still in hospital. She had learned that evil was a tangible reality. 'When that happened it was a confirmation for me that evil does exist. There was no reason to put this plot together. Whoever did it, I don't know. But it still feels like it was politically motivated. It's too big to be some ordinary gangster thing.'

The big question was whether the 'Smile Jamaica' concert would still feature a performance by Bob Marley and The Wailers. Family Man was nowhere to be found: he had stashed himself away at a Nyabinghi grounation which was taking place on the beach at Bull Bay – 'with the fishermen, burning fire and playing drums, singing chant music, giving joy to the Father.' Marcia Griffiths had also gone into hiding. Nevertheless, the rest of The Wailers expected to be playing the show. But it was up to Bob: what did he feel?

No one knew. Meanwhile, Judy went to the hospital to look for Rita. As soon as Rita saw her she told the doctor she wanted to be discharged. Still wearing her hospital 'duster', she was driven home to Bull Bay.

She found Tony Spaulding at her house, speaking on a walkie-talkie to Bob at Strawberry Hill. 'He was telling him he has to do the concert; the people were waiting for him; he had to show them he had overcome this,' said Judy. 'Bob was kind of iffy . . .

'But I knew that really his mind was already made up, because of the people. If it means his life, he would do it. Still, Bob was asking everybody's opinion. He asked me: "Judy, wha' ya t'ink?"

'I said, 'If you're going to do it then I'm there with you.' Rita said the same. "We don't want you to do it. But if you feel in your heart you should, then we're here with you, to support you one hundred per cent."'

Rita and Judy were driven to Strawberry Hill. 'When the hour came to do it,' said Judy, 'police cars came and Bob went in the lead police car. His friend Dr Fraser – Pee Wee – had a Volkswagen and so Rita and myself went in that behind the police car. The road from Strawberry Hill has about a million corners, and the police car was driving at about 120 miles an hour around these bends. And Pee Wee was following in his little car. We got to a square and a JLP meeting was going on. We were so frightened: "Jesus, this is an ambush," we said. The police siren was going and the lights flashing. But the people cheered and in a couple of minutes we get to Heroes Circle.

'I don't see Bob because people had him and they lift him up and pass him from man to man until they put him onstage. Before we even get to the stage we hear Bob singing "Curfew". We just take the mike – Rita in her hospital bedclothes. That night I thought Rita was in the spirit, because she sang the loudest I have ever heard her sing.

'While the show was going on there was a helicopter flying over. I myself started wondering if they had a gun with telescopic sights who could just shoot us on the stage.'

After the show Bob and Neville Garrick sneaked out of the island on a chartered Lear jet to Nassau. It was to be almost eighteen months before Bob Marley returned to Jamaica.

In the first week of 1977 Bob Marley and The Wailers flew to London, taking up residence in a house rented for them at 42 Oakley Street in Chelsea. Bob's presence therefore added to the collective energy in a city whose artistic life was undergoing a profound shift through the catalyst of Punk. At first, however, Bob strongly resisted

what he perceived to be simply another manifestation of Babylon. To counteract the effects of living in the British capital, he would spend time with his brethren at the Twelve Tribes headquarters in Kennington, south London.

After the Lyceum shows in 1975 a young dread named Don Letts, who had been deeply inspired by Marley's music, followed Bob and The Wailers back to the apartment where they were staying in Harrington Gardens, Earls Court. Slipping behind the musicians and other assorted London dreads into the living-room, Letts sat in a corner listening to the assorted reasonings. Needless to say, as daylight was breaking the inevitable occurred: Bob ran out of herb. Letts proffered his own small, humble supply and entered into a long discussion with his hero about Rastafari.

BOB MARLEY WITH DON LETTS, TAKEN ON LETTS' POLAROID.

So began a relationship of sorts. Whenever Bob was in London he would come and check Don Letts at Acme Attractions, the cutting edge clothing store he ran; Letts, after all, could always turn him on to the best source of sensi in town.

By the beginning of 1977 Don Letts was learning to become a film director. Having been DJ at the Roxy Club, he shot as much as he could of the emergent punk groups, only too aware of their spiritual connection with followers of Rastafari like himself.

But when he turned up in Oakley Street to see Bob, wearing a pair of bondage trousers, the Gong was shocked. 'What yuh wan' look like all them nasty punk people feh?' he demanded.

Letts told Bob he was wrong, that punk was a positive, creative spirit that was confronting the system and should be respected. They had a small argument, and agreed to differ.

After being in London only a few months, Bob

Marley had changed his mind. He saw the importance of the punk movement. With Lee Perry producing, and Aswad as backing musicians, Bob recorded 'Punky Reggae Party'. This became the definitive celebration of the punk-reggae fusion that was taking place in 1977, the year when the two sevens clashed. ('Two Sevens Clash' was the title of a big-selling Jamaican hit in which the vocal trio Culture, celebrated this long predicted time of change.)

As soon as they had arrived in London, Bob and the group locked themselves away in the basement rehearsal room at the headquarters of Island Records, which had now moved to St Peter's Square, west London. Company employees were sworn to secrecy: there were fears that further attempts could be made on Bob's life. It wasn't until the end of March, when Bob and Neville Garrick, out walking along Fulham Road, ran into a journalist called Vivien Goldman, who specialised in writing about reggae, that there was any media awareness at all that Bob Marley was living in London.

Bob had hit another level in the public consciousness. The attempted shooting of this Third World superstar undeniably created a frisson of outlaw romance. But it was a romance of the heart that was garnering as much media interest for Bob Marley: his affair with Cindy Breakspeare, the beautiful Jamaican woman who had been crowned Miss World the previous November, provided ample material for front-page features in the European popular press.

Working away at Island Records, Bob appeared oblivious to this. He was on a creative high, as though the shooting had only strengthened his resolve; Bob was also now working closely with Tyrone Downie who was becoming more prominent as the group arranger than Family Man had been. By the end of February Bob was ready to lay the tracks down and the group moved to Basing Street to record. Songs had flown out of these sessions, many of them inspired by events around the shooting. The new album was to be called *Exodus*, decreed Bob, even though that was one of the only songs he hadn't yet written.

There was one problem within The Wailers,

however: they no longer had a guitarist. Al Anderson had left to join Peter Tosh, and now his replacement, Donald Kinsey, had also defected to Tosh's group.

Junior Marvin, a guitarist friend of the group Traffic, was introduced to Bob, and they jammed in Chelsea at Oakley Street on 14 February 1977. 'We kinda clicked right on the spot and to my amazement Bob said to me, "Welcome to the Wailers". They were my favourite group: I was delighted that I even had the chance to meet them, much less play with them.'

'Bob and Junior got on well: they liked each other,' says Chris Blackwell. 'And Junior was very good for Bob: he was a good communicator in the outside world, whereas Bob was very quiet. Junior and Tyrone were very valuable in that respect.'

Bob was in high spirits, as Junior Marvin observed. 'I guess he was happy to be alive. He was writing a lot, writing every day. He seemed to be having a great time.' The guitarist immediately saw one of the reasons why Bob was so great a songwriter: 'He worked so hard at it. He tried to write a song every day. Out of every hundred songs he wrote, he would end up with just ten to fifteen, the ones that had a certain magic.'

Marvin's own magic came from several years of paying his dues. Born in 1947, he had left Jamaica for England with his parents when he was nine. Like countless other British teenagers, he had been inspired by Hank Marvin, lead guitarist with the hugely successful instrumental group The Shadows, and the source of Junior's stage name. Junior and a friend went out and bought guitars and formed a group. Later he moved to the States and played with Billy Preston, Ike and Tina Turner, and T-Bone Walker. In 1972, ironically, he spent time hanging out with Al Anderson; he was playing with a jazz organist called Larry Young who came from the same town in New Jersey as Anderson.

The fact that Junior Marvin moved around a lot onstage gave Bob a chance to cool out during his performance. Junior's joining the group was nevertheless a contentious matter for purists. When *Exodus* was released, the reviews criticised his rock-style guitar-playing, although

CINDY BREAKSPEARE

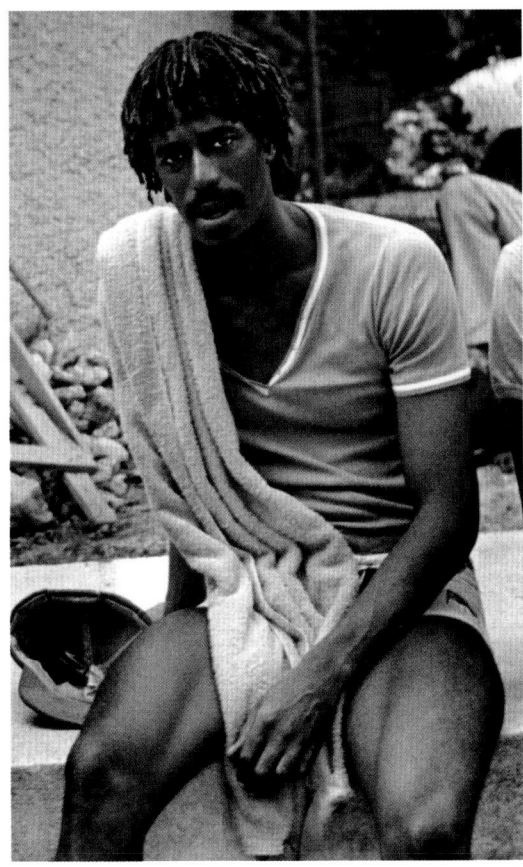

JUNIOR MARVIN: RECRUITED IN LONDON AFTER BOB HAD GONE INTO TEMPORARY EXILE, JUNIOR'S HENDRIX-LIKE PLAYING WAS TO PROVE INVALUABLE IN THE GRAND LIVE EXTRAVAGANZAS OF THE FUTURE.

his Hendrix-like approach was one of the reasons he had been chosen. 'There were a few people who wanted the music to be strictly one style, but Bob said to me, "How can I be free if they want it to be strict? Music has got to have some kind of freedom."'

He started working on the new songs straight away. Things had hardly changed from the days when the Soulettes were drilled by Bob at Studio One. 'It was very intense and disciplined. There wasn't much fooling around. They gave me a whole load of old Wailers albums to listen to. And I jammed on some of the new songs with Bob and Tyrone, just the three of us.'

There was only one unfortunate break in the routine of recording. On 6 April 1977, Bob was fined £50 at Marylebone Magistrates Court in west London for possession of cannabis. Family Man was fined £20 for a similar offence. The pair had been pulled over in a spot-check by Notting Hill police as they were driving back to their apartment from Basing Street late one night in their Ford Cortina station wagon: they had been passing the police station at the bottom of Ladbroke Grove. To the police searching their vehicle, they were just another pair of local dreads. It was only when they were taken into the police station that Bob's identity was revealed.

By the end of March all the songs for *Exodus* seemed to have been recorded, but the group worked on in the studio, completing a total of twenty-four songs. These were quickly weighed up: the tone of ten of them was perfect for *Exodus*, whose first side was given over to

songs about the shooting. The rest, lighter and more mystical in vein, were put aside for the next album, *Kaya*; *Kaya* was mixed at Criteria in Miami, a conscious and successful effort to give the record a different feel and sound.

The epochal *Exodus* album was released in May 1977. A month later Bob and The Wailers began a European tour in Paris, 200 miles from the Tuff Gong's temporary home in London. The tour took in dates in France, Germany and Scandinavia, before heading back to the United Kingdom.

The on-the-road discipline had intensified. It was, noted Judy Mowatt, like taking a church on tour. 'It was a crusade, a mission. We were like sentinels, like lights. On tour the shows were like church: Bob delivering his sermon. There were mixed emotions in the audience: you see people literally crying, people in a frenzy, on a spiritual high. I remember one night in Canada a woman gave birth in the audience. These concerts were powerful and highly spiritual. There was a power that pulled you there. It was a clean feeling: you leave a concert as though you have learned something, you have gained something. For months and maybe years it stays with you.'

Although there would always be one suite in every hotel set aside for hanging out, serious partying rarely took place. Bob was more interested in sitting down with the group members and listening to the previous show than in going to night-clubs.

After the chaos of the Hammersmith Odeon dates, the Rainbow in Finsbury Park became the only

venue in London willing to put on a series of four Bob Marley shows, beginning on 1 June 1977. It was only six months since the shooting in Jamaica and there was maximum security at the shows. Both Bob and Don Taylor were worried that some brethren of the Kingston gunmen might emerge out of the shadows of London's

Judy Mowatt: 'If you went to Bob's room at midnight, one o'clock, three o'clock, Bob would be playing a song. As the great philosopher said, "Height of great men were not attained by sudden flight, but while their companions slept they were toiling through the night."

'Most of those songs of Bob that we hear and make us feel so joyful in our hearts, he wrote late, late at night. Sometimes you'd be passing his room and you'd hear the guitar playing. You would hear him singing quietly in the still of the night.'

Paris: Ray Coleman in *Melody Maker*. 'Marley says he's added Junior Marvin so that he can be freer to move around the stage as a singer. Nowhere was this more in evidence than during his exotic, dervish-like dances on "Lively Up Yourself".

'We know Marley to be an athlete – a strong footballer, he gets up at home in Jamaica every day at 5 a.m. to go running – but his energy and surprisingly inventive dancing here was a joyful sight, perfectly in the mood of the song. Arms and dreadlocks flailing, he was a magical picture.'

Munich: Vivien Goldman in *Sounds*. 'It throbbed and burned forward, as natural and irresistible as the moon tugging the sea.

'It's a natural mystic flowing through the air. Let Jah be praised. And when he sings, "Forget your sorrows and dance", your heart swells so much you're hardly aware that you're dancing, feet and soul.'

Bob to Ray Coleman: 'People want to listen to a message, word from Jah. This could be passed through me or anybody. I am not a leader. Messenger. The words of the songs, not the person, is what attracts people.'

large Jamaican community. All backstage passes included a photograph of the holder, and the only people permitted in the backstage area were members of the group – Mick Cater and Don Taylor stood at the stage-door vetting everyone entering the building.

Each day Bob arrived at the venue at 4 p.m. in a black London taxi. On the second day at the Rainbow, as he was coming through the stage-door, a burly West Indian tried to follow him into the building. Taylor and Cater went to hold the man back, but he pulled out a gun and fired four shots in their direction. All those standing around the door fell back like dominoes, and the gunman ran off.

That evening it was discovered that the incident had been something of a false alarm: the shots were only blanks, the weapon a starting-pistol, and the man doing the shooting had tickets to that night's performance. But because Cater had been worried about some incident occurring, he had had metal detectors installed at the main entrance to the Rainbow: and the starting-pistol was immediately detected.

A tour of the United States was scheduled to begin in August. However, on 20 July 1977, Don Taylor announced to the US promoters that the tour was being postponed until the autumn. Bob's foot injury meant he was in no fit shape to tour. Instead he bought a large villa on Vista Lane in south Miami.

His mother sold her home in Wilmington and moved to Florida to this new house. Until she arrived, at the beginning of October, Bob had been staying at Don Taylor's Miami residence, moving into the villa on the day Cedella Booker arrived. 'Bob was recuperating from the toe there,' says his mother. 'Then he decide that the toe start to feel a little better. Because they cut some out and grafted some on. I remember him say, "Every time I'm to do a tour here in the US something happens."'

The cancellation of the US part of the 'Exodus' tour had a bad effect on the sales of *Exodus*, which had been bubbling in the charts, awaiting the major promotion that a tour would give it. Although there was no way this

In a football game in Paris between the Wailers and a group of French journalists, Bob was given a hard tackle. His right foot was badly hurt and the nail torn off the big toe. That toe was already vulnerable: Bob had first injured it in 1975; it had been slashed by another player's pair of rusty running spikes while he was playing football on the Boys Town recreation ground in Trench Town. Although he tried to clean up the wound with cotton and antiseptic, he never went and had an anti-tetanus shot. That wound never really healed (Cedella, his daughter, would dress it for him in the evenings).

The doctor Bob saw in Paris told him he must stay off his feet, but the Gong didn't heed this advice. The only compromise he made was to wear a large bandage on his right foot for a while. The Tuff Gong even played some shows with Bob wearing sandals and the bandage.

Bob was determined to get through his tour . . . Sometimes following a show, he would find his boot filled with blood, which happened after one of the London dates at the Rainbow Theatre. Those around him noticed that Bob had to keep changing the bandage; evidently the wound was not healing.

In London Bob went to see a Harley Street specialist with Junior Marvin. The doctor told him the toe should be cut off; it had become contaminated and the infection could get into his bloodstream. He also warned him of the danger of cancer. Everyone around Bob began to offer an opinion: he was advised that having his toe removed could ruin his career, and to get a second opinion. Then a doctor in Miami told Bob that a skin graft would cure the problem, to which he agreed.

cancellation could have been avoided, Bob's reputation with US promoters was harmed. 'It affects people a lot when tours get cancelled,' says Chris Blackwell. 'If it's an English rock act, that's one thing: it does you a lot of harm. But when it's a Jamaican act then it's much worse: people say that there's no point in booking it because you know these Jamaicans: they're never going to turn up. So you get a credibility gap you have to get over,which is very hard.'

Bob spent close to five months in Miami. Here he lived a life very similar to the one he would pursue in Jamaica. Rising at five or six in the morning, he would brew up some bush tea and then wander out to sit on the stoop in the back yard. There he would play around with tunes and sing until around eight or so. Much of the time Neville Garrick was with him. 'Him used to like sing in the morning, because him voice sound more hoarse, throaty. I never saw him record then, though. I remember him writing "Misty Morning" in Delaware after the "Natty Dread" tour. We wake up one morning. Everywhere she live Mrs Booker always plant a big garden: she even have a breadfruit tree in Delaware. We are out there: cloudy, cloudy morning. 'Im say, "It so dark up here." Then him just sing: "Misty morning, don't see no sun/I know you're out there somewhere/Having fun". And him work on it for next two hours: it just come like that.'

Exodus: Movement of Jah People

In Berlin on the 'Exodus' tour, Bob and The Wailers clearly felt very relaxed. Before going onstage they were given a bundle of their beloved Thai sticks. These presented Bob with a different perception of the evening's set. On the second encore he stopped the show and started the set again from 'Positive Vibration', which fell roughly a third of the way into the set. The group didn't come offstage until 2 a.m.

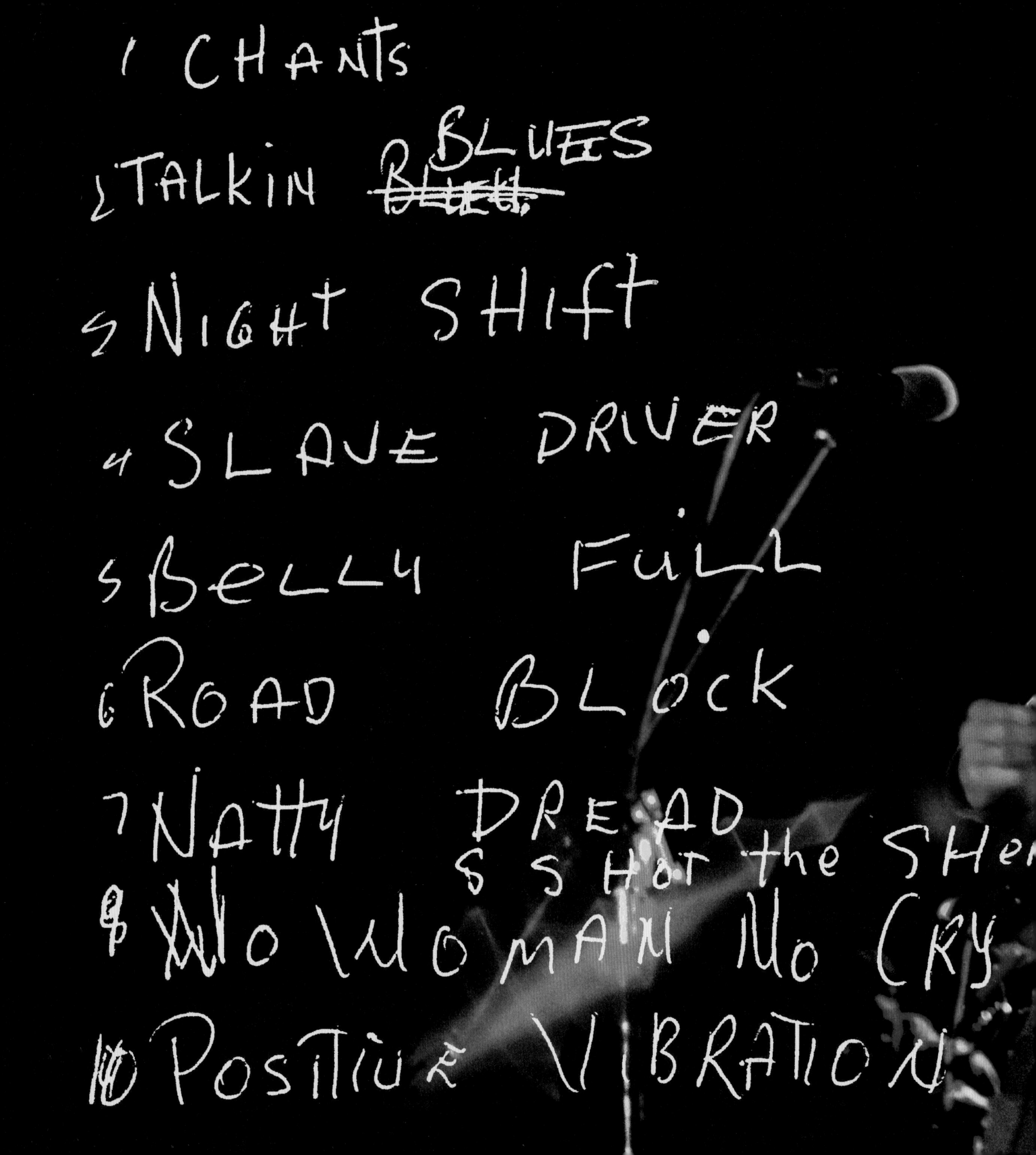

1 CHANTS

2 TALKIN ~~BLUE~~ BLUES

3 NIGHT SHIFT

4 SLAVE DRIVER

5 BELLY FULL

6 ROAD BLOCK

7 NATTY DREAD
9 SHOT the SHe...

8 NO WOMAN NO CRY

10 POSITIVE VIBRATION

KESKIDEE CENTRE

Located off Caledonian Road in north London is the Keskidee Centre. A former church, this building has played an inestimable role in the lives of London's Caribbean and African immigrants: as Britain's principal black arts centre, it is the country's main repository of African culture, as well as being the home of black theatre in Britain.

The Keskidee Centre also plays host to the Caribbean Artists Movement, in which many of the leading artists of the region have involved themselves. Prominent exhibitions of paintings, in addition to prose and poetry readings, are held at the centre, which boasts an extensive library, the largest collection of black cultural reading matter in the United Kingdom. In 1977 its librarian was a young black poet by the name of Linton Kwesi Johnson.

Linton was present when a video shoot was set up at the Keskidee Centre for Bob Marley's 'Is This Love'. The video was to be shaped around a children's party, in which Bob played the part of a kind of Rastafarian Pied Piper, even leading the children out of the building and away down the street; the party was entirely contrived, but a delight all the same for the underprivileged three-to twelve-year-olds of the area who were invited: they remained nonplussed by their famous host, but one and all were fascinated by Bob's dreadlocks.

Linton Kwesi Johnson was introduced to Bob Marley. 'He knew who I was, because I'd left a book of my poetry at Island for him. He wanted to know why I wasn't a Rasta. I said I wasn't religious. He asked why I was so angry. I said I was just expressing reality. He was a little, ordinary kind of guy, very affable, but very private.'

Later Bob was to acquire the Jamaican rights to Linton's records – as he also did to those of Steel Pulse – for the Tuff Gong label; although the records were ultimately never released.

The video shoot was thoroughly documented by

Adrian Boot, although the true importance of this
photographic session was not to be understood until
years later – 1984, to be precise, when the Island
Records art department was searching for a suitable
cover shot for the *Legend* compilation LP. It was a
shot from the Keskidee session, of Bob wearing the
ring that had formerly belonged to His Imperial
Majesty Haile Selassie, that was eventually chosen.

The video, ironically, was never shown at the time:
it was felt to conflict with a more militant image of
Bob that was then being put forward, and only became
available much later when a compilation of Bob
Marley videos was released by Island. Footage shot at
the event, however, was integrated into the video of
One Love/People Get Ready, made by Don Letts in
1984.

'Is this

love that

I'm

feeling?'

Bob Marley loved children, as should be apparent from the number of heirs he left. And at the Keskidee video shoot it soon became evident that the children present also loved Bob.

o n e

love

Chris Blackwell on *Legend*: 'I wasn't terribly keen on putting together a *Best of Bob*. We didn't put anything together after he died. In 1984 Dave Robinson was running the company. He thought we should do it. I said I didn't really want to get involved in it, and he said he would do it himself. He worked a lot with Trevor Wyatt in putting together the compilation.

'He approached the whole thing very professionally and very well. He even did some market research on it, finding out what the

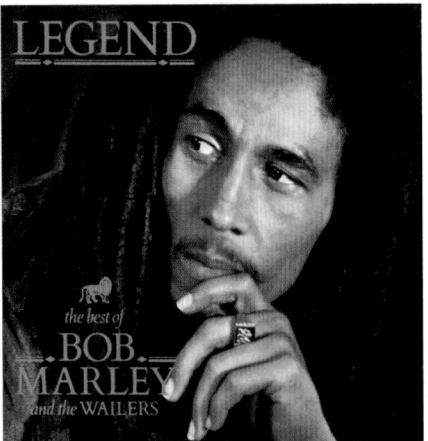

general public in England thought about reggae. Did they know about Bob Marley? What did they think about him? Did they like him? Not the sort of thing I would have done: I was too close to it, I think.

'Through all that research he finally came up with what the album cover and title should be. He learned that you should keep the word "reggae" out of it. Reggae had a mixed reaction: some people liked reggae, some people hated it. A lot of what people didn't like about Bob Marley was the threatening aspect of him, the revolutionary side.

'So the picture chosen was one of the softest pictures of Bob. It was a very well conceived and thought-out package. And a very well put together-record. It's an undeniable success. It was Number One in Britain for months. And it's one of the Top Three catalogue records of all time.'

THE PICTURE CHOSEN FOR THE COVER OF LEGEND, *TAKEN AT THAT CHILDREN'S PARTY AT THE* KESKIDEE *CENTRE IN* LONDON.

PEACE CONCERT

At the beginning of 1978 in Kingston, there were only two real topics of conversation: the increasing shortage of goods on sale in the island's stores, the consequence of Washington's efforts to bankrupt the Manley government; and the imminent return of Bob Marley to Jamaica, a hero coming back from his self-imposed exile following the attempt on his life in December 1976.

'If you see somebody setting up a fight against black people, you know that this guy got orders from big, big place or from low, low place. But if them look on us as inferior species, we look on them as nothing.'

The shooting of Bob Marley had been but the most public example of an extraordinary outbreak of murders in Jamaica. Gun law ruled the island. Both political parties, the ruling People's National Party and the right-wing Jamaican Labour Party, had hired ruthless teams of ghetto gunmen – some of them, like the JLP's Claudie Massop and the PNP's Bucky Marshall, began to take on an almost superstar status.

Bob's flight touched down at Kingston's Norman Manley airport on 26 February 1978; as it coasted to a halt he was aware that this return was only worthwhile as a direct effort to end the escalating violent hatred that was tearing Jamaica apart and terrifying its population.

Already the seeds for an end to this state of affairs had been sown. In London earlier in the month, at the video shoot at the Keskidee Centre, Bob had been approached by Claudie Massop, Bucky Marshall and another PNP shock troop commander, Tony Welch. They had asked Bob if he would agree to take part in a 'One Love Peace Concert' to help bring an end to the island's murderous political rivalry. It was to be held in Kingston on 22 April, under the auspices of the Twelve Tribes of Israel. Even these 'rankin'' gunmen had become aware that matters in Jamdown were getting out of hand.

The political parameters that exist in Jamaica are hardly the same as those of the United States or western Europe: they are more akin to those of a banana republic. Jamaicans, moreover, adore spaghetti westerns; it often seems as though some islanders have utterly misunderstood the dividing line between reality and art, allowing it to become blurred and

THE PEACE CONCERT MARKED BOB'S RETURN TO JAMAICA FROM HIS SELF-IMPOSED EXILE FOLLOWING THE ATTEMPTED ASSASINATION IN DECEMBER 1976. NOW, IN APRIL 1978, EVEN IN HIS YARD AT 56 HOPE ROAD THERE WERE MEMBERS OF THE SECURITY FORCES INTENT ON PROTECTING JAMAICA'S KING OF THE GHETTO.

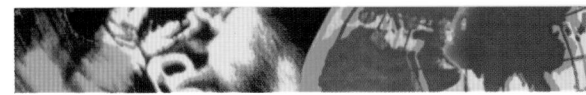

indistinct. Life in the ghetto area of west Kingston can seem as though it is being lived in a Sergio Leone film, with the body count as high. Suddenly, violence of an extraordinarily desperate and vicious nature can erupt, only to evaporate again within minutes.

But flying in the face of most predictions, the concert on 22 April was a resounding success, a focus for the media of the western world. Sixteen of the island's most significant reggae acts, including Jacob Miller and Inner Circle, The Mighty Diamonds, Trinity, Dennis Brown, Culture, Dillinger, Big Youth, Peter Tosh and Ras Michael and The Sons of Negus appeared. To coincide with the event, a new album was released by Bob Marley and The Wailers – *Kaya*, a collection of love songs and, of course, a homage to the power of ganja. The album was also to provide a couple of chart singles, 'Satisfy My Soul' and the beautiful 'Is This Love'.

During the concert, Peter Tosh harangued Michael Manley and Edward Seaga for persecuting ghetto sufferahs for their fondness for herb, and lit up a spliff onstage.

Bob, however, seemed in a state of transcendental bliss. Instead of attacking the prime minister and the leader of the opposition, he attempted to bring them together. During 'Jamming' his dancing delivery and skat extemporising on the lyrics showed someone taken over by the spirit:

'To make everything come true, we've got to be together, yeah, yeah. And to the spirit of the most high, His Imperial Majesty Emperor Haile Selassie I, run lightning, leading the people of the slaves to shake hands . . . To show the people that you love them right, to show the people that you gonna unite, show the people that you're over bright, show the people that everything is all right. Watch, watch, watch what you're doing, because . . . I'm not so good at talking but I hope you understand what I'm trying to say. I'm trying to say, could we have, could we have, up here onstage here the presence of Mr Michael Manley and Mr Edward Seaga. I just want to shake hands and show the people that we're gonna unite . . . we're gonna unite . . . we've got to unite . . . The moon is high over my head, and I give my love instead. The moon is high over my

LEFT: THIS CLASSIC SHOT BY ADRIAN BOOT SHOWS THE VERY MOMENT WHEN BOB MARLEY BROUGHT TOGETHER PRIME MINISTER MICHAEL MANLEY AND EDWARD SEAGA, THE LEADER OF THE OPPOSITION. AS BOB PERFORMED THE SONG 'JAMMING', HE SEEMED TRANSFIXED, AS THOUGH THE SPIRIT WAS UPON HIM. THEN, FROM EITHER SIDE OF HIM, HE PULLED THE TWO POLITICIANS TOGETHER.

head, and I give my love instead.'

As ghetto gunmen hovered on the edge of the stage, Bob brought the hands of Michael Manley and Edward Seaga together. And held them firmly together.

'Yes, the Peace,' he said later. 'Is really the Youth of Jamaica started it really. Asked me to help and get it together, y'know, knowing that I was one of the victims during the time of the politics. This peace work, it don't stop . . . it never stop . . . We know it never stop. That mean, we the youth got a work to do.'

KAYA

The Peace Concert was the opening salvo of the first Bob Marley and The Wailers world tour, which had the promotion of the new *Kaya* album as its hook. Tuff Gong gone outernational . . .

The Wailers were now exhibiting what was possibly the first example of twin lead guitars in reggae. Al Anderson had come to Bob and told him he'd like to play with the group again. Bob had asked Junior, 'What shall we do about Al?'

'I said, "If you want to get him back it will be a good thing because you can get the same sounds on the tracks he plays on records, and the same thing on the ones I play on." So Al came back and it was really cool – it made the group stronger.

'Bob would say, "We'll have a guitar night tonight." Sometimes he would make a joke, "Tonight the guitar player dem take the stage." We felt very secure musically, everyone playing to their best abilities. There were two keyboard players that were really good – Tyrone and Wire, and they would try and push each other to do better. The same thing happened with myself and Al. We both wanted to sound as good as we could. So competitively it was good. So Bob got the best of everyone.'

The American leg was scheduled to begin in Tampa, Florida, in May 1978. But it ran into difficulties: Junior Marvin was initially refused a US visa, his 'numerous drug convictions' cited as the reason.

The Tampa concert had to be cancelled four hours before showtime, leaving a local promoter furious. But the Florida dates and others in the American south were rescheduled and the tour began at the Music Hall in Cleveland, Ohio, on 19 May, moving on to Columbus and then to Chicago. In the Windy City Bob, whose reading matter was usually restricted to the Bible and music publications, visited a number of black

bookshops. He bought a large quantity of black consciousness literature, including various biographies of Malcolm X and work by Angela Davis. Davis had been a professor and friend of Neville Garrick's, Bob's art director; for the rest of the tour Garrick would see Bob devouring these volumes at every opportunity. 'You can see how his lyrics matured in terms of clarity over the next records. From *Natty Dread* to *Survival* is a big leap.'

The tour continued through Milwaukee and Minneapolis. In June it hit Pittsburgh, Rochester, Detroit, Philadelphia, Boston and Montreal, arriving at Toronto Maple Leaf Gardens on Friday, 9 June. After two more shows, in Buffalo and Washington DC, Bob Marley and The Wailers arrived in New York City. Here they played a Saturday night show at Madison Square Garden, where they were supported by Stanley Clarke, and drew a sold-out, racially diverse crowd of over 18,000. As befitted these larger venues that Bob and the group were now playing, the shows were an exaggeration of their predecessors, heavy with rock guitar from Junior Marvin, and almost histrionic in their presentation. Bigger-than-life, the message came across to an audience that was often more used to the melodrama of big rock shows. Bob and Chris Blackwell had made a conscious decision that this was the way to get

'You can't show aggression all the while. To make music is a life that I have to live. Sometimes you have to fight with music. So it's not just someone who studies and chats, it's a whole development. Right now is a more militant time on earth, because it's Jah Jah time. But me always militant, you know. Me too militant. That's why me did things like *Kaya*, to cool off the pace.'

'People don't understand that we live in this earth too. We don't sing these songs and live in the sky. I don't have an army behind me. If I did, I wouldn't care, I'd just get more militant. Because I'd know, well, I have 50,000 armed youth, and when I talk, I talk from strength. But you have to know how you're dealing. Maybe if I'd tried to make a heavier tune than "Kaya" they would have tried to assassinate me because I would have come too hard. I have to know how to run my life, because that's what I have, and nobody can tell me to put it on the line, you dig? Because no one understands these things. These things are heavier than anyone can understand. People that aren't involved don't know it, it's my work, and I know it outside in. I know when I am in danger and what to do to get out. I know when everything is cool, and I know when I tremble, do you understand? Because music is something that everyone follows, so it's a force, a terrible force.'

'I don't come down on you really with blood and fire, earthquake and lightning, but you must know seh, that within me all of that exists too . . .'

REASONING AT NINE MILES, SO NAMED BECAUSE THIS IS THE DISTANCE FROM ST ANN'S BAY IN THE PARISH OF ST ANN. BOB WOULD VISIT NINE MILES FIVE OR SIX TIMES A YEAR, OFTEN WITH SEECO, GILLIE AND NEVILLE GARRICK; HE WOULD SLEEP IN THE SMALL HOUSE, ONCE HIS GRANDFATHER'S.

John Rockwell's review of Madison Square Garden in *The New York Times*: 'The concert was a triumph . . . for reggae in general but for Mr Marley in particular. There were plenty of non-West Indians on hand, for one thing. And for another, after a slightly slow start, the concert built to a climax that was really wonderful in its fervor and exultation . . . By the final number, 'Jamming', and especially in the encores of 'Get Up, Stand Up', 'War' and 'Exodus', Mr Marley was extraordinary. Who would have believed Madison Square Garden would have swayed *en masse* to a speech by Haile Selassie, the words of which Mr Marley incorporates verbatim into 'War'?'

'To a casual listener the steadily rocking, offbeat accents of the music could seem too unvarying, especially with the minimal pauses between numbers and the frequent running together of one song into the next . . . But the band members overlay the pulse with solos in the traditional jazz and rock manner, and the order is determined with an air for variety.'

Madison Square Garden, *The Black American*: 'The crowd was near peaceful hysteria when Marley put down his guitar and did his patented herky-jerky dance across the stage as The Wailers ran through three rhythmic breaks that would have made the best of the disco groups envious.

'Marley finally danced into the wings while The Wailers kept "Jammin" onstage. By now, however, Marley's crowd was too far gone to stop dancing. Cries of "more, more" began to rise until the noise became deafening. Then a thunderous train-like sound grew as people began stomping their feet in delight. It was really breathtaking.'

the message across on an even larger scale. After a final East Coast date in Lenox, Massachusetts, the tour headed off across the Atlantic for shows in Paris, Ibiza, Stockholm, Copenhagen, Oslo, Rotterdam, Amsterdam, Brussels and Bingley in Staffordshire – slap-bang in the middle of England. After faulty planning resulted in three bus-loads filled with media arriving long after Bob's set had begun, the reviewer in *New Musical Express* assessed the British concert under the headline of 'Babylon by Bus'. After it was brought to Neville Garrick's attention, this became the title of the double live album of the tour that Chris Blackwell put together.

At the end of the 1978 tour of Europe, Bob caught a flight to Ethiopia. His old friend Alan Cole had been living there since 1976, coaching a local football team, and Bob seized the time to visit him in this holy land. Although he was only there for four days, during which time he wrote the song 'Zimbabwe', Bob didn't mind leaving: he knew he would be going back there very soon.

The tour then swung over to the American west coast. Bob Marley and The Wailers played in Vancouver, Seattle, Portland, San Francisco, Los Angeles and Santa Barbara. Then they wheeled through the dates in the US south that had been cancelled at the beginning of the tour. And finally the Bob Marley posse returned to Jamaica.

While he was back in his country, Bob spent time with his old spar Scratch Perry. Having linked up again with the increasingly eccentric producer to record 'Punky Reggae Party', their relationship had revived. Now, in one day, Bob cut four tunes out at Black Ark: 'Black Man Redemption' and 'Rastaman Live Up', both of which came out as singles on Tuff Gong, and which were a marked departure from the softer subjects of *Kaya*: the militancy of these two songs pointed the way ahead to Bob's next two albums. 'Who Colt the Game' and 'I Know a

Place Where We Can Go', two recordings that were never released, were also made on this occasion. All four songs were mixed at Tuff Gong.

In September 1978 Peter Tosh was badly beaten by police, suffering a broken right hand. He had been arrested in Half Way Tree whilst smoking a spliff, but it was widely believed that this arrest was in revenge for his pro-herb tirade from the stage of the Peace Concert. Bunny Lee heard the whole story: 'Bob come and go to the police and make them drop the charge. But Peter was kind of big-headed, too. Bob said he was going to take it to court. But the policeman said to him, "Bob, you can take it to court. But remember when they call your and Peter name they are going to hear, 'Deceased, your honour.'" But eventually they decide to withdraw the charges.'

In the autumn Bob and The Wailers headed across the Pacific to Australia and New Zealand. From all over the island Maoris had journeyed into the New Zealand capital of Auckland. At a ceremony of greeting, they awarded Bob Marley a name which, translated into English, means the redeemer. Bob made sure he spent time at a couple of Maori youth centres.

The most memorable of the shows on this leg of the tour was at Western Springs, a natural amphitheatre in Auckland. This scenario was given passionate back-up by Victor Stent, an enormous fan of reggae. In a competition between the various Island outlets to boost sales of reggae, Stent who ran the label in New Zealand, easily outstripped all the overseas competition.

In Japan, where he played four shows, Bob Marley met an extraordinary reception. At the concerts the audiences showed they knew every song, and could sing every word of the lyrics.

In subsequent years reggae has enjoyed immense popularity in Japan, and this may be directly traced back to Bob's only visit. But how did the Japanese perceive Bob? A little girl, for example, came up to him and bowed down reverentially. 'No, no: that's not for me – that's for the almighty God,' Bob felt obliged to say.

There was one problem, however: the almost

zero availability of herb in this notoriously drug-free country. To alleviate the situation, a member of the touring party had to travel to Japan ahead of the group. Such matters were always the responsibility of the local promoters, but this proved not to be understood in Japan.

Alternative arrangements were made, and when Bob and The Wailers arrived in Tokyo they were presented with fifty Thai sticks. The group retired to their hotel, surprised at the minute proportions of their rooms: as a security measure the floors directly above and below them had also been booked.

As was their wont, the group had virtually consumed all the Thai sticks by the time they went onstage. The next morning more were obtained from US marines. The Japanese were amazed: they thought that such a lifetime's supply of Thai sticks would certainly last Bob and The Wailers the entire tour.

WHEN BOB VISITED NINE MILES HE WOULD DINE ON SIMPLE COUNTRY FOOD: ROAST YAM AND RICE WERE A PARTICULAR FAVOURITE. THE YOUTH SAW HIM VERY MUCH AS BIG BROTHER FROM THE CITY, AND EVENINGS WOULD BE SPENT SMOKING HERB AND REASONING WITH THEM.

Rita Marley: 'Japan was memorable. We had a lot of press there saying how well they thought it would be doing there in ten years time: how it would be taking over Japan. And we said that it never would! They loved Bob, and Bob played a big part in their absorbing reggae as they have done.'

56 HOPE ROAD

When Bob was preparing for a tour, he and his football cronies would follow a strict régime of physical exercise. He would leave Hope Road late at night and drive down to Rita's place at Bull Bay. Bob rarely lived there himself, and would stay in a room round the back of the house when he did. Rising at 4.30 or 5.00 a.m., he would rendezvous with Skill Cole, who lived in Bull Bay with Judy Mowatt. Then the two of them would link up with Bunny Wailer, at whose place Neville Garrick was likely to have passed the night.

There were two possible runs: the mile and a half along road and track to Cane river, where they would wash their locks in the waterfall, or a hard sand run along the beach to Rock, about a mile or so from Bunny's house. If they bought fresh fish from the fishermen who were just coming in with their catches, they would go by Bunny's and fry up the doctor or parrot fish or snapper.

If they drove back into Kingston straight away, they would probably stop off at Hope Gardens. Here a woman kept a dozen or so cows, and they would buy fresh, warm milk from her. Back at 56 Hope Road they would make green banana porridge. Skill Cole and Gillie, meanwhile, might get into one of their juice-blending competitions, both being connoisseurs.

By ten in the morning the permanent hustle that was rarely absent from the yard would be underway. The Tuff Gong record store would have opened and ghetto rankin's and junior rankin's would be coming up to check Bob or to hustle him for money, or just to cool out: 56 Hope Road was about the only uptown place that a ghetto youth could hang in without experiencing the wrath of the police. During the time of the Peace Concert even Michael Manley passed by to idle away an hour or so. Bob was also extremely welcoming to the 'mad' people – a feature of Jamaican life – who would peer through the white fence, pouring out their stream-of-consciousness rants. 'It a mad man,' Bob would say, always eager to hear an extreme point of view, 'send him in for a reasoning.'

Bob used to like holding court in the shade of the awning over the front steps. Serious football, meanwhile, would be in progress on the grass-covered front yard. Sometimes a man would come up with large quantities of fish or fruit for Bob. If there was enough fish to go round, they would wrap it in foil, put it out on a sheet of corrugated zinc, and light a fire underneath.

As the voice of the ghetto, Bob could not help attracting gangsters and gunmen, who have always been fond of mingling with entertainers. Alan Cole's position as a sports superstar held a similar appeal. Those around Bob believe he also liked mixing with notorious characters. But Bob could be ruthlessly tough himself: on one occasion he was seen beating a man after he had been caught stealing money from a visitor.

Money was always an important issue. On Fridays, in particular, there would be long lines of people waiting for Bob's charity, each with a story to bend his ear. When the school term was about to start, 56 Hope Road yard would be packed with mothers, pleading with Bob for money to buy school uniforms. Sometimes he would distribute between $20,000 and $40,000 at these sessions.

After the Peace Concert many of the gunmen felt such a debt of gratitude to Bob that they were even more in evidence at 56 Hope Road, to the point where their presence became a problem, even sometimes a threat. Who could tell what nefarious deals were taking place away in some corner under the shade of a mango tree?

'But as a Rasta you can't dismiss people,' pointed out Neville Garrick. 'Him only shield him could wear was him noted screwface: the screwface alone would turn people away. But then Bob love people and always want to help them. Him can empathise with everything. Bob don't have no easier life than any of them. Him kinda raised on the streets.'

'He grew up with a lot of these guys,' said Junior Marvin, 'and he wanted to straighten out

BOB 'BACK A YARD'.

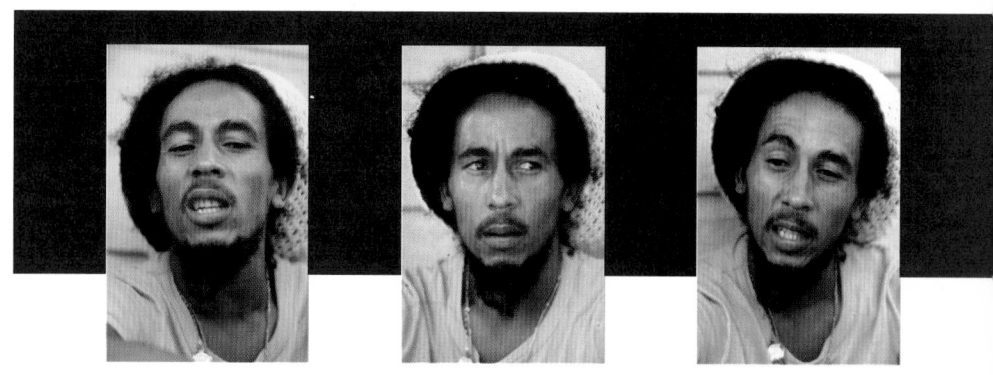

*BOB AT 56 HOPE ROAD
WITH THE 'RANKIN''
GUNMAN CLAUDIE
MASSOP.*

At the beginning of 1979 Claudie Massop was killed by what looked suspiciously like an official death squad. After the taxi in which Massop and two JLP brethren were travelling was stopped by police in downtown Kingston, Massop was discovered to be carrying a revolver and all three of them were shot dead.

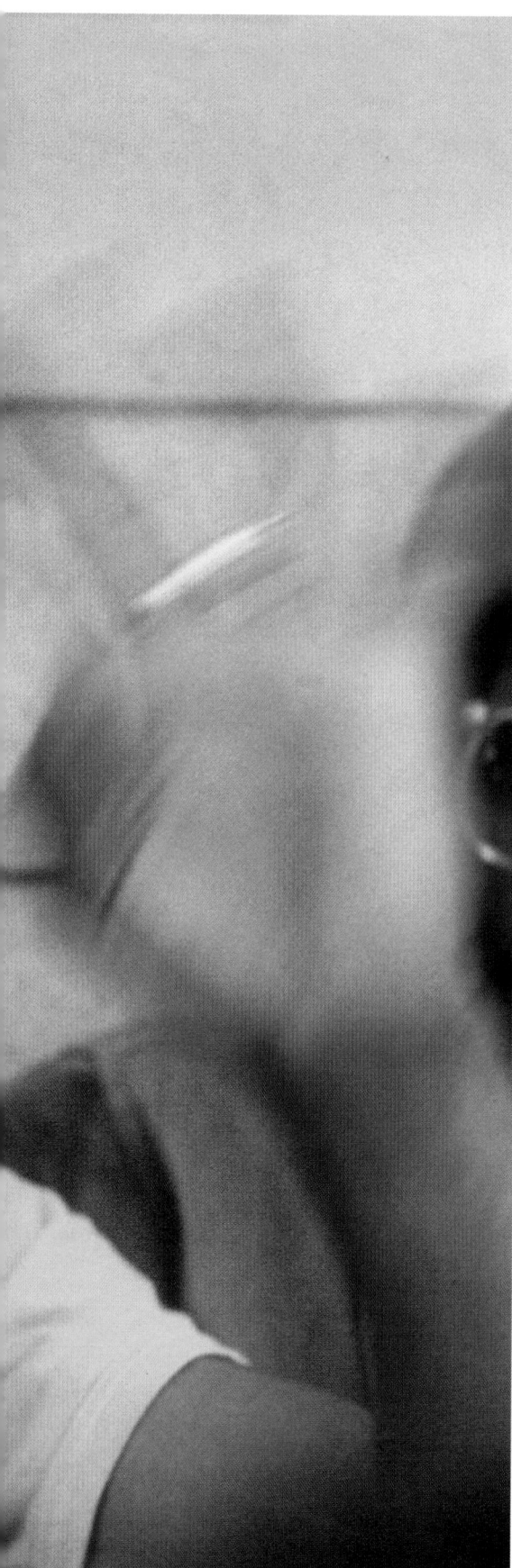

a lot of them. He was trying to help them. He was trying to say, "Look you don't really need violence; if you've go that kind of power, you don't have to use it: you can divert it into another kind of positive energy."'

In the evenings, however, a different life would go on. Round the back of the house, Bob would sit with his close brethren. Strumming his guitar, he would pick away at new or sometimes old songs. At these, the finest times, a peace of almost visible proportions would descend. And, protected by Jah, Bob would be in touch with the deepest source of his creativity.

PARTAKING OF THE CHALICE WAS AN INTEGRAL ASPECT OF DREAD CULTURE. HERE BOB INHALES A BOWLFUL OF SENSI WITH HIS BRETHREN GILLIE AND ALVIN 'SEECO' PATTERSON, THE WAILERS' PERCUSSIONIST AND BOB'S LONGTIME SPAR AND MENTOR FROM THE DAYS OF TRENCH TOWN.

AT 56 HOPE ROAD BOB HANGS WITH HIS CLOSE FRIEND AND CONFIDANTE, DENISE MILLS, A PERSON CRUCIAL IN ALL ASPECTS OF HIS CAREER.

BOB WITH JUDY MOWATT
AND CHILDREN.

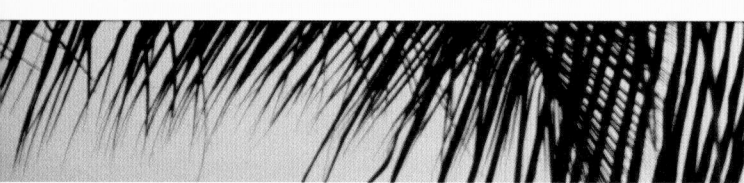

*THE TUFF GONG SHOP, TO
THE LEFT OF THE MAIN
HOUSE AT 56 HOPE ROAD,
ADDED AN ELEMENT OF
COMMERCIAL SELF-
SUFFICIENCY TO THE
ASSORTED REASONINGS
AND HUSTLINGS THAT
TOOK PLACE IN BOB'S
UPTOWN YARD.*

joe higgs & bob

FOOTBALL

Bob balancing and bouncing a football on his thighs; Bob dribbling in a spray of dust through the dirt of some anonymous yard in Jamaica; Bob knocking a ball down with his chest, trapping it with his inside foot; Bob hammering a ball into the back of a net with what seemed a flick of a toe . . . Images almost as archetypal as some of his dramatic stage postures . . . Bob Marley him just love football – everyone know that.

As his musical stature grew, Bob increasingly confided in his close friends that perhaps he should have been a soccer player instead.

And he always did. From as far back as anyone could remember, even when he was a lickle youth in Nine Miles, Bob could be content kicking a dried-up watermelon around the lop-sided patches of waste-ground that are scraped out of St Ann's hillside. Bob Marley loved that game. Was it any surprise that later one of his closest spars should turn out to be Skill Cole, a player with the Jamaican national team? Skillie was rarely absent from the yard at 56 Hope Road; it was he would rally round the various teams from the posse at the Tuff Gong headquarters, or join Bob in his morning 'eye-opener' runs in Bull Bay.

Living with Bob in London, or on the road in Europe or the States, Alan Cole was like a personal trainer to Bob. Rising as early as the skipper, he would run and work out with him and organise the endless matches that were a daily part of life on the road. An on-the-ball player, one of those footballers for whom the ball seems magnetically attached to their feet, Bob favoured the fluid, melodic Latin version of the game: the European-style of play, with its hard, knock-down tackles, was not to his liking. His favourite team was Santos of Brazil, and in 1978 Bob flew down to South America and met Paolo Cesar, the Brazilian captain. Bob and his posse attributed an almost Zen-type quality to soccer, sufficiently so for a French production crew to make a film in 1987 with the self-descriptive title *Rasta and the Ball*, a half-hour TV documentary exploring those connections.

Bob's heroes were the soccer players in Brazil. It was a feather in Bob's cap when the five-a-side team he put together on his visit to Brazil in March 1980 beat all the opposition in a tournament put together by Ariola, the local record company. Jim Capaldi from Traffic was living in Rio and played for The Wailers team, along with Bob, Junior Marvin, Jacob Miller and a Traffic roadie.

The event led to Bob musing on the possibilities that might have been his, had he gone into football full-time instead of music. 'I think he wanted to be a football player more than anything, more than being a musician or a songwriter,' said Marvin.

On wet, wintry days in Europe Mick Cater, the group's agent, would find hotel suites depleted of every stick of furniture – which he then discovered temporarily stacked neatly in other rooms taken by the group – as indoor pitches were improvised.

Not all The Wailers shared Bob's enthusiasm for the game, and none equalled his ability. Tyrone Downie, Al Anderson and Junior Marvin might energetically engage in a knock-about tussle, but they were hardly guaranteed to make the first team. 'The group themselves weren't really good players,' according to Neville Garrick, the group's art director.

So when it came to crucial matches in London, Bob's Rastafarian brethren were frequently enlisted: Trevor Bow and Derek, members of the Sons of Jah, would be in there with the main eleven. For a series of five-a-side matches, the team comprised Bob, Seeco, Gillie the cook, Skill Cole and Neville Garrick.

In June 1977, Rob Partridge relinquished his title of news editor of *Melody Maker* and joined Island Records to head the label's press team.

'Why mi father like to be fit? Because when you fit, you feel nice.' – Ziggy Marley

'Bob

Marley him

just love

football –

everyone

know that.'

'The first thing I had to get right, within two weeks of joining the company, was playtime for Bob Marley. In fact, the first time I met him was on the football pitch.'

This 'playtime' consisted of organising a football match in Battersea Park, London. The opposing team to The Wailers was one comprised of Island Records employees; further matches were organised on a recreational ground near Island's west London base.

'Bob played everywhere,' Trevor Wyatt, an Island A and R man who played for the company's team, remembered. 'He was fantastic, as was his cook Gillie.

'Bob had a great touch. We couldn't get the ball – just watched them pass it around. You'd try to take them, but they'd just pass it about between themselves. One of the reasons, of course, that they were so good, was because they played all the time. But it was also because they were just born to the game.'

'It was a great match,' remembers Partridge. 'Seeco was a particularly dervish-like figure on the wing – he nearly killed a dog that tried to get the ball.'

As an admirer of the Latin style, Bob was a great fan of the Argentinian player Ossie Ardiles, who had transferred to London to play for Tottenham Hotspur. As an acknowledgement of this, Partridge bought the skipper a Spurs shirt which he could be seen wearing from time to time. 'I would videotape *Match of the Day* when Spurs were playing and send it to Bob.'

Not that Bob's love of football wasn't sometimes a mixed blessing. 'In 1978,' Partridge recalls, 'Bob was in Britain at the time of the World Cup, and he made sure he recorded every match he could. We even had to schedule interviews around the game.' Partridge remembers taking a *Daily Mirror* journalist to interview Bob between the rehearsals and his live performance on BBC's *Top of the Pops*. Unfortunately, Partridge had neglected to check whether Argentina was playing in a match that day: they were, and infinite patience was required to ensure that the interview took place at all.

This was nothing compared to the mood on Bob's next official visit to London, in the summer

*BOB'S TEAM FOR THE
BATTERSEA PARK MATCH
INCLUDED NEVILLE
GARRICK, GILLIE, BOB'S
SPAR TREVOR BOW AND
DEREK FROM THE SONS OF
JAH.*

of 1980, at the end of the 'Tuff Gong Uprising' tour. Bob plumped not to do any interviews at all – just to play football matches with assorted teams from the media. Accordingly, a succession of matches was arranged at an indoor sports stadium next to Fulham football ground in west London. Among the five-a-side teams played by Bob and his crew were representatives of *Record Mirror* and Ice Records, captained by the Guyanese star, Eddie Grant.

'I was football fixtures secretary,' Rob Partridge recalls. 'Every day I picked Bob up from his apartment at Carlos Place and drove him down to Fulham.'

Football also played another important role in Bob Marley's life that summer. With the Wailers, he played a show at the San Siro stadium in Milan, a venue shared by the top Italian soccer teams AC Milan and Inter Milan, to the largest audience of his career.

RICO
m
RICO

RICO
m
RICO

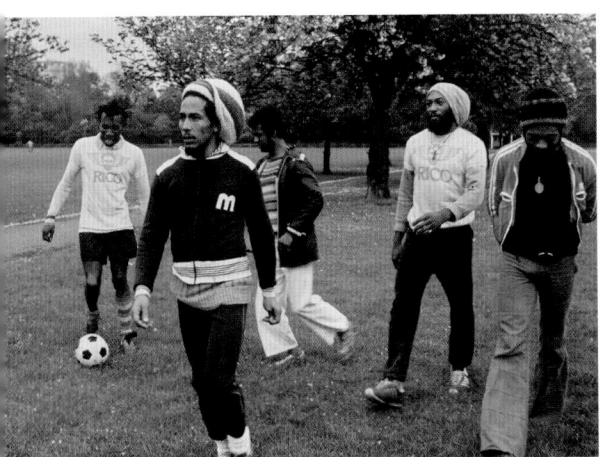

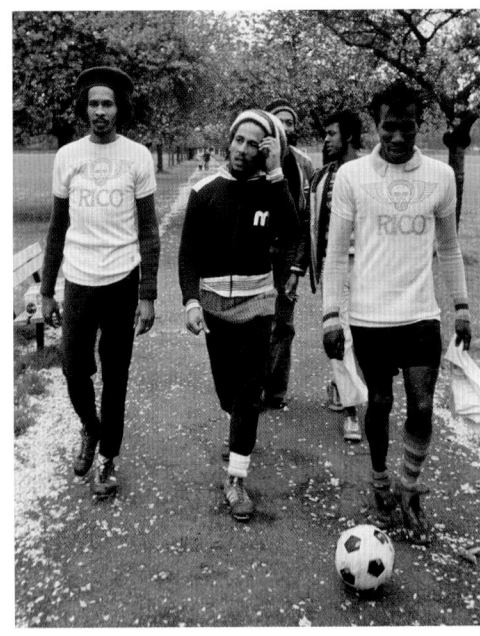

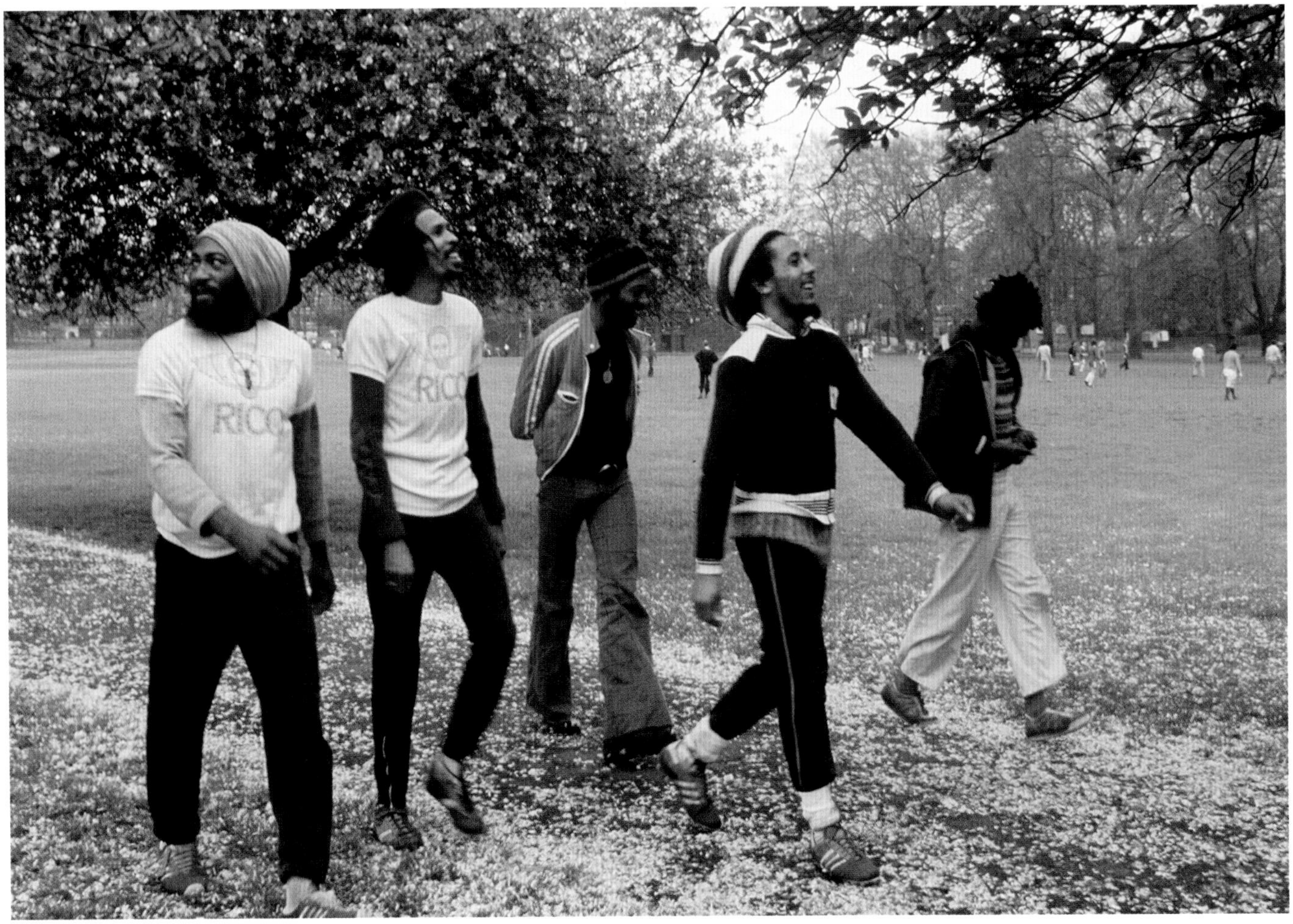
RICO
RICO

*BOB WITH SOME OF THE
ISLAND TEAM, INCLUDING
TREVOR WYATT (ON HIS
LEFT) WHO HELPED PUT
TOGETHER THE LEGEND
COMPILATION.*

SUNSPLASH

Early in July of 1979 Bob and The Wailers played their first show in Jamaica since the Peace Concert. It was early in the morning when they went onstage at Jarrett Park in Montego Bay, topping the bill for the Tuff Gong evening of Reggae Sunsplash II. It was a reasoning at 56 Hope Road between Bob, Family Man and the event's promoters that led to the first Sunsplash. Away on tour and unable to perform that year, Bob was determined the group should play this time to give the festival a boost.

Their performance was more like a mudsplash than a sunsplash. It had been raining so hard before the group performed that there was mud all over the stage: Junior Marvin's shoes filled with it, and the audience assumed his slipping and sliding was part of the act.

'I got war in my shoes!' cried Bob, turning this onstage problem around, in between verses of 'Lively Up Yourself', before playing a new tune, 'Ambush in the Night', from the soon to be released Survival LP. The venue was rammed, not just with Jamaicans, but with the Americans and Europeans who were now pouring into Jamaica; a potent consequence of Bob's ambassadorship was that the Isle of Springs had joined India, Morocco and Bali as a spiritual power-point for the counter culture. He had consciously played Reggae Sunsplash II to help Sunsplash become a recognised event in the reggae calendar; Bob's altruistic thinking paid off, for the festival was considered a serious fixture from then on.

Early the next afternoon, at a fenced-off part of the main beach in Jamaica's principal resort town, Bob was presiding over his court at the regular party held to celebrate the event. All the Wailers were present, as well as Burning Spear, Bunny Wailer, Jacob Miller and a host of local luminaries, some 500 people when the party was kicking at its peak. It was a fabulous daytime rave, bright and breezy, and the group stayed on the beach the entire day. Jamaica adored Bob. Reggae was gaining international respect; there was a feeling of growth, a mood that this was the time to seize opportunities.

In October 1979, Bob Marley and The Wailers began a seven-week tour of the United States – they were set to play forty-seven shows in forty-

Interview in *NME* with Neil Spencer at the time of the Apollo dates.

What do you feel happiest about that you've achieved so far? That you've maybe woken people up?

'Yeah, me feel good that plenty people is aware that there is something happening. Man can check it out cos I know Rasta grow. I don't see it deteriorate, I watch them and they grow more and more. It might not be in the headlines every day but dem grow.'

You've never seen it as a race thing?

'No, it's not really a race thing on that sense because a whole heap of people from all nation, kindred and tongue follow the Rasta movement. Is dat the Bible seh. But is really a black man organisation cos the white man nah know about it in that sense. The black man have the knowledge to hold that thing there while the white man him study fe mek all things a go to space. 'Im study too much, 'im get lost . . . but today there's no turnin' back, come too far and turn back now, it just mus' have fe go . . . But some people a go save still and all these people are one people who believe in something, believe in God, fear of true conscience and the works of Ras Tafari.'

nine days. The performances began with 'Natural Mystic', a tune that was a virtual celebration of Bob's very existence, and ended with an intensely militant trio of songs: 'Get Up, Stand Up', 'War' and 'Exodus'. On the road Bob was playing with the structure of a new number he was writing called 'Redemption Song'.

These US dates kicked off at the legendary Apollo Theater in Harlem. Here, in the venue where Marcus Garvey had preached, Bob and the group played seven concerts in four days.

The dates at the Harlem Apollo had been specifically requested by Bob. He was concerned, even distressed, that the black American audience remained elusive; this tour

THE SALES OF BOB'S RECORDS WERE BY NOW SO STRONG THAT EVERYWHERE HE TOURED THERE WOULD BE PRESENTATIONS OF GOLD RECORDS.

had specifically targeted this market. In Chicago he paid a long visit to Johnson and Johnson Publications, the publishers of *Essence and Ebony*; despite this, nothing appeared in these magazines about Bob Marley. Black radio programme directors still considered that reggae was 'jungle music' and that it didn't fit into their formats. *Kaya* had deliberately been a commercial album, in order that albums like *Survival* could follow. In the United States, however, getting the message across continued to be a struggle.

Rita Marley: 'That was an exposure, the pinnacle of all that Don had been doing over the years. Bob was the kind of man who doesn't really look into documents and contracts, which was very trusting of him. So Don was having a ball. For example, he set up a travel agency with his wife April, and she would take care of all the tickets that we would need to do tours. So we'd be flying to Miami via California and Australia, because they could do better on the tickets that way. He was making big bucks out of it. He was very dangerous.'

Judy Mowatt: 'Bob tried to keep it as covered up as he could, but we knew what was going on. Don got a licking and a kicking from Bob that day, man. For stealing money.'

Still Bob relentlessly plugged The Wailers on every local radio station he could get to visit. He was also disguising the fact that for much of the time he was operating in a state of sheer exhaustion, so much so that Tyrone Downie had to accompany him on press interviews to answer the more mundane questions on Bob's behalf. By the end of this tour many of those travelling with Bob were extremely worried about his health.

1980 began with Bob and The Wailers playing live; this time in Africa, for the very first time. On 1 January the group had flown to London and then on to Gabon in West Africa. They were scheduled to play for the birthday party of President Omar Bongo. Although this seemed a strange show for the group to be playing, Bob was delighted to have at last been asked to play in Africa. In fact,

he had volunteered to play for free, but Don Taylor told him that they had been offered a forty-thousand dollar fee, which they should take as it would cover their expenses.

After the group had played two shows – disappointingly, to small audiences of Gabonese high society – they remained in Gabon for a further two weeks. They stayed in a charming hotel on the beach, and all-night reasonings would be held with the local youth on matters of spiritual importance.

However, as they were about to leave Gabon, what was initially a small dispute emerged over Bob's fee. The problem soon escalated, and in the discussions that took place, all the dirt came out: Bob accused Don Taylor of receiving sixty thousand dollars and not forty thousand – the manager was defrauding Bob who was furious at this betrayal. He and the group had been humiliated in Africa the first time they had travelled there to perform. In a three-hour confrontation, Taylor was made to confess how, for years, he had held back large amounts of concert fees, and how he had played around with Bob's money on the Jamaican black

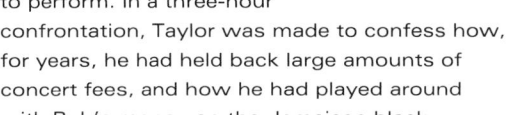

Family Man: 'We were in the next door room, Gillie, Neville Garrick and myself. After a while we hear some hard talking, so Neville go outside to see what is happening. Then I see Neville coming back looking for a baseball bat. He can't find it, so he is looking for a pickaxe stick, and I hide the stick. So Gillie and I decide to walk over there and listen and we hear Bob and Don Taylor talking. Then we hear some money business mentioned, and some feisty chat. Then we hear the whole thing. That wasn't really my department.'

WITH THE APPEARANCE OF BOB AND THE WAILERS AT SUNSPLASH IN 1979, THE EVENT BECAME ESTABLISHED AS AN ANNUAL CULTURAL EVENT IN JAMAICA. AT THE PARTY ON THE BEACH THE DAY AFTER HIS PERFORMANCE, BOB SPENT MOST OF HIS TIME WITH JACOB MILLER (BELOW, LEFT), THE SUPREME MUSICAL ARTIST IJAHMAN AND JUNIOR MARVIN.

'Mi see myself as a revolutionary. Who don't have no help and take no bribe from no one and fight it single-handed – with music.'

market. Outraged, Bob attacked Taylor.

After returning to Kingston and working on the sessions for the new *Uprising* album, Bob went to his home in Miami during February. He needed a rest, but while he was in Florida he also had discussions with Danny Sims, his former manager, about the future of his career.

In March Bob flew down to Rio for five days with Junior Marvin and Jacob Miller. Bob was in great shape on this trip, writing almost non-stop with Junior and Jacob. They wanted to set up a South American tour following the dates already scheduled for the summer and autumn in Europe and the United States. Miller's Inner Circle group were to support The Wailers.

Two days after they returned to Jamaica, the charismatic Jacob Miller was tragically killed in a car crash on Hope Road near Halfway Tree. Tired from the trip to Brazil, he lost his concentration. Chewing on a piece of sugarcane, driving, and looking after his two kids who were seated in the rear of the vehicle was too much for him and Jacob drove into a lamp-post. He broke his neck and died instantly. 'He was a very kind man,' said Junior Marvin. 'I've seen him give hundreds of dollars to hungry kids, and then just laugh when he realised he had no more money left to buy his own food.'

ZIMBABWE

It was 14 April 1980, the end of a hard week, around 4.00 p.m. on a Friday afternoon. Mick Cater was in his office, thinking about maybe leaving early for the weekend. Then the phone rang.

Bob Marley was calling from the Tuff Gong International offices in Kingston. Could Mick organise a crew and all necessary equipment and fly to Salisbury in Rhodesia over the weekend? On Tuesday, 18 April, the country was changing its name to Zimbabwe, and the city would be renamed Harare. Bob had two officials from Zimbabwe's government elect in his office with him, and they had invited him to perform at the Independence ceremonies. Cost was to be no barrier: Bob, whose 'Zimbabwe' tune had proved inspirational to the ZANLA [Zimbabwe National Liberation Army] freedom fighters, was paying for it all out of his own pocket. He would be playing amidst the ruins of Great Zimbabwe, an enormous pyramid built by Solomon and Sheba.

At the Island Records offices in west London, Denise Mills received a similar call. 'Bob said he was flying into London over the weekend and wanted to continue straight on to Africa. Could we arrange it?'

Within two hours of the call, Cater had booked his crew and PA equipment. More importantly, he also had a chartered 707 waiting on the tarmac at Gatwick airport. The next day the plane took off from Gatwick, carrying the agent, the lighting, the soundmen and the sound equipment.

The advance party for this Bob Marley expedition to Africa caused much bewilderment when it arrived at Salisbury airport, as it was then still

known. 'The import people hadn't a clue what to do, how to deal with us,' Cater said. 'What got us and everything through was a huge bag of Bob Marley T-shirts that I had sensibly persuaded Island to give me before I left. These were liberally dispensed all around. And it also helped enormously that I was wearing an "Exodus" tour jacket, which was my passport to everything.'

The only contact Cater had been given was an address in the capital: Job's Nitespot, a club run by one Jobs Kidengu, a second-hand car dealer who worked for ZANU (the Zimbabwe African National Union), and who had somehow become the promoter. Kidengu passed Cater on to a certain Mr Edgar Tekere, the Minister for Planning and Development. At 3.00 a.m. on Sunday morning Cater was driven in a taxi to Tekere's bungalow to wake him and receive instructions.

A bleary-eyed Tekere directed Cater to the Rufano Sports Stadium on the edge of Harare where the Independence ceremony was to be held. When he and his crew arrived there, a team of night-watchmen loomed out of the darkness, trying to chase them off.

Within hours Cater had secured the services of a squad of soldiers and a scaffolding company to build the stage. 'But the wood we had been given was green and came from a damp warehouse. As the sun came up and dried it, the planks turned rotten. We laid down tarpaulin, but we kept having to make chalk-marks where the holes were. I saw two wooden gates, and had them taken down and they became the PA stage.'

But there was still no electrical power and there seemed little hope of the promised

THE IMAGE OF ROBERT MUGABE, THE FIRST PRIME MINISTER OF ZIMBABWE, WAS OMNIPRESENT IN THE NEW NATION; BUT SOME OF HIS SUPPORTERS WERE VEXED THAT PORTRAITS OF BOB WERE BEGINNING TO RIVAL THOSE OF THE COUNTRY'S LEADER.

generator arriving to provide it. 'However,' Cater remembers, 'we found a cable running underneath the pitch. It provided the electricity to a nearby village. So this guy jumped in and cut it for us to tap into it. And as he did so you could see all the lights go out in the village.'

There were no hotels booked for the Marley party. Everywhere was full, booked up weeks before to accommodate the visiting dignitaries who were coming from all over the world for the Independence ceremony. Although he temporarily managed to secure a hotel room, Mick Cater was kicked out of it at gunpoint by several soldiers.

Bob and the Wailers were taken to a guest-house twenty miles out of town; even so, there were not enough rooms for the group and Bob shared his room with Neville Garrick, Family Man, Gillie and Dennis Thompson, the engineer.

Bob took a commercial flight to Nairobi. As he waited in the transit lounge for his plane, he received an unexpected message from a royal equerry: Prince Charles was waiting in the VIP suite; would Bob care to come and join him and pay his respects? Bob's reply was immediate. If Prince Charles wanted to meet him, he should come out there and check him with all the people. Needless to say, Bob's invitation was not accepted.

Some time later, as Bob and The Wailers sat by the window of the departure lounge, they saw the royal party crossing the tarmac in the direction of the royal jet. When Prince Charles had walked only a few yards, however, he turned and looked up at the window where Bob was sitting. Looking directly into Bob Marley's eyes, Prince Charles smiled broadly. Then he continued on his way.

Bob and his party flew into Harare in the early evening of Sunday, 16 April. With him were

Denise Mills, and Rob Partridge and Phil Cooper, respectively the heads of press and international affairs at Island Records in London.

'The most amazing thing,' Denise remembers, 'was the arrival at the airport. Joshua Nkomo, who was Minister of Home Affairs in Robert Mugabe's new government, and various cabinet officials had to line up and shake our hands. I couldn't believe it: there were about twenty-five of us, and I'm sure none of these people had a clue who we were.

'Then we went to tea at the palace with these drunken soldiers and the president. It was so English and colonial: cucumber sandwiches and lemonade – all considered a bit off by The Wailers.' However, Bob sang 'No Woman, No Cry' at the piano for the president's family.

What no one had thought to inform Bob and his team of was the precise nature of the first show they would be playing: it was scheduled for the slot immediately following the ceremony in which Zimbabwe would receive its independence and was to be performed in front of only the assembled dignitaries and media. As well as the party faithful, the international luminaries included Britain's Prince Charles and India's Indira Gandhi.

Such a scheduling implied that the events would have an exact order. But instead, Mick Cater said, 'it was complete anarchy. Bob went on immediately after the flag-raising ceremony. We'd arrived at 8.30 in the evening, and were leisurely getting ready. We hadn't realised just how suddenly they expected us onstage. When they announced us, we weren't ready at all.' In fact, the first official words uttered in Zimbabwe, following the raising of the new nation's flag, were, 'Ladies and gentlemen, Bob Marley and The Wailers.'

Twenty minutes later Bob and The Wailers started their set. As soon as the first notes rang out, pandemonium broke loose in the enormous crowd gathered by the entrance to the sports stadium: the gates shook and began to break apart as the crush increased, the citizens of Harare both excited and angry at being excluded from seeing these inspirational musicians. The too hasty response of the security forces? To fire

At 10.14 p.m. Bob and The Wailers arrived onstage. Bob's first words were 'Viva Zimbabwe!' Then it was straight into 'Positive Vibration'; followed by 'Them Belly Full'. At the beginning of the next number, 'I Shot the Sheriff', tear-gas flew around the stadium, fired by the trigger-happy police; Bob and The Wailers left the stage.

   Order was only restored when ZANLA (Zimbabwe National Liberation Army) guerrillas marched through the stadium with raised clenched fists. Bob and the group returned to the stage shouting 'Freedom!' and a crisp English voice from the other end of the stadium announced: 'Bob Marley, you have exactly two minutes left.' Bob responded with 'War'. The audience jumped and chanted, shouting 'War!'

   Then came 'No More Trouble'. Dennis Thompson frantically mixed the sound that poured out of the twenty-foot-high speaker boxes. Now running a quarter of an hour over their allotted two minutes, The Wailers performed 'Zimbabwe', with the entire audience joining in the chorus line.

BOB MARLEY & THE WAILERS
ZIMBABWE

tear-gas directly into the crowd.

As clouds of gas drifted almost immediately into the stadium itself, the audience on the pitch fell to their knees in an attempt to protect themselves. The group-members tasted their first whiffs of the gas and left the stage, their eyes already streaming. 'All of a sudden,' said Judy Mowatt, 'you smell this thing taking over your whole body, going in your throat until you want to choke, burning your eyes. I looked at Rita and Marcia and they were feeling the same thing.'

'I feel my eyes and nose,' remembered Family Man, 'and I think, "from when I was born, I have to come all the way to Africa to experience tear-gas".'

Bob Marley, however, seemed to have moved to a transcendent state. His eyes were shut, and for a while the gas didn't seem to affect him at all. Then he opened his eyes and also left the stage.

Backstage the group had taken refuge in a truck. Outside they could see small children fainting and women collapsing. It looked like death personified to Judy Mowatt, who briefly wondered whether they had been brought to Zimbabwe to meet their ends.

She persuaded someone to drive her and the other I-Threes back to the hotel, only to discover on the television that the concert had resumed. After about half an hour Bob and the Wailers had gone back onstage. They ended their set with 'Zimbabwe', a song Bob had begun to work on during his pilgrimage to Ethiopia late in 1978, and which became arguably his most important single composition. Bob was just coming offstage as Judy and her fellow women singers returned to the stadium. 'Hah,' he looked at them with a half-grin, 'now I know who the real revolutionaries are.'

It was decided that the group would play

another concert the following day, to give the ordinary people of Zimbabwe an opportunity to see Bob Marley. Tommy Cowan, for long a senior figure in Jamaican music, had come on the trip as tour manager. He was elected to be in charge of ticket sales at the main turnstile – not the best of decisions, according to Rob Partridge: 'Unfortunately, Tommy's understanding of the local languages was non-existent. After about fifteen minutes the barrier fell down and it became a free show.'

Over 100,000 people – an audience that was almost entirely black – watched this show by Bob and The Wailers. The group performed for an hour and a half, the musicians fired up to a point of near ecstasy. But Bob, who – uncharacteristically – hadn't bothered to turn up for the soundcheck, was strangely lack-lustre in his performance; a mood of disillusionment had set in around him following the tear-gassing the previous day.

After the day's performance the Bob Marley team were invited to spend the evening at the home of Edgar Tekere, the Minister of Planning and Development. This was not the most relaxed of social occasions. As his henchmen strutted around with their Kalashnikovs, Denise Mills was informed by Tekere ('real sleaze' according to her) that he wanted Bob to stay in Zimbabwe and tour the country. 'Bob told me to say he wasn't going to, but the guy didn't want to hear me.'

While Bob remained in the house, Rob Partridge and Phil Cooper sat out in the garden. 'I could hear,' said Cooper, Island's head of international affairs, 'Tekere saying to Bob, "I want this man Cooper. He's been going around putting up your image everywhere. He's trying to portray you as a bigger man than our President." I could hear all this.

'Then Bob came out and said to us, in hushed, perfect Queen's English, "I think it's a good idea for you to leave." Rob Partridge and I went and packed, and took the first international flight out, which was to Nairobi. About five months later Tekere was arrested and put in jail; he'd been involved in the murder of some white settlers.'

The next day Mick Cater found himself being cajoled in the way Denise Mills had been. 'Jobs Kidengu told me there was a show in Bulawayo we had to do. But I was signing for trucks on behalf of the Minister of Development – Tekere, in other words. So we drove out to the airport with all the gear, loaded up the plane we'd chartered and left the country.'

Returning to England, Bob was photographed with the entire group for the sleeve of the *Uprising* album. The shot was taken by Adrian Boot in the lift of the Kensington Hilton Hotel, west London, and was, strangely, the first group shot since *Catch a Fire*. In the picture Bob looks exhausted, his face lined and drawn. This has often been cited as proof of precisely how ill the Tuff Gong had become. Yet Junior Marvin gives another explanation: 'The reason Bob looks so tired and I'm looking to the left, to disguise my tired face, is because on the way back from Zimbabwe we'd stopped off in Paris for a couple of days. We'd been up all night talking to people about Zimbabwe on the first night; and on the second night we'd hung out with some people from Gabon – the royal family and the president's family – making music and talking. Neither of us had slept – that's the only reason we look so tired. Bob had asked me to hang out with him just writing songs and rapping to people. Both of us paid a penalty for it: by the time we got to London and the pictures were taken we looked really haggard.'

UPRISING

The 'Tuff Gong Uprising' tour began in May 1980, in Zurich. It continued at a gruelling, breakneck pace: in six weeks the group was to play to more than one million fans in twelve countries; it was to be the largest grossing tour of Europe up to that point. As the bus had left 56 Hope Road for Kingston airport at the beginning of the journey to Europe, Mortimer Planner was standing by the gates, bidding farewell and good luck to his brethren. As the vehicle pulled past him, Bob's eyes momentarily caught Planner's. From nowhere a thought ran through the dread elder: 'I won't see you again.'

The highest point of the tour was when Bob and The Wailers drew 100,000 fans to Milan's San Siro soccer stadium, the venue shared by the teams AC Milan and Inter Milan. A stupendous performance, it presented Bob Marley at the peak of his power. Considering the history of Italy earlier in the twentieth century, it was ironic that so many Ethiopian flags should have been flying in the audience that day.

Backstage a pair of Italian youths approached Bob: 'We are not responsible for what Mussolini did to the Ethiopians. But we want you to know that we are friends of the Rastafarians, and that God has accepted us.'

This magical show was reprised the next day by another with a slightly smaller audience, at the grounds of the Turin football team.

After the Paris date, Phonogram, Island's French licensees, held a party on a boat travelling down the Seine. As a chic way of showing their respect to Bob, it had been arranged for all the buildings to be lit along the banks of the Seine. This spectacular light show had cost over £10,000. But Bob never noticed it: he was slumped in the back of the boat, smoking a giant spliff.

Many of the shows on the tour were opened by a set from the I-Threes; in Germany, Marcia Griffiths introduced the group in German; she had worked there frequently in the past. On many nights after the shows, the I-Threes would find themselves back in Bob's hotel room, working out the harmonies on a new song he had written called 'Leah and Rachel', based on the biblical story about Jacob's concubine and his wife Rachel. Judy Mowatt would often be yawning, wanting to go to her bed. 'But Bob would insist that we learn this song: he is always a perfectionist. It was not fun sometimes. But when you go onstage you feel as though you are in your backyard: you are so comfortable with what you are doing, because you know what you're doing.'

After playing to 100,000 people in an open-air show in Dublin, the entourage moved on to London for another outdoor concert, at the Crystal Palace Bowl in south London. Separated from his audience by a small lake, Bob and The Wailers performed a show of sterling professionalism that climaxed with Bob's solo acoustic version of 'Redemption Song'. But you could not help noticing the exhaustion and pain that hovered like an aura about the Tuff Gong.

There was an early evening curfew on shows at Crystal Palace and it was still daylight as Bob and the group rushed from the venue to catch a flight to Munich for their next show. At Munich airport, however, they found themselves trapped all night when no transport turned up to take the tired musicians to their hotel. At the next day's performance they were playing a festival in which they were jointly topping the bill with Fleetwood Mac. A major argument took place between the production crews of the Wailers and Fleetwood Mac: Mick Fleetwood's drum riser, the Jamaicans were told, was out of bounds to Carlton Barrett. However, reason eventually prevailed.

Then when Bob and the group went onstage

Family Man: 'I can recall myself, Tyrone and Neville walking through these strange towns to look for magazines. And every one we pick up has a promotional piece on Bob Marley and The Wailers. It really looked as though we were the most popular group in Europe.'

THE TOUR IN SUPPORT OF THE UPRISING ALBUM PLAYED TO THE LARGEST COMBINED AUDIENCES A MUSICAL ACT HAD ENJOYED IN EUROPE UP TO THAT POINT.

Neville Garrick: '"Redemption Song" is one of the most profound and important statements Bob ever uttered. One of the most celebrated things Marcus Garvey ever said was "Up ye mighty race: you can accomplish what you will." To me, "Redemption Song" is an update of that: it really lies with you; you have to make the move; you have to free your mind first, before you can attain anything.'

Family Man: 'We played at this place called Crystal Palace, where there was like a pool in front of the stage. And I tell you, when the music get started, I don't see no pool. People in them suit is in the water to the waist.

'I tell you that show was a show, man. There was a lot of colours: I never see so much red, gold and green. Each of us have three sweat-suit on that tour: a red and a gold and a green sweat-suit, and a red, gold and green jacket and scarf and tams. The whole scene was colourful, I tell you.'

David Corio: 'I remember being slightly disappointed by the actual gig. As it was the only time I'd photographed him, and I'd looked forward to photographing him for so long, it seemed a shame.

'I was doing it for *NME*. I was twenty and it was one of the first big gigs I'd done. I was on the side of the stage and I thought the only thing to do was to wade

into the lake. I got a plastic carrier bag and put one camera and some film into it.

'There was me and one other photographer in the water. It was up to my chest. And there was a muddy bank in front of the stage and I kept slipping back.

'The shot with the flailing locks was the last one on the film, the 37th or 38th exposure. I was holding out for that shot. I knew I'd got it when I took it. You can't make out his face, but everyone knows it's Bob.

'After I came out of the lake I went backstage. Bob was still onstage, but the cars were set up for his departure. I went round there, and prepared myself for him coming offstage. There were a lot of dreads hanging around. But Bob came off and was whisked away. Shapewise, that was the closest to a portrait that I got. It gives a nice shape, the way the lines lead. Considering how ill we later discovered he was, he looked very well.

'In some of the pictures it's depressing to look at him - he seems so tortured. I wish I could have photographed him in more intimate surroundings.

'I went home on the tube, covered in green slime, shivering. But I was so up from the gig, really charged up, that I went off to see U2 in a pub, which was where Chris Blackwell was, watching them for the first time.'

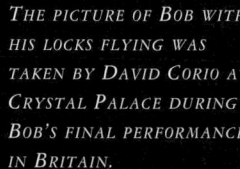

THE PICTURE OF BOB WITH HIS LOCKS FLYING WAS TAKEN BY DAVID CORIO AT CRYSTAL PALACE DURING BOB'S FINAL PERFORMANCE IN BRITAIN.

rain began pouring down on to the 50,000-strong audience. But instead of being daunted by it, the fans turned it into a virtue, luxuriating in the downpour as though it was a tropical thunderstorm. That is, until the end of The Wailers' set, when the audience suddenly shrank to 20,000; it was as though Fleetwood Mac were being taught a lesson for their belligerence towards Jah people.

Returning to London at the end of the six-week

tour, the group settled down for the games of five-a-side soccer that were organised for them at the sports hall in Fulham.

In London Bob considered his next moves. A tour of the United States was scheduled to begin in the middle of September, and The Wailers were flying back to Jamaica until it was time to head north again. But Bob Marley was warned off from any return to the Isle of Springs. Jamaica was riven by pre-election civil war and Bob was tipped off that the attempt on his life in December 1976 would be brutally repeated if he returned home now. Instead, he flew to Miami and tried to rest up for the beginning of the US tour. To all those around him, Bob seemed very tired.

The American tour began in Boston on Sunday, 14 September. Then the Wailers touring party drove south to New York City, where they were scheduled to play a pair of shows that weekend, on 19 and 20 September, at Madison Square Garden, sharing the bill with The Commodores, in an attempt to broaden Bob's American audience.

Bob checked into the Essex House on Central Park south, the hotel he usually stayed at in Manhattan; with him were Alan Cole and assorted members of his inner circle. The Wailers, along with Rita Marley and the I-Threes, however, were lodged further downtown, at the Gramercy Park. Here they were removed from the mood of decadence that had not previously been seen on Wailers tours.

At the Essex House champagne and fine wines were being ordered up on room service. Pascaline, a daughter of the Gabonese president who was Bob's latest girlfriend, was ensconced in his suite with him. Limousines followed the tour bus wherever it went, like some anti-Exodus. New York-based Jamaicans flooded into the various suites; cocaine free-basing was openly practised; good-time girls were sprawled about the rooms. Everything seemed to be disintegrating, just falling apart. Bob tucked himself away in his bedroom, often aghast at the bedlam taking place outside his door. As he himself would have said, it was too much mix-up, mix-up.

Subsequently, those who were lodged at the

Gramercy Park have voiced their theories as to why the band was separated from Bob in this way. Some saw it as a conscious attempt to isolate Bob from those who had always been around him. Danny Sims seemed to be advising Bob about his business affairs, and some thought they detected some kind of conspiracy between Sims and Alan Cole.

Although he doesn't go as far as this, Junior Marvin was surprised that they were not all staying at the same hotel. 'I started to feel a bit isolated, as though we were losing that sense of security when all of the band were together. When we were all together people wouldn't come in on us so fast: you could tell that it was definitely a group. When we were apart it was certainly much easier for people to infiltrate it. It was easier for people to get to Bob, whether it be fans or hustlers.'

Alan Cole has a simple explanation as to why the rest of the group weren't checked into the Essex House: the hotel was full, and only had enough rooms for Bob and those immediately around him.

On the Saturday afternoon Bob paid a surprise visit to the West Indian-American Day Carnival Association at the Brooklyn Museum, appearing onstage briefly with The Wailers. He also posed for pictures with the finalists of the Miss West Indian-American Beauty Pageant. In the Carnival parade there was a Bob Marley float, with a fifty-foot-high version of the *Uprising* logo; Bob had intended to parade through the streets of Brooklyn on the float, but when he realised how near he would be to the huge crowd, he changed his mind and returned to the Essex House.

As expected, the Madison Square Garden shows were a huge success. Although Bob and The Wailers weren't given a full soundcheck, the performances were tremendous, as was the audience response. From the first note everything fell into place, Al Anderson in particular showing superb authority in his musicianship. 'We were ready for that tour,' said Family Man. 'We and Stevie Wonder were supposed to tour the US. We were going to break reggae big-big in the States just like in Europe. Then suddenly something came up.'

The dates seemed to be taking an unexpected toll on the Tuff Gong: on the Saturday morning, after the first concert, he was almost beside himself with exhaustion. He managed to recover his energies for the evening's performance, but afterwards left the Negril reggae club early and went back to the Essex House.

The following morning, Rita called Bob, asking him to accompany her to a service at the Ethiopian Orthodox Church, as was their custom when they were in New York. The man she spoke to didn't sound like the Bob she knew. 'What happened?' she asked him. 'You didn't sleep last night?' Bob told his wife he didn't feel well and wouldn't be going to church with her, but that he would send a car to pick her up. When the vehicle arrived, Rita told the driver to take her to the Essex House instead. 'When I got there  he wasn't looking his normal self. I thought he must be out partying with girls and the usual hang-on things that happens sometimes after a concert.'

Rita left the hotel and took the car on to church. Bob felt nauseous and wanted some fresh air. Attempting to kick-start his life-force with some light running, Bob and Alan Cole and a few friends jogged into Central Park, opposite their hotel. Before they had gone far, however, Bob started to collapse, calling out for Cole who caught him before he slumped to the ground. Bob's body seemed to be rigid, and he couldn't move his neck which hurt terribly. Helped back to the hotel, he recovered after a couple of hours. The incident had nevertheless shaken him to his core, and he still felt great pain in his neck region.

A security blanket was thrown around news

BOB WITH THE LINE-UP OF
THE WAILERS AT THE
TIME OF UPRISING.
BELOW; TOP ROW FROM
LEFT: CARLTON 'CARLY'
BARRETT, BOB, ALVIN
'SEECO' PATTERSON, AL
ANDERSON; BOTTOM ROW
FROM LEFT: EARL 'WIRE'
LINDO, TYRONE DOWNIE,
ASTON 'FAMILY MAN'
BARRETT, JUNIOR
MARVIN.

BOB'S DRAWN APPEARANCE IN THIS ADRIAN BOOT PICTURE SESSION, HELD IN AN ELEVATOR AT THE KENSINGTON HILTON IN LONDON, HAS BEEN CITED AS PROOF OF HOW HIS ILLNESS WAS TAKING ITS TOLL ON HIM; BUT JUNIOR MARVIN INSISTS IT WAS THE CONSEQUENCE OF TWO NIGHTS OF PARTYING IN PARIS.

*BOB IN A SERIES OF
PICTURES TAKEN BY
ADRIAN BOOT IN HIS LAST
INTERVIEW, FOR THE FACE
MAGAZINE WITH
JOURNALIST ROS REINES
AT THE ESSEX HOUSE
HOTEL IN NEW YORK.*

BOB ONSTAGE AT THE FINAL MADISON SQUARE GARDEN SHOWS.

of Bob's illness. Family Man expected to see Bob come by the Gramercy to eat at their mobile ital kitchen. 'When I don't see him come for his food, I think maybe he's gone to do some TV or radio interviews. But then this youth called Ian Winter carried the food for Bob up to the Essex House. Him say when him reach the door, them just take the food from him and lock up the door. I said, "If you told me, I would have personally carried the food." A separation go on. We were always close: mi check with Bob before show, after show. Before soundcheck, after soundcheck. Before bedtime.'

So successful was the secrecy surrounding the incident that the following day The Wailers, still staying downtown at the Gramercy Park, left Manhattan and travelled to Pittsburgh for the next night's show. 'After Bob collapsed,' said Junior Marvin, 'it was more evident that things were getting a bit weird: we weren't even in the same hotel to find out how he was. We didn't know if he was OK or not.'

Bob didn't accompany them on the tour bus to Pittsburgh; instead, he was taken to see a neurologist who rapidly diagnosed the problem: Bob Marley was suffering from a terminal cancerous brain tumour.

Rita Marley wasn't even aware that her husband had collapsed, and it was only on the bus that she discovered what had happened to him the previous day: nevertheless, the general opinion seemed to be that it was a result of

exhaustion. All the same, the vibes on the bus were strange: Rita didn't even know where Bob was or why he hadn't accompanied them.

'I said something is not right. I kept saying it, and I'm still saying it.'

For a long time Chris Blackwell had kept an apartment on the top floor of the Essex House. Late on the Monday morning his doorbell rang. It was Bob. He told Blackwell the news: that he was suffering from what was apparently an incurable brain tumour and had been given no more than three weeks to live.

Blackwell was shaken by the news. Terrible remorse, even self-recrimination, came over him. He remembered how Bob had been told by the doctor he saw in 1977 that he should have a check-up every three months. 'Everybody kind of forgot about that. But when something like that happens it rushes back. I felt I should have reminded him. I should have insisted he had the check-ups. If only he had, they could have caught it a lot earlier: if he'd had his toe amputated in the first place, it probably would have saved his life.'

But what has to be has to be. Before he departed for Pittsburgh, Bob suggested that he and Blackwell have their picture taken together. Blackwell had always disliked the clichéd schmooze picture of the record-company man with his arm around his artist: he felt it was antithetical to the spirit of a rebellious music; and he was also wary of any suggestion of racial condescension that might be implied by a picture of himself with Bob in such a pose. Accordingly, he did not possess a single picture of himself with his most valued and loved artist. When this had been rectified, Bob left for Pittsburgh, arriving at the group's hotel that evening. 'What happened?' asked Rita.

Bob gave her a half-explanation: that he hadn't known what was happening; how people were doing cocaine all around him; so he had gone for a run. 'And 'im feel like somebody hit him in the back. And he turned around and couldn't find him speech. He said he didn't know

Judy Mowatt: 'I would say that Bob gave his life for his people. Because it was when he was working that he got sick. I don't think he gave any thought to his toe. He never hopped, he never limped. And when you look at the shoes Bob used to wear onstage, it was boots up to here. So there was no air at all given to the toe. And he worked and he worked and he worked relentlessly, and nobody knew until it got out of control.'

'One heart, one destiny. Peace and love for all mankind. And Africa for Africans.'

BOB LEAVES THE ESSEX HOUSE HOTEL FOR THE MADISON SQUARE GARDEN SOUNDCHECK; CENTRAL PARK, WHERE HE WAS TO COLLAPSE THE MORNING AFTER THE SECOND SHOW, IS ON HIS LEFT.

Judy: 'Now I realise what he went through. Alone, because it had to be alone. We did not know how he was hurting. We did not know the pain he was going through. We did not know if he was afraid. We did not know if he was wondering if he could do the show or not. He didn't say anything to anybody. But he did do the show. And then they said that that was the last one, because he couldn't go on anymore. It was very, very, very sad.'

what happened.

'Then I was totally confused. So I insisted on hearing what this doctor said.'

Rita had a dream that night: Bob was wearing a hospital robe and talking to her through a fence, all his hair cut off. The dream deeply worried her.

At the soundcheck at the Stanley Theater in Pittsburgh the next afternoon, Bob seemed distant, not present in either his body or his mind.

At the group's hotel earlier in the day there had been a dramatic confrontation between Rita and Alan Cole. 'Why don't you stop the tour?' she had demanded. 'If Bob has a brain tumour why are we even having a show tonight? Stop the show!'

'Cool it, man: I feel all right,' Bob had told his wife. But Rita could see that her husband was virtually in another world.

When they got to the venue, Rita called his mother in Miami. 'I don't like what's happening with Bob here,' she told her. 'It doesn't feel right. I think we're going to come straight home.'

When Rita put the phone down, she ran into Bob's dressing-room. 'Stop the fucking tour now!' she begged him, becoming almost hysterical when she heard that the neurologist had advised Alan Cole that Bob might as well complete the tour; he was going to die anyway. When Rita learned that the doctor was a specialist recommended by Danny Sims, she felt

she was beginning to unearth a plot. She called Sims and cursed him down the phone. Then she telephoned those group members who were still at the hotel. 'They are telling me Bob is this sick, but we should go on with the tour . . .'

Instead of the usual four songs that were tried out at a soundcheck, Bob only performed a long version of an old Wailers tune, 'Keep On Moving', sitting for much of the time on the drum-riser beside Carly. Although it involved only the one song, it was the longest soundcheck any of the group could remember. Most of them felt very sad indeed.

That night's show was extraordinary. Bob came onstage unannounced and the group played a ninety-minute set that exploded into a succession of encores: 'Redemption Song', 'Coming In from the Cold', 'Could You Be Loved', 'Is This Love' and 'Work'. This was literally what he was doing. 'Work' was the last song Bob Marley ever performed onstage, and he gave his absolute best. 'That show had to be great,' said Junior Marvin. 'Everyone was aware that Bob wasn't at all well and that it could be the last show. We were just hoping that it wouldn't be.'

Later that night, at Rita's instigation, a press release was put out. Bob Marley and The Wailers' 'Tuff Gong International' tour of the United States was cancelled. The reason? Bob Marley was suffering from 'exhaustion'. The group returned to Miami, and then dispersed.

'BOB IS SOMEBODY WHO WAS AN INCREDIBLE ROLE MODEL. ANYBODY YOU TALK TO, WHO HAS WITNESSED HIM, KNOWS HE REALLY LED BY EXAMPLE. HE WAS ALWAYS ON TIME FOR THINGS — WHICH IS HARDLY A JAMAICAN TRAIT. I WENT ON A LOT OF THE 1980 TOUR AND HE WAS ALWAYS THE FIRST ONE ON THE BUS. TRADITIONALLY, THE STAR IS THE LAST ONE ON THE BUS, IF HE ISN'T GOING IN A LIMO. IF THERE WERE A LOT OF PEOPLE AND THEY HAD TO FLY ECONOMY, HE WOULD TRAVEL WITH THEM. HE NEVER PUT HIMSELF IN A POSITION WHERE HE WOULD BE SEEN AS BEING DIFFERENT FROM ANYBODY ELSE. IN THAT RESPECT, HE WAS SOMEBODY WHO LIVED UP TO THE EXAMPLE OF THE LEADERS OF ALL THE MAIN RELIGIONS: THERE IS ONE QUALITY ALL SUCH FIGURES HAVE, WHICH IS HUMILITY. AND BOB REALLY HAD THAT NATURAL HUMILITY. HE ALSO WAS A NATURAL LEADER. ABSOLUTELY, TRULY NATURAL.'

CHRIS BLACKWELL

'HE IS NOT GONE, MAN: HIS WORK IS HERE. HE IS ALIVE. WHENEVER YOU CALL HIS NAME, YOU BRING HIM ALIVE. THE RESERVOIR OF MUSIC HE HAS LEFT BEHIND HIM IS LIKE AN ENCYCLOPAEDIA: WHEN YOU NEED TO REFER TO A CERTAIN SITUATION OR CRISIS, THERE WILL ALWAYS BE A BOB MARLEY SONG THAT WILL RELATE TO IT. BOB WAS A MUSICAL PROPHET.'

JUDY MOWATT

'BOB NEVER LOST HIS INNOCENCE.'

DIANE JOBSON

'BOB WILL COME AGAIN. LIKE CHRIST HE SHALL COME IN A NEW NAME.'

RITA MARLEY

'Redemption Song'

Old pirates yes they rob I
Sold I to the merchant ships
Minutes after they took I from the
Bottomless pit
But my hand was made strong
By the hand of the almighty
We forward in this generation triumphantly
All I ever had is songs of freedom
Won't you help to sing these songs of freedom
'Cause all I ever had redemption songs,
redemption songs

Emancipate yourselves from mental slavery
None but ourselves can free our minds
Have no fear for atomic energy
'Cause none a them can stop the time
How long shall they kill our prophets
While we stand aside and look
Some say it's just a part of it
We've got to fulfill the book

Emancipate yourselves from mental slavery
None but ourselves can free our minds
Have no fear for atomic energy
'Cause none a them can stop the time
How long shall they kill our prophets
While we stand aside and look
Yes some say it's just a part of it
We've got to fulfill the book

Won't you help to sing these songs of freedom
'Cause they're all I ever had, redemption songs
All i ever had, redemption songs
These songs of freedom, songs of freedom.

Alleyne, Mervyn *Roots of Jamaican Culture* (Pluto)

Baldwin, James *The Fire Next Time* (Penguin)

Barrow, Steve *The Story of Jamaican Music* (book contained within Island Records 4-CD box set)

Bible

Boot, Adrian and Goldman, Vivien *Bob Marley, Soul Rebel–Natural Mystic* (Eel Pie)

Black, Clinton V. *History of Jamaica* (Longman Caribbean)

Dr Paul Brunton *A Search in Secret Egypt* (Rider)

Budge, E. A. Wallis *The Egyptian Book of the Dead* (Routledge and Kegan Paul)

Campbell, Joseph *The Hero with a Thousand Faces* (Paladin)

Campbell, Mavis C. *The Maroons of Jamaica 1655–1796* (Africa World Press)

Clarke, Sebastian *Jah Music* (HEB)

Davis, Stephen *Bob Marley* (Plexus)

Davis, Stephen and Simon, Peter *Reggae Bloodlines* (Anchor Press/Doubleday)

Davis, Stephen and Simon, Peter *Reggae International* (Thames and Hudson)

Garvey, Marcus *Philosophy and Opinions of Marcus Garvey* (Atheneum)

George, Nelson *The Death of Rhythm and Blues* (Omnibus Press)

George, Nelson *Where Did Our Love Go?* (St Martin's Press)

Gillett, Charlie *The Sound of the City* (Souvenir Press)

Henzell, Perry *The Power Game* (Ten-A Publications)

Imperato, Pascal James *African Folk Medicine* (York Press)

Insight *Guide to Jamaica* (Insight Guides)

Jones, Simon *Black Culture, White Youth: The Reggae Tradition* from JA to UK (MacMillan)

Longmore, Zenga *Tap-Taps to Trinidad: A Journey through the Caribbean* (Arrow)

Masimba, Ras Mweya F. *I Forward the Sword for Nyhabingy Warriors of Rastafari* (I Forward The Sword Publications)

McCann, Ian *Bob Marley in his Own Words* (Omnibus Press)

Mockler, Anthony *Haile Selassie's War* (Oxford University Press)

Owens, Joseph *Dread – The Rastafarians of Jamaica* (Sangster Books)

Ritz, David *Divided Soul: The Life of Marvin Gaye* (Michael Joseph)

Senior, Olive *A–Z of Jamaican Heritage* (HEB)

Sidran, Ben *Black Talk* (Da Capo)

Tafari, Seko *From the Maroons to Marcus* (School Times Publications)

Thelwell, Michael *The Harder They Come* (Pluto)

Thomas, Michael and Boot, Adrian *Babylon on a Thin Wire* (Thames and Hudson)

Tompkins, Peter *Secrets of the Great Pyramid* (Penguin)

White, Timothy *Catch a Fire* (Omnibus)

ARTICLES

Material has been gleaned from countless publications. These include Bob Marley archivist Roger Steffens' admirable *The Beat*; also *Billboard*, *Black Echoes*, *Black Music*, *Crawdaddy*, *Cream*, the *Daily Gleaner*, *The Face*, the *Guardian*, *High Times*, *Jahugliman*, *Melody Maker*, *New Musical Express*, the *Observer*, *Q*, *Rolling Stone*, *Sounds*, the *Sunday Times*, *The Village Voice*.

The following articles have proved particularly informative:

Bradshaw, Jon 'The Reggae Way to Salvation', *The New York Times* (14 August 1977)

Coleman, Ray 'Marley: Still a Life and Death Struggle', *Melody Maker* (21 May 1977)

Davis, Stephen 'The Last Interview', *Black Music* (July 1981)

Goldman, Vivien 'Bob Marley in his own backyard', *Melody Maker* (11 August 1979)

Goldman, Vivien 'Dread on Arrival', *Sounds* (28 May 1977)

High Times interview 'This Man Is Seeing God', reprinted in *The Best of High Times* 14.

McCormack, Ed 'Bob Marley: Rastaman with a Bullet', *Rolling Stone* (12 August 1976)

O'Brien, Glen 'So Much Things to Say', interview (July 1978)

Occhiogrosso, Peter 'Marley Moves to a New League', *Soho Weekly News* (22 June 1978)

Spencer, Neil 'Jamaican Lion Inna Concrete Jungle', (10 November 1979)

Steffens, Roger 'In the Beginning: Coxsone Dodd', *The Beat* (issue no. 3, 1994)

Steffens, Roger 'Cuisine Heart', *The Beat* (issue no. 3, 1994)

Thomas, Michael 'Jamaica at War', *Rolling Stone* (12 August 1976)

Williams, Richard 'The First Genius of Reggae', *Melody Maker* (24 February 1973)

White, Timothy 'Bob Marley and the Reggae Rebellion', *Crawdaddy* (January 1976)

White, Timothy 'Jump Up', *Rolling Stone* (16 April 1981)

ADRIAN BOOT After graduating from university, Adrian Boot moved to Jamaica to teach physics in the late 1960s. In the early 1970s, in conjunction with writer Michael Thomas, he shot and published *Babylon on a Thin Wire*, a study of the island. Soon afterwards Boot moved back to Britain. There he became chief photographer for *Melody Maker*; his most noteworthy shoots included The Clash in Belfast, the Sex Pistols on tour, and Grateful Dead's historic trip to Egypt. He also covered the 1980 Jamaican elections, and photographed Baby Doc in Haiti for the British national press. Adrian Boot photographed pictures for Bob Marley extensively, and took the *Live at the Lyceum* and *Legend* record covers. He travelled in Africa, the Caribbean and South America, photographing most of the leading musicians of those areas. His published books include *Jah Revenge*, *Bob Marley: Natural Mystic* with Vivien Goldman, and a photo-study of the Soviet Union with Chris Salewicz. Boot has worked extensively for most major publications throughout the world.

DENNIS MORRIS Dennis Morris had his first photograph published at the age of eleven on the front page of the *Daily Mirror*. When he was eighteen years old he became the youngest black photographer to receive a grant from the Arts Council, to document the Asian community of Southall. Morris studied at Twickenham Art College in London. His work has been published variously by the *Sunday Times*, *Rolling Stone*, *Time Out*, *City Limits*, *NME*, *Melody Maker* and many other publications. He took the original shot of Bob Marley that was used for the sleeve painting of *Natty Dread*. For two years Morris ran the Island Records Art Department: he was instrumental in campaigns for Marianne Faithfull's Grammy-nominated *Broken English* LP as well as all of Linton Kwesi Johnson's recordings on the label. He has also fronted his own groups, including Basement Five, the highly influential first black rock band. Morris has published *Bob Marley – Rebel with a Cause* as well as *Reggae Rebels* and *Rebel Rock*, the latter photo-documenting the Sex Pistols on tour. He has also worked in film, notably as director of a documentary on the independent dance scene for French television. In Belgium, Dennis Morris was a recipient of the prestigious Diamond Award; he has also exhibited in Brussels.

NEVILLE GARRICK Neville Garrick is a graphic designer with a fine arts background. He first met Bob Marley in early 1974 when he was Art Director for the *Jamaican Daily News*, a post he had taken after graduating from UCLA. Shortly after Neville resigned to work full-time with Bob Marley. Over the years, Neville graduated from playing occasional percussion and taking on-the-road pictures of the band to creating and supervising the graphic images that surrounded Bob Marley and The Wailers; he was responsible for the celebrated Marcus Garvey and H.I.M. Haile Selassie I stage backdrops as well as providing all of the concert lighting. Neville Garrick is Executive Director of The Bob Marley Foundation.

MICHAEL PUTLAND In 1966, at the age of nineteen, Mike Putland's first magazine commission was a session with Mick Jagger for the now defunct British pop weekly, *Disc and Music Echo*. By the turn of the decade, Putland had toured with the Rolling Stones, T. Rex and The Carpenters while shooting portraits of subjects as diverse as John Lennon and Herb Alpert. Relocating to New York, he worked with *Time* and *Newsweek* magazines as well as with key American music magazines. Opening his own agency, Retna, he quickly established it, and by 1985 he had opened Retna's London office. Mike Putland opened his third office in Los Angeles in 1990.

ARTHUR H. GORSON Photographer/film-maker Arthur H Gorson's lasting involvement with Jamaica began in the early 1970s as a stills photographer for director Perry Henzell on *The Harder They Come*. In 1972/73 he covered the emerging energy of Jamaica for several publications; on one such trip his guide was Bob Marley. Bob took them through Trench Town, allowing them privileged access – the photos included here are a result of that visit. Arthur H. Gorson's technical credits include the introduction of the Dolby System for film sound; as a record producer he made over twenty albums by artists as diverse as Phil Ochs, Tom Rush and Golden Earring. As a concert promoter Arthur was the first to present The Who and Cream in America. In 1980 he founded the Los Angeles based production company, Dreamstreet, where he worked with directors Tony Scott and Andrei Konchalovsky. Arthur H. Gorson is President of Ventane Films.

PETER MURPHY AND CLAIRE HERSHMAN Peter Murphy's photographic career with Claire Hershman began because he knew the music and she had the equipment. They sold their first ever set of photographs for a rushed-out, minor label live reggae album. They spent the 1970s indulging in their twin passions, music and travel. The music provided a direct route to the heartbeat of societies as far flung as Jamaica and Nigeria; Bob Marley and The Wailers were the kingpins of the international reggae scene and provided highspots for the Murphy/Hershman partnership. In 1986 Murphy was lighting cameraman for the award-winning dramas *Passing Glory* and *Before I Die Forever*. Murphy handled the same role for the title sequence for the film *Batman*.

STEPHANIE NASH Formerly a director of Island Art, Stephanie Nash is a partner at Michael Nash Associates and is based in London.

DAVID CORIO Corio completed his degree at Gloucester College of Art, and quickly established himself in the British music papers. Over the past years, Corio has travelled extensively, expanding his photographic horizons. He has worked throughout the Caribbean. His pictures have appeared on a plethora of album covers. Corio regularly contributes to *Vox*, *Echoes*, the *Guardian*, and *The New York Times*; he now lives in Manhattan.

VICKY FOX Vicky Fox has worked at London's specialist record store Rock On for the past twelve years. For the last two years she has also worked as a darkroom assistant, specialising in hand-tinting and electronic imaging.

JAH BOBBY Jah Bobby was until recently resident painter at The Bob Marley Museum in Kingston, Jamaica. Besides contributing to many Tuff Gong record sleeves, Jah Bobby is a mural specialist, his larger-than-life work crucial to the museum's exhibits. He has recently moved to New York, proclaiming, 'Ghetto means get out'.

CHRIS CRASKE Chris Craske has worked in all spheres of music photography. His picture of Bob Marley was taken at Brighton Centre. Craske works at the London design house Stylo-Rouge. He specialises in abstract work, multiple-exposure images and constructivist art.

EXPORT TUFF GONG
45 RPM
KINGSTON 12 SHUFFLE
U ROY & BOB MARLEY
Peter TOSH

TUFF GONG
ASCAP
Produced by
Tuff Gong
Records
127 King St. Kgn.
45 RPM
KNOTTY DREAD
(Bob Marley)
BOB MARLEY
WAILERS
&
I THREES

Beverley's
RECORDS
135
ORANGE
STREET
KINGSTON
JAMAICA
W.I.
MADE IN
JAMAICA
LM 052
COPYING OF
THIS RECORD
IS PROHIBITED
ONE CUP OF COFFEE
[R. MARLEY]
BOBBY MARTELL
BEVERLEY'S ALL-STARS

TUFF GONG
Tuff Gong
Production
Pub. By Tuff
Gong Music
45 RPM.
RAT RACE
(R. MARLEY)
Bob Marley and The Wailers

CoxSone
RECORDS
C 110
SIMMER DOWN
BOB AND THE WAILERS

CoxSone
RECORDS
A Studio One
RECORDS
ONE LOVE
(C. DODD)
The Wailers

CoxSone
RECORDS
MR. TALKATIVE
THE WAILERS

UPSETTER
RECORDS
PRODUCED
AND DIRECTED
PERRY
Peter TOSH
DREAMLAND
(BUNNY)
THE WAILERS

STUDIO
MADE IN JAMAICA
Monroe Music
JAIL HOUSE
(Sarstoo)
THE WAILERS

No. 1 STUDIO
ST. 27
PLAYBOY
(R. Marley)
THE WAILERS
RECORDED BY JAMAICA RECORDING STUDIO 13 BRENTFORD ROAD

Solomonic
PUB.
NO.11
MUSIC
PROD.
TUFF
GONG
SIDE 1
R.P.M.
TIME: 3.10
PASS IT ON
J. Watt
WAILERS

Supreme
RECORDS
417
WHITE CHRISTMAS
(IRVING BERLIN)
BOB MARLEY & THE WAILERS

Beverley's
RECORDS
135
ORANGE
STREET
KINGSTON
JAMAICA
W.I.
MADE IN
JAMAICA
COPYING OF
THIS RECORD
IS PROHIBITED
JUDGE NOT!
(R. MARLEY)
ROBERT MARLEY
BEVERLEY'S ALL-STARS

Supreme
RECORDS
WHAT'S NEW PUSSY CAT?
(David Bacharach)
BOB MARLEY AND
THE WAILERS
RECORDED BY JAMAICA RECORDING STUDIO 13 BRENTFORD ROAD KGN.

TRADE
Bob
MARK
WAIL
SOUL
Bob Marley
and The
Wailing Wailers
18A Greenwich
Park Road,
Kingston 5
N
M
BUS DEM SHUT

CoxSone
RECORDS
509
RUDE BOY
(BOB MARLEY)
THE WAILERS